Collection fondée en 1981
Directeur Wolfgang Leiner

| 124 | **BIBLIO 17**

Ziad Elmarsafy

# The Histrionic Sensibility
Theatricality and Identity from Corneille to Rousseau

Ziad Elmarsafy

# The Histrionic Sensibility

## Theatricality and Identity from Corneille to Rousseau

Biblio 17 – 124

gnⱴ  Gunter Narr Verlag Tübingen
2001

Die Deutsche Bibliothek – CIP-Einheitsaufnahme

**Elmarsafy, Ziad M.:**
The histrionic sensibility : theatricality and identity from Corneille to Rousseau /
Ziad M. Elmarsafy. – Tübingen : Narr, 2001
  (Biblio 17 ; 124)
  ISBN 3-8233-5536-8

# Biblio 17

Suppléments aux *Papers on French Seventeenth Century Literature*
Directeur de la publication: Wolfgang Leiner
Secrétaire de rédaction: Isabell' Kopp
Romanisches Seminar – Wilhelmstraße 50 – D-72074 Tübingen

© 2001 · Gunter Narr Verlag Tübingen
P.O. Box 2567 · D-72070 Tübingen

ISSN 1434-6397
ISBN 3-8233-5536-8    1002279067

T

# Contents

Acknowledgements     9

Introduction     11

Chapter One:
Gemini:
Corneille's Histrionics     23

Chapter Two:
Molière: Imagination and Its Discontents, or,
When Is a Self Not a Self?     67

Chapter Three:
The Impostor and the King:
Thomas Corneille and the Ruses of the Romanesque     93

Chapter Four:
The Eighteenth Century     117

Chapter Five:
Marivaux:
How One Becomes What One Is     135

Chapter Six:
Crébillon fils:
Carnal Knowledge and Narrative Knowledge     167

Chapter Seven:
Rousseau:
Being Supreme     193

Bibliography     233

*To my beloved parents, Aya and Magdy*

# Acknowledgements

My thanks, first and foremost, to the two who supported and encouraged this project right from the start, and have yet to stop: Josué Harari and Ora Avni. Among the many who read, listened to and commented on various chapters and extracts, Alain Viala, Thomas Pavel, Richard Macksey, Thomas Kavanagh, Kathryn Hoffmann, Volker Schröder, Malina Stefanovska, Michael Randall, Alice Jarrard, James Petterson, Stephen Bold, Vinnie Datta, Stephen Schwartz, Daniel Desormeaux, and Thoraya Tlatli all deserve special mention.

On a more personal note, thanks are due to the many friends and colleagues—too numerous to mention here—who encouraged my research on an almost daily basis. I am especially grateful to my two families, the El-marsafys and the Shius, and most of all to Jachi Shiu for efforts on my behalf that were nothing short of extraordinary. This book could not have been written without them.

Last, but by no means least, my thanks to Wolfgang Leiner and the members of the Biblio 17 editorial team—past and present—for their warm reception of my work and help with the publication process. May the world's *dix-septiémistes* enjoy their support for many years to come.

# Introduction

> J'ay mis tous mes efforts à former ma
> vie. Voylà mon mestier et mon ouvrage.
> (*Essais*, II.xxvii)

> The French transform every aspect of
> life into a ceremony. (Sanche de Gra-
> mont, *The French*).

"The real person comes first." "To thine own self be true." "I've gotta
be me." And so on. These phrases, clichéd and common as they are, be-
speak a culture based on certain assumptions about identity. Chief among
them seems to be the belief that we are each endowed with a "self" that
precedes the trials and tribulations of our lives, and that it is incumbent upon
each and every one of us to make that self manifest in all of life's situations.
Rarely, if at all, is the possibility of that self's being a mere role (social or
otherwise) addressed, and when it is, it is usually in negative terms that
depict this role-based self as being inauthentic, hypocritical and illusory.

Our contemporary post-Romantic obsession with authenticity and devotion to "being ourselves" reinforces the belief in the priority of the "real
person", before time and circumstance throw that person into any number
of social and theatrical roles. And yet, it is difficult to accept such assertions
uncritically. Does the axiomatic priority of person over role expressed in my
opening truisms bear close scrutiny? Or could it be that the "real person" is
only conceivable as a reflection or by-product of a given theatrical role, an
illusion? Moreover, what happens when these questions are put in historical
perspective through a given literary corpus? For example, when and where
does this conceptual apparatus appear in the Western literary tradition? With
what consequence? Put more broadly, what is the significance, then as well
as now, of an "authentic" self mediated by "illusions"?

These are the questions I would like to address in the following study. I
shall examine this dogma of the self as a standard feature of modernity (a
period which, for the purposes of this study, I assume begins in the Renaissance) through a series of readings of literary texts written between the six-
teenth and late eighteenth centuries. As I tackle these issues, I hope to provide both a reading of the early modern "self" and to highlight its influence

on contemporary discourses of individuality. Far from being an attack on authenticity (or a defence of hypocrisy), this project aims at emphasizing the extent to which any understanding of the individual self is indebted to role-playing, doubling, and storytelling, all of which I shall examine under the rubric of "histrionics."

\*

\*   \*

Montaigne's *Essais* mark an interesting moment in the history of French letters. Doubtless Montaigne was not the first to think of writing as a means of self-formation, although the magnitude and style of his project certainly set it apart. What makes Montaigne's case especially interesting is the use he makes of the saying that all the world's a stage. He did not invent that particular adage, either, but it takes on added weight in his case due to its importance in the auto-formative process at the heart of the *Essais*.[1]

Consider his essay on the rearing of children (I.xxvi.) In this account, addressed to the Countess of Gurson as an advisory piece on how best to bring up her children, Montaigne takes his own case as being especially worthy of note. Through an imitative ethos he hopes to establish himself as an example. This practice of mimicry also regulates Montaigne's own up-bringing, since his earliest memories are those of play-acting:

> Mettray-je en compte cette faculté de mon enfance: une asseurance de visage, et souplesse de voix et de geste, à m'appliquer aux rolles que j'entreprenois? Car avant l'aage, *Alter ab undecimo tum me vix ceperat annus*, j'ai soutenu les premiers personnages és tragédies latines de Bucanan, de Guerente et de Muret, qui se representerent en nostre college de Guienne avec dignité. En cela, Andreas Goveanus, nostre principal, comme en toutes autre parties de sa charge, fut sans comparaison le plus grand principal de France: et m'en tenoit-on maistre ouvrier. C'est un exercise que je ne meslouë poinct aux jeunes enfans de maison: et j'ay vu nos princes s'y adonner depuis en personne, à l'exemple d'aucuns de nos anciens, honnestement et louablement.[2]

Not only does Montaigne imitate insofar as he play parts, but in doing so he also imitates his masters, whose salient qualification has more to do with appearances than anything else; "car les principales parties que mon pere

---

[1] For a useful history of the idea of *theatrum mundi* in European literature, see Ernest Curtius, *European Literature and the Latin Middle Ages*, trans. Willard R. Trask (New York: Pantheon, 1953), 138-144.

[2] In *Les Essais*, Pierre Villey ed., P.U.F. 1924, 175-177.

cherchoit à ceux à qui il donnoit charge de moy, c'estoit la debonnaireté et facilité de complexion." As he plays, Montaigne effects a *mise en scène* of Latin, his mother tongue and the idiom of his formation; he forms himself—linguistically and intellectually—through these theatrical games. Thus the man who wrote the *Essais* started his life as a child who played parts.

The fact of the matter is that Montaigne's dramatic activity never came to an end. Whereas once it had been a very effective way of practicing the idiom in which he was schooled, it becomes, later on, a means of self-recitation, a direct route to the completion of his project of dynamic self-documentation. In his deft analysis of "Du repentir", Erich Auerbach points out that the word *essai* is to be taken in the context of Montaigne's adaptation to his subject, that it would best be rendered by "self-tryouts" or "self-rehearsals."[3] This tendency goes beyond mere self-indulgence. Montaigne fully embraces the stoicism of his day and age. He draws a strong distinction between his public and private life, with a view to privileging the latter as the one that enables the processes of thinking, writing and self-cultivation. And if he thinks, writes or cultivates himself it is with a view to living a good life and rehearsing a proper death. Indeed, he devotes an entire essay to the fact that "philosopher, c'est apprendre à mourir." Not atypically, Montaigne approaches death theatrically; for him, it is an "acte à un seul personnage." (979)

Despite his originality, Montaigne is not without his predecessors. First, there is the ancient stoic ideal of separating public from private life by considering one's life a play.[4] The following passage from Epictetus' *Encheiridion* best sums up this attitude:

> Remember that you are an actor in a play, which is as the playwright wants it to be: short when he wants it short, long if he wants it long. If he wants you to play a beggar, play even this part skillfully, or a cripple, or a public official, or a private citizen. What is yours is to play the assigned part well. But to choose it belongs to someone else.[5]

It bears pointing out that Epictetus uses the figure of the actor as a metaphor to be adopted in reaction to life's trials and tribulations, rather

---

[3] Erich Auerbach, *Mimesis: The Representation of Reality in Western Literature*, trans. Willard R. Trask (Princeton: Princeton UP, 1953) 293.

[4] I am grateful to Thomas Pavel for bringing the importance of stoicism and neo-stoicism in early modern France to my attention.

[5] Epictetus, *Encheiridion* § 6 (in *Handbook* (Nicholas White trans., Indianapolis, in: Hackett Publishing Co., 1986), 16).

than an activity to be taken up voluntarily. He reminds the reader that all decisions about the nature or quality of the part one is meant to play (the life one leads) are in the hands of a higher power. The best that one can do is play it well.

Second, the notion of private self-cultivation (or self-governance) stands as an ethical ideal and an important step on the path to the good life. Once again, we are dealing with a theme dear to antiquity. In addition to Epictetus, who treats it extensively, we might mention Seneca, in whose *Letters to Lucilius* and *De tranquilitate animi* formulae of self-mastery, belonging to one's self, and being made one's own (suum fieri, suum esse) occur with some frequency.[6]

Finally, Montaigne revives the ideal of self-spectatorship: one cultivates oneself by examining oneself. In this he is the inheritor of a tradition extending to Erasmus' *In Praise of Folly*, whereby the reign of *homo ludens* is celebrated and self-consciousness through a separation from oneself is valourised as the apex of human development[7].

As he implements his ambitious undertaking, Montaigne becomes a divided entity: in order to get at himself he necessarily plays actor and spectator to himself, as described by Michel Jeanneret:

> L'accouchement de la pensée par le dialogue est une action avec mise en scène et personnages. A la fois acteur et spectateur, l'être qui se surprend dans ce processus de création accède à l'une des formes les plus exaltantes de la conscience d'exister.[8]

---

[6] On the ancient ideal of self-cultivation as part and parcel of the "art of living", see Michel Foucault, *Le Souci de soi* (Paris: Gallimard, 1984) 57-85. The late Foucault's description of the practice of philosophy as a spiritual exercise of the self recalls Montaigne's: "L'"essai"—qu'il faut entendre comme épreuve modificatrice de soi-même dans le jeu de la vérité et non comme appropriation simplificatrice d'autrui à des fins de communication—est le corps vivant de la philosophie, si du moins celle-ci est encore maintenant ce qu'elle était autrefois, c'est-à-dire une "ascèse", un exercise de soi, dans la pensée." (*L'Usage des plaisirs* (Paris: Gallimard, 1984), 15). On the ancient view of philosophy as a rupture with the quotidian and self-cultivation as spiritual exercise, see Pierre Hadot, *Exercises spirituels et philosophie antique* (2nd. ed., Paris: Etudes Augustiniennes, 1987) 13-74 and 196-227.

[7] The farthest-reaching analysis of this episode in the seventeenth-century context is Marc Fumaroli's "Microcosme comique et macrocosme solaire: Molière, Louis XIV et *L'Impromptu de Versailles*" where the aim of the theatrical representation of madness is summed up thus: "[S]e connaître comme sujet d'illusion, et persister cependant à partir de cet acte d'humilité, à poursuivre patiemment et fidèlement cette vérité sans laquelle l'illusion ne serait pas connue comme telle; ainsi peut se résumer la leçon du jeu de la folie" in *Revue des sciences humaines* 145 (1972): 97.

[8] Michel Jeanneret, "Rabelais et Montaigne: l'écriture comme parole," *L'esprit créateur* 16.6 (1976): 83.

This intellectual genealogy—stretching through the European Renaissance to the stoics—enables Montaigne to expound the links between theatricality and pedagogy (understood as formation or *Bildung*). The rhetorical skill that he describes in "De l'institution des enfans" and that he embodied so well (the "asseurance de visage et souplesse de voix et de geste à m'appliquer aux rolles que j'entreprenois") aims primarily at creating identities through the ritual of performed utterance. *Qua* master-playwright and actor, Montaigne enacts for his readers the process of coming into one's own by faithfully representing oneself to oneself, and, consequently, to the world. Montaigne produces himself by theatrically reproducing himself; the book of his rehearsals (his *Essais*) is part and parcel of himself ("je suis moymesme la matière de mon livre") and he becomes himself once he accomplishes the final act.[9]

*<br>*   *

Montaigne's individualism was of a piece with his age, and the one that followed it. The period between the end of the French wars of religion and the end of the Fronde coincided with the absolutist experiment in French politics, an experiment whose success was made manifest in the persona of the Sun King. This installation of a totalitarian regime wherein power emanated from—and only from—the crown led to a hierarchical society where the intellectual's lot was lonelier than ever:

> There was little evidence of what might be called a "communitarian ethic" among Frenchmen who expressed themselves about ethics and politics. The ancient view, revived during the Renaissance and again during the eighteenth century, of man as a social and political animal who found his individual realization in the community, was absent. In its place was the radically individualist ethic of the "dissociated man." This is one aspect of what historians have described as a "separation between civil society and the state" in seventeenth-century France; on the one hand, ordinary people going about their business, a business to which politics had only a peripheral and formal relevance, and on the other hand, the absolutist regime working to consolidate the machinery of state (primarily to make war more effectively), with little integration between state machinery and social activity.[10]

---

[9] On the relationship between Montaigne and his mask, see Starobinski, *Montaigne en mouvement* (Paris: Gallimard, 1982) 260.

[10] Nannerl Keohane, *Philosophy and the State* (Princeton: Princeton UP, 1980), 122.

As a result, there arose two distinct schools of social thought, one conformist and the other oppositional. Both set in motion the same topoi as Montaigne and the stoics. The oppositional group includes the neo-Stoic philosophers who wrote in the late 1500s and early 1600s (Justus Lipsius, Guillaume du Vair, Pierre Charron) as well as the free-thinkers (*libertins*) who followed them later in the century (La Mothe le Vayer, Naudé and Gassendi). All were writers who took to heart the stoic distinction between public and private life, argued for private authenticity and public deceit, and hid their reservations about absolutist rule under a mask of serious professional dedication. The "conformists", on the other hand, seem to have taken their cue from Castiglione and Graciàn, writing texts that offered advice on adapting to the new realities of political life by succeeding at the court—now the focus of all worthwhile social activity—and capitalised on the aristocratic craze for finding meaning in a human life by turning it into an art form.[11] Surprisingly enough, texts from both camps sound remarkably similar. Consider the following passage by the Chevalier de Méré, taken from a discourse on what he calls *le commerce du monde*:

> Je suis persuadé qu'en beaucoup d'occasions il n'est pas inutile de regarder ce qu'on fait comme une Comedie, et de s'imaginer qu'on joüe un personnage de theatre. Cette pensée empéche d'avoir rien trop à coeur, et donne ensuite une liberté de langage et d'action, qu'on n'a point, quand on est troublé de crainte et d'inquiétude.[12]

Méré's views can be compared to those advanced in the following passage from Pierre Charron's *De la sagesse*, a compendium of neo-stoic philosophy:

> Au reste, il faut bien sçavoir distinguer & separer nous mesme d'avec nos charges publiques; chacun de nous joüe deux roolles & deux personnages, l'un estranger et apparent, l'autre propre et essentiel. Il faut discerner la peau de la chemise: l'habile homme fera bien sa charge & ne laissera pas de bien juger la sottise, le vice, le fourbe qui y est. Il l'exercera, car elle est en usage en son pays, elle est utile au public, & peut-estre à soy, le monde vit ainsi, il ne faut rien gaster. Il se faut servir & se prevaloir du monde tel qu'on le trouve: Cependant le considerer comme chose estrangere de soy, sçavoir bien de soy jouyr

---

[11] Cf. Domna Stanton's analyses of *honnêteté*, aristocratic manner and the self-as-art in her *The Aristocrat as Art* (New York: Columbia UP, 1980) 1-30, 45-53 and 119-146.

[12] Antoine Gombeaud, chevalier de Méré, *Oeuvres* (Charles-Henri Boudhors, ed., Paris: Ed. François Roche, 1930) 3:158.

à part, & se communiquer à un sien bien confident, au pis aller, à soy mesme.[13]

Both Charron and Méré evince the same tendencies: a heavy individualist bent, a trenchant division between the public and private spheres and the ethics appropriate to each, and, finally, recourse to theatre and role-playing as the figure that best represents how a life is, or ought to be, lived.

This tendency to construe the self in theatrical terms is the central concern of the study that follows. The creation of the self in the space of language, the use of language as both mask and disguise, and the fact that this mask eventually becomes its bearer: all of these strands inform what Roger Shattuck (following Frances Fergusson) has called the histrionic sensibility, the construction of an identity through the adoption and practice of a given role.[14] Furthermore, the impact of this conception goes well beyond literary praxis, couched as literature is in the surrounding social matrix.

The first chapter covers the ways in which Corneille, a very close reader of Montaigne, implements this process both in his work and in his life. Corneille's dramaturgy, a product of Montaigne's individualism, neo-stoic scepticism and Jesuit rhetorical zeal, is meta-theatrical, haunted by the possibility of the theatrical construction of an identity.[15] His plays all approximate L'Illusion comique; they all stand as staged meditations on theatre and the theatricality of everyday life. His characters become what they are by actively assuming and vigorously performing the role that society

---

[13] Pierre Charron, De la sagesse, Book II, Chapter ii, (Amsterdam: Louys et Daniel Elzevier, 1662), 262-263.

[14] The term itself is coined by Francis Fergusson in The Idea of a Theater. Shattuck cogently explores its ramifications and relationship to our understanding of the concept of identity in his essay, "The Prince, the Actor and I: The Histrionic Sensibility" in The Innocent Eye. However, I take my distance from Shattuck on two counts, the one historical and the other theoretical. Shattuck's essay focuses on "the ways in which playacting and character formation have mingled in the modern post-revolutionary world." (122) I trace its development in the pre-revolutionary world. Moreover, Shattuck seems to assume the a priori existence of a "self", (as when he wonders whether we in the contemporary world have "lost touch with ourselves as selves" (150)) while I would contend that such an assumption is too strong not to require modification, if not relaxation, in light of the self's theatrical foundations.

[15] On Corneille's sources, see André Stegmann, L'Héroïsme cornélien (Paris: A. Colin, 1968, 2 vols.) Jean-Jacques Maurens' Une tragédie sans tragique. Le Neo-stoicisme dans l'oeuvre de Pierre Corneille (Paris: A. Colin, 1966) argues for an influential relationship between du Vair's ethics on Corneille, but Stegmann (2:212-218) calls this into question. On the importance of the counter-reformation, see Fumaroli, Héros et orateurs (Genève: Droz, 1990) 4-36.

assigns to them. The Cornelian hero strives to coincide with the mask or persona that is his social lot.

Corneille thus brings into play the same themes as his predecessors, but in doing so he manages to sublate them all into a new procedure. The individualist ethic reaches its apotheosis in the figure of the *généreux* hero, concerned more with his glory than his survival; the division between the public and private spheres translate into the tension between loyalty to the family and loyalty to the state that motivates, inter alia, *Le Cid* and *Horace*, and finally, the emphasis on self-mastery that comes through with particular clarity in *La Place royale* and *Cinna* (where Auguste barks "Je suis maître de moi comme de l'univers") echoes the Senecan ideals of being made one's own.

So far, so typical. Furthermore, Corneille's concern with the stage is not entirely exceptional: other writers in the seventeenth century capitalised on the public's interest in the theatre and the theme of theatricality. Several authors apart from Corneille—Baro, Scudéry, and, most significantly, Rotrou—made use of the stage-within-a-stage. Most of them were content to posit theatricality and role-playing as social survival strategies and ways of resigning oneself to life's trials and tribulations; all assume an a priori separation of public and private personae.

What sets Corneille apart is his use of role-playing as the essential mechanism for the *construction* of the self. In so doing he actually collapses the distinction between private and public: rather than advising his readers and spectators to behave one way at home and one way in public, Corneille argues for an identity that consists in a fusion of public and private, mask and player. His early plays (specifically the Roman trilogy) are all histories of the construction of identities. By the end of each tragedy, no distinction can possibly be drawn between the self formed in private and the self forged before a social public: at the end of the fifth act there is no difference between Rodrigue and Le Cid, Horace and "le bras de Rome", Octave and Auguste. Each of these characters wants to be seen in a certain way. In each case, someone plays a part, to which they sacrifice any private passions and preferences that do not conform to their conception thereof, and all are rewarded for their pains with a title, a rank, a social identity; a self defined by the adage, "I play a part therefore I am."[16]

Corneille thus establishes a paradigm to which his successors react. These reactions are treated in the second and third chapters. The idea of a self that

---

[16] The messianic aspect of this sacrifice approximates the sacrifice of private passion to public office that a king is supposed to perform according to the tenets of absolutist ideology. Corneille's conception of a world where all self-construction imitates royal self-construction is grandiose indeed. Cf. Apostolidès, *Le Prince sacrifié* (Paris: Minuit, 1983), 19-26 and 43-53.

never differs from itself, together with the concomitant collapse of the schizophrenic self expounded by the individualists and the neo-stoics, comes under very close scrutiny by other writers during the seventeenth century. Thomas Corneille[17], Pierre Corneille's younger (and far more successful) brother, uses the idioms of pastoral and *romanesque* theatre to extend the model to the identity of the king: what if, he asks, the absolute king, the hub of the social wheel and the determinant of every social identity in his kingdom, were just playing his part, too?[18] Thomas Corneille presents plays in which this question is raised again and again, either in the form of lost or false kings, only to settle the issue in a most conformist manner by having a "real" king emerge in a spectacular *deus ex machina* at the end of the play. Nevertheless, his insistence on the question, as well as the *romanesque* mould in which he casts it, reflects the dominance of the histrionic ideology in seventeenth century France, as well as the fact that absolute political systems do not allow easy answers to the question of identity: one is always, as it were, caught between the uncertainties of depending on the king's pleasure and the even greater uncertainties of the civil war that preceded the king's installation on the throne. Molière, on the other hand, uses the language of realism to re-assert the *libertin*'s emphasis on what people are like when they're at home, and calls Corneille's framework into question by asking what it would mean to live in a society where every self is defined by the part that it (ostensibly) plays. The establishment of identities and ranks through these theatrical procedures provides Molière with a very sharp tool with which to criticize his contemporaries. The radical nature of his critique calls attention to the limits—both conceptual and social—past which Pierre Corneille's histrionic paradigm no longer seems valid. Not, at least, without the addition of further elements that help delineate personal and social identity.

It is my contention that the missing element is narrative. The second part of this study traces the eighteenth century's cross-fertilisation of theatre with narrative history and describes the resulting conception of identity through the works of Marivaux, Crébillon *fils*, and one of the greatest actors of all time, Jean-Jacques Rousseau. During this period, narrative is used as a second generator of identity, one which eventually replaces theatre. In

---

[17] In order to avoid any possible confusion in the following chapters, the name "Corneille" will be used in reference to Pierre Corneille. Thomas Corneille will be referred to by his full name.

[18] It bears pointing out that Thomas Corneille was not alone in raising this question: Pascal raises it with the parable of the "lost king" in the first *Discours sur la condition des grands*, Pierre Corneille treats it in *Don Sanche d'Aragon* and *Héraclius*, and Molière presents many situations where he systematically demystifies the simulacrum of authority. We will return to these issues in the next three chapters.

Marivaux's plays, we see characters who construct their identities by
narrating their autobiographies, rather than bringing the script of noble
behaviour to bear on a given social situation, as Corneille's characters would
have done. Instead of "I play a part therefore I am," the adage that defines
them is, "I tell a story therefore I am." This process of self-construction
through storytelling is part and parcel of the social ethics of *le monde*, the
salon society of the eighteenth century, where power derives from control
over a given set of narratives. The principles that regulate this social system
are worked out in the novels of Crébillon *fils*. Finally, Rousseau's project of
auto-deification marks the return of a French classical sensibility in
eighteenth-century guise: he couples a concern with performance with the
social circulation of narrative in order to arrive at a position of radical
individuality, a self convinced of its own perfection. The consequences are
political as well as literary. Whereas in Corneille's theatre acting derived its
legitimacy from the political order, and the roles were scripted according to
the code of *noblesse*, Rousseau translates acting into a political exercise and
gives it a stamp of social legitimacy and moral superiority. The political
space described in his political writing only works because of the theatrical
endeavours of the legislator and his promulgation of the laws by
manipulating the general will. By this point, the political path is paved for the
spectacular social paroxysms that shook Europe at the end of the eighteenth
century, giving way to an entire society of self-legitimating actors who
follow Rousseau's example, from the early romantics to latter-day
intellectuals.

*

\*   \*

Finally, a brief comment on the presentation of the material and the
choice of authors would seem to be in order.

It is not my intention to exhaustively treat the issue of theatricality in the
seventeenth and eighteenth centuries, tempting though it might be to do so.
My focus is primarily on the relationship between theatricality and the
understanding of the self. Consequently I have dealt only with those who set
up and those who modify this literary paradigm. Thus Racine has been
excluded, not because he ignores Corneille's histrionism, but because he
perfects it without calling its axioms into question or modifying it substantially. His classical style is derived from the *romanesque* theatrical tradition
developed by Thomas Corneille and "purified" of its *romanesque* elements.
In fact, the relationship between classical "simplicity" and *romanesque*
complication has been commented upon by two of Racine's most astute
readers, namely Alain Viala and Georges Forestier. Alain Viala, for one,

traces *Liebesketten* and metaphors of worldly *galanterie* everywhere, from *Alexandre* to *Andromaque* to *Phèdre*:

> [On] a mis en rengaine la fameuse chaîne des amours non partagées dans *Andromaque*: Oreste aime Hermione qui aime Pyrrhus qui aime Hector. Mais on ne s'est guère avisé que cette structure est *la même* que celle d'*Alexandre*, la structure à cinq de la pastorale galante... Il [Racine] fut galant à fond, et fit naître le tragique du coeur de la galanterie: c'est la pastorale pervertie qui structure la pièce... On trouvait que ses vers n'avaient pas la force de ceux de Corneille: il laissa la force et fit dans le plus galant. C'est là une des innovations qui marquent l'*Andromaque*: au lieu de conter des fleurettes en des vers scandés, antithétiques, le discours des personnages s'y laisse emporter par la logique interne des métaphores amoureuses.[19]

And Forestier, for his part, sees in *Iphigénie* the same problematics of disguise and imposture as those underlying Pierre Corneille's *Oedipe* and *Héraclius*.[20] Coupled with our readings of the Corneilles and Molière, it is difficult not to conclude that Racine's "classical" theatre is little more than *romanesque* theatre that has forgotten its *romanesque* status.

Voltaire would have been an interesting choice for the second part of the book, since he adopted a stage-name ("jardinier", "malade", "suisse" and so on) with each of his correspondents and "initiés", and wrote parabolic stories in a code fashioned exclusively for those allowed entrance to his theatrical utopia.[21] Montesquieu's *Lettres persanes* and Casanova's memoirs both treat issues that are not unrelated to the problematic under consideration here. Once again, however, we are dealing with writers who perfect and polish a literary paradigm without really changing it. It was therefore deemed expedient to focus on those whose eighteenth-century au-thors whose work consistently engages with (rather than simply adopting) the concept of self-formation through theatrical endeavours: Marivaux, who effects the narrative "turn" in the process of self-formation, Crébillon, who describes the principles of its operation, and, finally, Rousseau, whose work represents the triumph of individualism that opens the modern era.

---

[19] *Racine. La stratégie du caméléon* (Paris: Seghers, 1990), 119-121.

[20] Georges Forestier, *Esthétique de l'identité dans le théâtre français (1550-1680). Le Déguisement et ses avatars* (Genève: Droz, 1988), 583-588.

[21] This aspect of Voltaire's writing has been studied decisively by Geoffrey Murray in his *Voltaire's Candide: The Protean Gardener, 1755-1762* (Geneva: Institut Voltaire, 1970).

# Chapter One

## Gemini: Corneille's Histrionics

### Introductory Remarks:

Readers of *Le Cid* will remember that Chimène articulates her predicament thus: "La moitié de ma vie a mis l'autre au tombeau." (800) The meaning behind her rhetorically loaded formulation is fairly straightforward: Rodrigue, her lover, her soul's better half, has killed the other half, namely her father.[1] Chimène's lament, however, goes beyond the level of rhetorical skill; it connotes an entire network of strategies and procedures by which identities are constructed in the texts of Corneille. These textual modi operandi enable the figurative component of Chimène's utterance, constituting as they do a system of doubling, internal reflection and role-playing through which selves are assembled in the space of the theatre.

In Corneille's work we see a synthesis of two thematic strands, one arising from the French Renaissance and the other from the Spanish baroque. From Montaigne he inherits a sensitivity to the ethos of being through doing, and to the possibility of fashioning, through his writing, a social persona quite different from his empirical self.[2] This stoic stance that foregrounds the difference between public persona and private self leads to a theatre where identities are thought through as parts to be played. Corneille's theatre, in addition to standing as a series of profound meditations on history and politics, centres on the issue of the theatrical construction of social identity through such filters as individual gallantry (the early comedies), individual "heroic" destiny (the Roman trilogy) and political

---

[1] A closer reading would discern echoes of the Horatian locution (via Montaigne) in which a close friend or lover is identified with half of one's soul. Cf. Horace, *Odes* I.iii.8 ("animae dimidium meae" being Virgil) and II.xvii.5 ("partem animae meae" being Maecenas) and Montaigne, *Essais* I.xxviii. ("De l'amitié"). References to the plays will be by verse number and title (where necessary) following Georges Couton's edition of the *Oeuvres complètes* (Paris: Gallimard, 1980). Other texts in this edition will be referred to by volume and page number.

[2] For a lucid and informative account of the influence of Montaigne and Corneille's "carrière héroïque" the reader is referred to Marc Fumaroli's *Héros et orateurs. Rhétorique et dramaturgie cornéliennes* (Genève: Droz, 1990), 17-63.

intrigue (*Rodogune, Don Sanche D'Aragon*). Throughout the course of Corneille's literary and social careers, being and doing cannot be separated:

> Ce que vous faites,
> Montre à tout l'univers, seigneur, ce que vous êtes. (*Sertorius*, 297-8)

Self-fashioning, both verbal and actual, is the quintessential undertaking of Corneille's characters. His protagonists make a name for themselves with the sort of rhetorical verve that Montaigne would have prescribed for his readers.

This verbal skill can be ascribed to the other baroque component of his work, from which he inherits the *topoi* of *theatrum mundi* and the mirror that both forms and informs its spectator.[3] The resulting *repli sur soi* pervades Corneille's work on both thematic and formal levels. Consequently, we see a sensitivity in Corneille's work to the theatricality of everyday life, to the continuities between the stage and the world. Consider *L'Illusion comique*, a text in which Corneille takes stock of his situation as a playwright. Corneille shows us a man, Pridamant, going to visit a magician, Alcandre, to help him find his long lost son, Clindor. The magician tells Pridamant to sit down and proceeds to turn his cave into a stage where Clindor's life unfolds. The last chapter in Clindor's life, the one that unfolds before his father's very eyes, is one where Clindor becomes a successful actor. So not only is the stage used as the locus of the revelation of distant, hidden truths about Clindor's life, but acting is represented as being the crowning achievement of a human life. Clindor acquires an identity when he becomes an actor. *L'Illusion comique* show us the history of the formation of that identity in the crucible that is the theatre.

---

[3] These sweeping claims need some qualification: the metaphor of the world as stage does antedate the Spanish baroque and can be traced at least as far back as Petronius. The seventeenth century is, however, unique in the use to which it puts this metaphor. Once the link between actor and spectator has been abolished and made purely visual (rather than physical and quotidian as it was in the passion plays), the theatre is put to more effective use as a locus for the creation of identities. This separation, coupled with the theme of *theatrum mundi*, also helps to explain the extensive use of the device of the stage within a stage: if all the world is a stage and the stage is the place best suited to the examination of human behaviour, then any statement made about the stage must be made onstage, as it were. It should also be noted that the use of contained stages in the early seventeenth century in France owes at least as much to the pedagogical influence of the Society of Jesus as any direct literary influence from Elizabethan and/or Spanish baroque playwrights. For a critical history of the device of contained stages, see Georges Forestier's *Théâtre dans le théâtre sur la scène française du dix-septième siècle* (Genève: Droz, 1981). For an account of the Spanish and Latin influences on French literature of the period, see A. Cioranescu's *Le masque et le visage* (Genève: Droz, 1983); Fumaroli, *Héros et orateurs* and Curtius, *European Literature and the Latin Middle Ages*.

All along the history of that formation, moreover, there seems to be a doubling, a kind of mirroring, between Clindor, the actor, and Alcandre, the magician and "director" or "playwright" that brings him to life. Neither without either could or would obtain; even their names are near anagrams of each other. So in addition to the theatricality of Clindor's life and identity, Corneille seems to be telling us something about the theatrical underpinnings of the writer's social situation in 1636, not only by the fact that the dramatist depends on his art, but that the making—social as well as literary—of the theatrical author depends on his characters.

Another relationship worthy of note is the one between Clindor and his employer, Matamore. The latter's status as a *miles gloriosus* in a play dealing with theatricality is not uninteresting; for here we see someone who is very good at playing parts (and Matamore is nothing if not histrionic: "le seul bruit de mon nom renverse les murailles"(233)) but who cannot live up to the parts he plays, who cannot make the mask stick, as it were. This stands in stark contrast to Clindor, who lives up to his promise, both martial and mercenary, and whose emergence as an actor thus seems more authentic because it establishes a continuity between his theatrical and extra-theatrical lives. Indeed, this continuity is what makes the play work: Pridamant, who represents the spectator in *L'Illusion comique*, does not realise that his son is an actor until the fifth act. Matamore is also a foil to the magician-playwright, Alcandre; the former's words are empty and meaningless while the latter's word is magical, creating by its very utterance a theatrical world of its own.[4]

The parallels between this theatrical world and the surrounding sociopolitical space are legion. Indeed, the latter is a space where looks can kill; for just as Matamore yells "le seul bruit de mon nom renverse les murailles," Louis XIV wins battles in Corneille's idiom by his mere appearance: "Louis n'a qu'à paraître, et vos Murailles tombent/ Il n'a qu'à donner l'ordre, et vos Héros succombent" ("Sur les victoires du roi en l'année 1677", 3:1317).[5] In the forty years that elapse between the composition of *L'Illusion comique* and "Sur les victoires du roi...", nothing shakes Corneille's faith in the theatricality of his social environment.

What *L'Illusion comique* foregrounds through the device of the contained stage is present implicitly elsewhere. The fake soldier casts a long shadow in Corneille's idiom, and is as we shall see, as close to Corneille's other theatrically constructed military heroes (Le Cid, Horace) as he is to

---

[4] On the contrast between the relationship between Matamore and Alcandre as one between verbal emptiness and plenitude, see Peter Bürger's *Die frühen Komödien Pierre Corneilles* (Frankfurt: Athenäum, 1971), 226-228.

[5] Cf. Jean Starobinski, *L'Oeil vivant* (Paris: Gallimard, 1961), 31-33.

Clindor. Corneille's characters are only too well aware of the fact that their status and identity depend on what part they play before other characters in a space where the metatheatrical dimension is as real as mass and momentum. Here character is determined by the paces that one has to go through. The acme of Cornelian authority consists of occupying the same position before the characters as God before the (theatre of the) world, and of subsequently manipulating the inhabitants of that stage space with divine impunity.

In addition to this conscious reflection on the facticity of the stage, Corneille's idiom underlines the importance of showing this reflection. It is not enough to postulate a link between being and doing or essences and appearances; their coincidence must be portrayed with spectacular *éclat*.[6] Thus Auguste's clemency in *Cinna* is a performed clemency, enacted for the viewing benefit of Cinna, of Rome and (in Octave's mind) of the entire universe. There is also a concern with oratory insofar as it constructs its colloquists. Corneille's theatre is one where the performative weight of language overtakes its constative function, and this performative function in turn acquires a certain constructive power by virtue of its performance. As one astute critic puts it, "the personnages of Cornelian drama literally talk themselves into irreconcilable hatreds."[7] They also talk themselves into themselves: in *Mélite*, Tircis rhetorically improvises his love for the heroine before our very eyes. The "art de parler" with which he taunts Eraste is merely the ability to enact and realise that which is uttered.[8] The performed language of Corneille's stage soon hardens into a verbal mask that identifies its bearer. The ideal way of making essences and appearances coincide in his idiom is the adoption of an appearance made of words that adequately translate the essence in question.

## On Stage:

The contained stage is not particular to Corneille. Its flourish as a theatrical device on the French stage of the 1630's, especially in the works of

---

[6] The farthest-reaching analysis of this aspect of Corneille's work is Jean Starobinski's essay, "Sur Corneille" in *L'Oeil vivant*, 31-67.

[7] George Steiner in *The Death of Tragedy* (New York: Knopf, 1961), 56.

[8] This process whereby a character improvises something into reality was relatively widespread in the literature of the seventeenth century, reaching its pinnacle in the treatment of the legend of St. Genesius' conversion onstage by Lope de Vega and Rotrou.

Scudéry, Gougenot, Baro and Charles Beys, reflects the self-consciousness of an art form coming to grips with itself.[9]

Corneille's case merits special attention because the implications of this device of contained stages are carried as far as possible in his work. In the Cornelian text the device of the contained stage becomes a lens through which the fashioning of a theatrical self is viewed. There is an overall *mise en abyme* inherent in Corneille's entire oeuvre that far surpasses *L'Illusion comique* and is evident in all of his plays. The terrestrial paradise that houses the heroes and heroines of the early comedies (the very titles of which are indicative: *La Galerie du palais, La Place royale*), as well as the rigid courts that bear witness to the making and unmaking of the later Roman heroes, can all be compared to a stage[10]. Seen against this background, *L'Illusion comique* presents us with a convolution of this topos; the stage that we see is a stage within a stage within a stage. Moreover, within these contained stages, characters are divided into those who manipulate and those who act, those who author and those who are authorised. Almost all of Corneille's characters fall to one side or another of the division represented by Alcandre and Clindor of *L'Illusion comique*; one is either author or actor. This hierarchy also reflects the social reality out of which Corneille's theatre grew: the aristocratic sector of seventeenth-century France tended asymptotically towards the apotheosis of court society.[11] This is a world in which situations impose roles on people, who then have to prove themselves worthy of the role in question. The theatricality inherent in the fabric of society extends to the playwright himself: through the influence of the academies and the networks of royal and noble patronage, a career in the theatre becomes, as was the case with Corneille, a path to the nobility.

Corneille's inclusion of a second stage by implication is not without significance as a reflection of the shifts in paradigms of representation current in seventeenth century France. With the advent of the classical *episteme*, Foucault tells us, the view of language, and consequently the view of the world, were altered radically: "A partir de l'âge classique, le signe c'est

---

[9] Cf. Forestier's *Théâtre dans le théâtre* as well as H.C. Lancaster's exhaustive *History of French Dramatic Literature in the Seventeenth Century* (Baltimore: The Johns Hopkins University Press, 1929-1942) vols. 1 & 2 for an account of the origins of this practice.

[10] Cf. Fumaroli, *Héros*, 36-45.

[11] Evidently, this tendency was not without its interruptions. For more detailed accounts of the development of court society see Norbert Elias, *Die höfische Gesellschaft. Untersuchungen zur Soziologie des Königtums und der höfischen Aristokratie* (Darmstadt: Suhrkamp, 1983) and Roland Mousnier, *Les Institutions de la France sous la monarchie absolue, 1598-1789* (Paris: PUF, 1974).

la *représentativité* de la représentation en tant qu'elle est représentable."[12]
Much the same can be said of what is represented by Corneille's theatre,
which stands (by different) means as a sign for theatricality itself. The om-
nipresent contained stages evince Corneille's preoccupation with the theatre as a means of investigating language, representation and subjectivity.

From this perspective, *L'Illusion comique* emerges as a meditation on
the confluence of these three vectors rather than the simple apologia for the
theatre that it is often made out to be. In calling his play an "étrange monstre" Corneille draws attention to what it demonstrates: that there is no end
to the stages contained in all walks of life and that even the most compelling situations are to be viewed with the stoic detachment of a spectator.
Under the auspices of this scheme Clindor himself becomes a sign. Readers
of the play will remember that before becoming an actor, Clindor spends
much of his time engaging in theatrical endeavours: in order to seduce
Isabelle, he pretends to seduce Lysis and takes advantage of his role as
Matamore's spokesman to the same end; when he "dies" he is only doing
so as he plays the part of Théagène and so on. Moreover, a literary historical view—the same perspective held by the audience who first witnessed
*L'Illusion comique*—would have recognised a plot typical of the early Corneille and of the French theatre of the 1620s and 1630s in the history of
Clindor and Isabelle.[13] Theatricality is everywhere and nowhere in this text,
and Clindor becomes an allegory of the actor per se; as his life unfolds before the spectator's (and Pridamant's) gaze, he enacts both the events of his
life and his capacity to reproduce them, in much the same way that he represents both Matamore and his own ability to seduce mentally when he
woos Isabelle.[14] That Clindor's trials and tribulations are rehearsals of a
future self that lives up to a pre-established role is attested to by Alcandre's
frequent use of the verb "se faire" and its variants to connote his self-fashioning: "Dedans Saint Innocent il se fit sécretaire" (173), "Et s'est fait de
Clindor le Sieur de la Montagne" (206) and so on. Moreover, Clindor's
formation is the end-product of a lineage running through the picaresque
novel as it existed in the 1630s. Commenting on his many misadventures,
Alcandre adds that "Enfin, jamais Buscon, Lazarille de Tormes/ Sayavèdre
et Gusman ne prirent tant de formes." (180-181) This genealogy suggests
that the histrionic self is necessarily created in the space of literary lan-

---

[12] *Les Mots et les choses*, 79.

[13] See Collette Scherer's "La Tragédie du cinquième acte de *L'Illusion comique* et
le théâtre du temps" in *Dramaturgies, langages, dramatiques. Mélanges pour Jacques
Scherer* (Paris: Nizet, 1986).

[14] For analyses of actors as tropes incarnate, see Anne Ubersfeld, *Lire le théâtre I*
(Paris: Editions sociales, 1977), 119-125.

guage, which consequently takes on added weight as being more real than reality itself. The dual register whereby we are shown both the theatre and its theatricality, both a character and his characterisation, operates as a means of auto-biographical presentation and as a means of re-constructing reality in light of the imaginary space, literary or theatrical. As Serge Doubrovsky points out, in Corneille's case "il ne s'agit pas d'utiliser le langage pour explorer le monde réel, mais d'utiliser le monde réel pour aboutir à un certain langage."[15]

The Cornelian project does not end with the invention of this idiolect, however. The "certain langage", the idiom of theatricality, is created with a view to re-inventing identity as its direct consequence. This construction of the subject in the idiom of Corneille's theatre functions on three concurrent levels: the linguistic, the rhetorical and the literary. On a linguistic level we are within the domain of general linguistics as mapped out by Emile Benveniste. We are dealing with the subject as an outcome of language:

> C'est dans et par le langage que l'homme se constitue comme sujet; parce que le langage seul le fonde, en réalité, dans *sa* réalité qui est celle de l'être... *Est* ego qui *dit* "ego"... L'installation de la subjectivité dans le langage crée, dans le langage et, croyons-nous hors du langage aussi bien, la catégorie de la personne.[16]

The link thus established between being, saying and identity (*Est* ego qui *dit* ego) creates an implicitly performative component of language which becomes the limiting test-case for Benveniste's theory.[17] In Corneille's theatre, every character is identified by his or her verbal output. By extending the frame of reference to linguistic and discursive production in general, one can say that like his characters, the subject Corneille (as a discursive locus) is produced by his literary output, thus re-confirming Valéry's dictum that "le personnage de l'auteur est l'oeuvre de ses oeuvres."[18]

The issue of linguistic analysis is further complicated when it comes to analysing theatrical discourse, as Anne Ubersfeld has already demonstrated. When an actor speaks, the resulting discourse is not enclosed in a constative function linked to a real referent. Similarly, when an actor says "I", the pronoun refers to a number of people all of whom speak through the actor at that specific moment: the author, the real actor, the character.

---

[15] In *Corneille et la dialectique du héros* (Paris: Gallimard, 1963), 17.

[16] *Problèmes de linguistique générale I* (Paris: Gallimard, 1966), 259-263.

[17] "*Je jure* est un engagement, *il jure* n'est qu'une description;" Benveniste, 265.

[18] Paul Valéry, *Carnets I*, qtd. Fumaroli, *Héros*, 17.

And yet, in order for theatrical presentation to cohere it is necessary that the first two be emptied of their subjectivity, which is then mapped onto the character. As a result there exists a certain lack of subjectivity in the theatre; "le discours théâtral est un *discours sans sujet*."[19] Theatre unfolds by constructing a referent for a discourse based on a series of shifters (I, here, now). This referent is cut off from the space of the real except insofar as theatrical representation is aimed at the spectator, who receives and re-confirms this relationship between a discourse without a subject and the imaginary subject constructed onstage. As for the character, he or she does not speak in his or her own name; in the space of the theatre "le je de l'énconciation *est* un autre."

In Corneille's theatre we see a certain manipulation of these conventions with a view to foregrounding their operation. Ubersfeld has pointed out how his characters' self-revelation does not convey much information over and above what the spectator already knows, often lapsing into blank tautologies: "Je suis Médée", "Je suis encore Sévère", "Je suis Romaine", "Souviens-toi seulement que je suis Cornélie" and many others following the pattern, "I am I."[20] This rhetorical *repli sur soi* of what should be the most informative utterance of all is really quite telling: the predicate of the phrase that starts, "Je suis…" is in fact the identity under construction, the identity whose construction only begins with the pronouncement of this seemingly blank self-revelation. If "le héros cornélien se satisfait de l'affirmation autosuffisante du moi et de son nom, sans aucune justification, sans aucune raison," it is because these self-revelations are not intended as constatives or observations. Instead, statements of this sort carry out a crucial performative function: the enactment of the theatrical self. Through this device, Cornelian theatre presents us with the spectacle of a subject bridging the gap between the "je de l'énonciation" and "l'autre," synthesising the two to produce a final "je."

The operation of this synthetic model applies to Corneille himself, who spends his entire career engaged in what Marc Fumaroli calls "literary heroism" with the ulterior motive of re-creating the subject lacking from theatrical discourse. Thus the dissolved self, both that of the author and that of the actor, is re-created as a result of the idiom of the theatre. The linguistic relationship between self and theatrical text thus re-enforces the

---

[19] Ubersfeld, 241. Emphasis in the original.

[20] See "*Je suis* ou l'dentité héroïque chez Corneille" in *Pierre Corneille. Actes du colloque tenu à Rouen* (Alain Niderst ed., Paris: P.U.F. 1985). In this text, Ubersfeld limits herself to a formal analysis of the topic. My aim is to go beyond her framework, to examine the actual formation of the self revealed in these apparent tautologies and draw the consequences.

need for multiple stages: the self that starts off as a mask can be staged only in Corneille's metatheatrical mould.

Corneille's verbal self-fashioning can be roughly divided into two steps: first, a given character will weave a verbal mask, a fixed set of claims in accordance with which he or she will act, such as Alidor's "Je veux la liberté dans le milieu des fers..../ et quand j'aime, je veux/ Que de ma volonté dépendent tous mes voeux."(*La Place royale*, 104-107) Second, he or she will act in accordance with the principles laid out in that verbal banner, conforming thereto as an actor would to a role, and thus make a name for his or herself. Corneille's heroes become themselves by enacting themselves, by playing the part that they become. It would be difficult to imagine any of them—Rodrigue, say—saying, "cogito ergo sum." If anything, their attitude would be summed up by something closer to, "I play a part, therefore I am."[21] This part creates and overtakes the character in question, usually with tragic results: the name that Horace makes for himself on the battlefield catches up with him when he kills Camille. Thus Corneille's theatre presents us with the most paradoxical of tricks, the creation that re-casts its creator in its own light.

Hence the concern with the rhetorical operation of language in Corneille's theatre. It is there from the very beginning of his theatrical output: *Mélite* revolves around the "art de parler" that divides Eraste and Tircis. (Not coincidentally, Eraste, the better orator, tries to author his own drama involving Tircis and Melite and, in going mad, endows all of his "characters" with new identities.) His characters have nothing but their verbal masks, whose power is not to be underestimated: "Que ne peut l'artifice et le fard du langage?" (*Othon* 114) Corneille puts oratory to the same ends as those to which it was put in Roman public life (and in the exercises of the Jesuit college at Rouen): it is, first and foremost, a language used for the construction of those who use it. The speech or soliloquy of a character becomes a mask that allows the law of ostentation, the law of the revelation of identities, to operate effectively. Like an orator in a judicial context, an actor speaks for another: "l'orateur, parlant à la place d'un autre, devient un des personnages impliqués dans le drame judiciaire, dont il n'est maître que

---

[21]There is not space enough to launch a discussion of the relationship between Descartes' cogito and Corneille's theatrical self-conception here. I would like to mention, however briefly, Jean-Luc Nancy's definitive analysis of the theatricality of Descartes' position in his *Ego sum* (Paris: Aubier-Flammarion, 1979), 63-94. Nancy paraphrases Descartes' phrase, "larvatus prodeo", as "Je ne me masque que pour m'apparaître et me voir, et me voir entendre;" (69) and concludes that, "[L]e *cogito*, en tant qu'il a ou qu'il fait figure, est excogité—il ne se pense qu'en s'exposant, en feignant de s'exposer et en exposant sa feinte, sa fiction, son extravagance." (77)

très partiellement, et à sa place."[22] In so doing, the actor creates himself.
Corneille's oratorical self-fashioning can be used to explain three tendencies. First, it helps to explain characterisation: styles of speech are
bound inextricably with the characters to which they are linked. The verbal
tours de force by which crises are precipitated and resolved are the same
ones that make or break their creators. (A more localised instance of the
auto-constructive use of deliberative rhetoric is to be found in the tribunal
scenes of *Le Cid, Horace* and *Cinna*.) Rhetoric creates the *éclat* that sus-
tains the *evidentia* of a given character's case. Second, it helps to explain a
certain *bovarysme avant la lettre* operative in Corneille's theatre and fundamental to the procedure of verbal self-fashioning: his characters exist
through their speeches. André Gide sums up the situation quite nicely:

> Le héros français, tel que nous le peint Corneille, projette devant lui
> un modèle idéal, qui est lui-même encore, mais lui-même tel qu'il se
> souhaite, tel qu'il s'efforce d'être... nous ne sommes pas très loin de
> ce que M. Jules de Gaultier appelera le *bovarysme*—Nom qu'il donne
> à cette tendance qu'ont certains à doubler leur vie d'une existence
> imaginaire, à cesser d'être qui l'on est, pour devenir qui l'on croit être,
> qui l'on veut être.[23]

This representative model of the self translates into both a pre-scribed
role that requires playing and a double that both precedes and defines the
self under construction. Furthermore, by setting in motion the free play of
rhetorical style and substance, the playwright necessarily evokes the common memory of idealised exempla, ethopoetic paradigms that dominate a
given verbal mask. The playwright thus emerges as a storehouse of rhetorical and oratorical paradigms, which, in turn, form the matrix of subjectivity
by dictating the rules that govern the construction of the verbal mask. Insofar as his characters are part of his enunciation, the orator-playwright can
be read as a product of these paradigms. "Corneille" is the name of a mask
containing masks.[24]
Finally, Corneille's oratorical self-fashioning helps to explain the use of
the term, "loi" in his theatre. Alidor expresses his ideal of independence as
a situation where, "C'est de moi seulement que je prendrai la loi." (*La
Place royale*, 1506) An identity is contracted, as it were, through a law set

---

[22] Fumaroli, *Héros*, 300.

[23] André Gide, *Dostoïevsky. Articles et causeries* (Paris: Plon, 1923), qtd. Starobinski, 54.

[24] "[Le]... personnage classique...est un visage à la recherche de son masque
définitif, et ce qu'on appelle sa psychologie est la palpitation même des *personae* possi-
bles qui s'offrent à lui en route, jusqu'à ce qu'il trouve celle qu'appelait sa vocation, li-
brement consentie chez Corneille, prédéterminée chez Racine." Fumaroli, *Héros*, 311.

forth at some point and in accordance with which a given character proceeds to act. The law, in other words, is the role pre-scribed for that character. Every play will contain its playwrights or internal dramatists, theatrical legislators who (ostensibly) create roles for all the other characters. It is not for nothing that Corneille was a lawyer. The converse is also true: much hesitation in Corneille's theatre is occasioned by the speaker's taking stock of the higher powers that manipulate him or her. The voices of conventional wisdom in his tragedies never tire of telling us that one's life and one's self are not things that one necessarily owns:

> Vous n'avez pas la vie ainsi qu'en héritage;
> Le jour qui vous la donne en même temps l'engage:
> Vous la devez au prince, au public, à l'état. (*Polyeucte*, 1203-5)

If the Cornelian hero can be said to have a "mission" of mastery, it is aimed at being his or her own playwright, the author of one's existence. In Corneille's theatre, the question of the voluntary assumption of an identity imposed by others (the king, lovers, rivals, the social system) is translated into the quest for a self-sufficient manipulation of the self by oneself. The same can be said of Corneille himself; the end of the *Excuse à Ariste* bears out this structure of idealised self-manipulation:

> Laissez-la [ma muse] toujours libre, agir suivant son choix,
> Céder à son caprice et s'en faire des lois. (1:781)

This is not easily accomplished, however; to enter this mode of self-mastery one necessarily separates from oneself. Being one's own manipulator is an idealised final step that can only be realised once one becomes both self and other vis-à-vis oneself. Identity only becomes real once one mirrors oneself back to oneself, thus becoming both playwright and manipulated character at the same time.[25] For Corneille, this mediation is provided by his characters. This truism holds true from the start of his career. In the *Excusatio* that he wrote to the Archbishop of Rouen in 1633, he attributes his success to the actor Montdory. Despite Corneille's putative "modesty", Montdory is only mentioned after a lengthy description of Corneille's works up to this point in time (from *Mélite* to *La Place royale*),

---

[25] One final link is missing, namely the self as spectator of this scenario, but this is an ideal rarely realised, if at all. Indeed, it is the need for a spectator that drives Corneille's characters to behave as they do, *pour autrui*. Even the final state of self-mastery has to be witnessed. Cf. Marc Fumaroli, "Microcosme comique et macrocosme solaire" where the subject is treated through the tri-partite structure of actor-spectator-*magister ludi*.

leaving us with a fitting precursor to the *Excuse à Ariste* (1634). Still, the terms in which Montdory ("Roscius") is praised are not insignificant:

> Sed tamen hic Scaena est, et gestu et voce juvamur,
> Forsitan et mancum Roscius implet opus.
> Tollit si qua jacent, et toto corpore prodest,
> Forsan et inde ignis versibus, inde lepos.
> Vix sonat a magno divulsa Camoena theatro,
> Blaesaque nil proprio sustinet ore loqui. (1:465)

The actor literally fills out the gaps left by the author in the work at hand, a step without which neither dramatic creation nor creator would exist. Now, this goes against the grain of the rest of the poem, where Corneille speaks of himself as a playwright second to none as well as the haughty tone of the *Excuse à Ariste* and its most frequently quoted verse, "Je ne dois qu'à moi seul toute ma renommée." The impasse is resolved, however, if the term "moi seul" is read in relation to what this *moi* does, as a playwright whose characters function as autobiographical reflections or second selves that condition his self-construction.[26] It is no accident, therefore, that the following confession appears in verse during a rare moment of autobiographical candour;

> J'ai la plume féconde et la bouche stérile,
> Bon galant au théâtre et fort mauvais en ville
> Et l'on peut rarement m'écouter sans ennui,
> Que quand *je me produis par la bouche d'autrui.* (3:11)

The theatre, in other words, provides Corneille with his (other) self. It is this scenario of self-construction through the combined mechanisms of role-playing and the discovery of the self as other in Corneille's work that will concern us here.

### The Subject in Society

This concern with mastery obviously echoes the social realities of the day. The hierarchisation of the stage and the division of the characters into

---

[26] Further evidence for this reading of the *Excuse à Ariste* can be adduced from the verses that follow "Je ne dois qu'à moi seul toute ma renommée": "Et pense toutefois n'avoir point de rival,/ A qui je fasse tort en le traitant d'égal". Corneille, therefore, exists as a function of his rivals. He underlines his self-sufficiency only as a first among equals, equals that operate as doubles and render his identity intelligible to him. The authorial persona that he creates escapes neither the logic of the mirror nor the twinning imperative in which his characters are caught.

agents and objects of manipulation clearly reflects the hierarchies that were hardening into the social structures of seventeenth-century France. In what follows I should like to argue for two principal processes in the operation of this society: first, the importance of rank (or order), and second, the extent to which power translated into authority, the power to manipulate those who were not as powerful. The society of orders[27] was structured so as to allow identity to depend, in the first place, on rank. Rank, in turn, was calculated as a function of the distance from the central locus of power, the court. The court itself was similarly arranged, with power varying in inverse proportion to distance from the throne. On a strictly formal level, at least, we are not very far from the stage-within-a-stage arrangement.

Now, rank and social role were synonymous. Social identity was therefore part and parcel of the function one performed qua occupant of a given location within the hierarchy, both within and outside the court.[28] This aspect of social interaction was not without its consequences. With social role as the primary determinant of social subjectivity the entire social system depended almost totally on its centre, the king. Hence the eventual translation of this state of affairs into a powerful popular myth proclaiming the king God on earth.[29] The king himself, in view of his dual capacity as *rex et sacerdos*[30], is engulfed by this process: the continuity of the royal function, the royal role, was a fundamental law of the state as a result of the edict of April 1403. New kings did not go into mourning for their predecessors. "Le roi est mort. Vive le roi:" the repetitive syntax of this proclamation (together with the associated truism, "En France, les rois ne meurent pas,") attests to the predominance of social role as a concept on whose basis, both figurative and real, an entire state was founded. The king, or rather the

---

[27] The term is Roland Mousnier's. The following sketch of the social landscape of the seventeenth century is by no means exhaustive. It is much indebted to Mousnier's work, as well as Apostolidès' *Roi machine* and Elias's *Die höfische Gesellschaft*. Also helpful were Mousnier's *Histoire générale des civilisations. Les XVIe et XVIIe siècles* (Paris: P.U.F., 1962) and *Etat et société en France au XVIIe et XVIIIe siècles* (Cours de Sorbonne; Paris: Centre de documentation universitaire, 1968); and Ernst Kantorowicz's landmark study of *The King's Two Bodies: A Study in Mediaeval Political Theology* (Princeton, N.J.: Princeton UP, 1957).

[28] The most incisive analysis of this aspect of society's functioning in absolutist France is in Elias's *Die höfische Gesellschaft*,78-116. Elias reminds us that Louis XIV managed to consolidate his power by giving a specific role to every individual lord—and lady-in-waiting. Yves-Marie Bercé traces this image of society as a pyramid of roles to Zuccolo in his *Naissance dramatique de l'absolutisme* (Paris: Seuil, 1992) 217-218.

[29] Mousnier, *Institutions*, 1:519.

[30] On the dual status of the king, see Kantorowicz, *The King's Two Bodies*, 42-192, and Apostolidès, *Le Prince sacrifié*, 11-26.

royal role, was the state. As such the theatrical basis of his construction was very much in the foreground. The king's situation as master of the state that creates him in turn echoes the highest ideal of Cornelian self-affirmation, "Je suis maître de moi comme de l'univers." Coupled with this state of affairs was the king's contingent status as a human being in flesh and blood who would, one day, come to dust. In this there was a parallel between his situation and that of the lowest sub-order of the nobility; namely those who were ennobled as recognition for services rendered. In both cases we have a temporary fulfillment of a social rank that is also rendered contingent, in the first case by death and in the second by death or royal edict.[31] The overall social format was therefore marked at its limits by the tension between two ethical outlooks, the one equating being with birth and the other equating being and doing, the former postulating the irrevocable nature of social rank and the other liberating the forces that motivated social mobility.

The impact of these forces was not negligible. French society at the end of the civil wars was in a state of "permanent unrest"[32] where the boundaries separating good from evil, true from false and noble from commoner were far from clear. Corneille wrote amidst a strong current of stoic individualism running from Montaigne through Du Vair and Justus Lipsius to Guez de Balzac. Within this tradition two contradictory tendencies were emphasised, the first stressing the individual's self-containment and his total separation from public life, and the second bridging the gap through total submission to the will of the monarch in affairs of the state. Once a person's service has been recognised and legitimised by the king, a new identity is forged. Rodrigue, Horace and Polyeucte all make a name for themselves in this way. This tradition also informs Corneille's mapping of public self-fashioning (qua soldier, king or whatever) onto private spaces. It is from the incongruity of this mapping in certain cases that the tragedy of *Horace*, whose protagonist behaves at home in the same way that he does on the battlefield, is derived. It is not only the king who plays a part, it is every member of the state and, moreover, they both employ the same mechanisms in doing so. The Clindor of *L'Illusion comique* is emblematic

---

[31] Mousnier, *Institutions*, 1:105-110.

[32] This term, too, is Roland Mousnier's. See his "The Fronde" in *Preconditions of Revolution in Early Modern Europe* (Robert Forster and Jack P. Greene, eds. Baltimore, MD: The Johns Hopkins University Press, 1970), 136.

of this current in the French social format of his day.[33] Corneille concerns himself less with *le roi soleil* than with *le moi soleil*.[34]

Nevertheless, there is no denying the sheer weight and consequence of the absolute monarchic principle. Court life, as we have seen, was eminently theatrical: it could not be otherwise under the carefully organised scrutiny of the absolute monarch.[35] As a result of the theatrical bases on which life at *la cour et la ville* was predicated, the court (or, for that matter, any space associated with the king) became a virtual space in which act and representation were one: people were defined and ranked by the steps that they went through and the lines that they recited. The relationship between the court and the stage goes beyond isomorphism pure and simple: once the court has undergone this translation into a virtual space, the spectacular overtakes the actual. The nobility now found itself engaged in exploits of a more spectacular sort, and feudal battles were replaced by paradigms of showmanship such as tournaments, carrousels and jousts. Literature became the basis for these politico-spectacular forms, rather than the passive incantation of past glory.[36] Thus the texts of Corneille, to a certain extent, and those of his successors (Molière, Quinault, Thomas Corneille) to a larger extent, operate within the economy of the virtual space where noth-

---

[33] For an account of the actor's proverbially rapid social mobility and the possibility of making a name for oneself in the theatre of seventeenth-century France see Jean Duvignaud's *L'Acteur. Esquisse d'une sociologie du comédien* (Paris: Gallimard, 1965), 39-119.

[34] The term is A.J. Krailsheimer's. See his *Studies in Self-Interest: Descartes to La Bruyère* (Oxford: Oxford UP, 1962).

[35] This behaviour was also linked to one's quintessential identity, which link is reflected in the myth that people became transparent in the presence of Louis XIV. Insofar as he was supreme *suzérain* and master of fealties, his subjects made a gift of their person to the king, which gift led to his omniscience: "Le sujet-roi exige, outre une fidélité inconditionnelle, un état de transparence éliminant tout obstacle entre vassal et suzerain... Dans son *Art de Régner* le Père Lemoyne développe le thème de l'impérialisme oculaire: les individus sont mis en perspective par le regard monarchique; aucun obstacle ne résiste à l'oeil qui éclaire en même temps qu'il dévoile." (Apostolidès, *Le roi-machine*, 47). Conversely, the king's appearance was both inscrutable and omnipotent: "Louis n'a qu'à paraître" for wars to be won. This aspect of the "heroic" subjectivity is mirrored in Mélite's impact on Tircis, who improvises his love for her immediately after seeing her. Cf. Starobinski, *L'Oeil vivant*, 31-43.

[36] "La littérature prend à la cour une place nouvelle; elle ne constitue plus un écho dans les livres des exploits féodaux, elle est la source où les seigneurs puisent pour représenter des pseudo-exploits qu'ils n'ont pas la possibilité d'accomplir en dehors du théâtre." Apostolidès, *Le Roi-machine*, 97.

ing exists but everything means, where objects function semiophorically[37] and every subjectivity exists with the express purpose of mediating another.

In addition to his post as supreme spectator, the king was endowed with creative powers that enabled those of his subjects. As Perrault puts it, the king was the "père de tous les arts;"[38] his invisible hand moved those of the sculptor, the painter and the writer.[39] In his capacity as master of fealties, and therefore as every subject's "better half" (fealty being the state that obtains when master and *fidèle* become the same man in two bodies[40]), the king was the supreme author/manipulator whose power regulated artistic production as it would any of the state's resources. From this perspective artists stand in the same relationship to the king as actors to their author; they effectively become passive instruments, "qui résonnent quand le roi les touche."[41] The king thus becomes a supreme *magister ludi* who regulates the systems of artistic production and reproduction within the stage-space of the court, the city and the state.

It is this aspect of the royal function that brings the king—qua royal epitome of authority and creation, as master puppeteer of the subjects that he creates through his sovereignty—closest to the situation of the playwright. This makes Corneille's case all the more interesting: the playwright who builds an entire career on the ethos of self-mastery and self-sufficiency ("Je ne dois qu'à moi seul toute ma renommée") is really attempting to multiply the royal function by several factors and partake of its power. Refracted through the filter of the theatre, Corneille's position is superimposed on that of the king. The paradigm of subjectivity based on histrionic self-mastery that exists in Corneille's theatre leads to a space in which every identity thus constructed emulates the royal function. The tension that exists in his theatre is not merely one between actors and authors or sovereigns and subjects, but among the sovereigns themselves: *Le Cid* is as much a play about teaching Chimène to accept the king as mediator as it is about Rodrigue becoming himself. As he makes his way in the virtual space, and in using the world of the court to create his idiom, Corneille

---

[37] The term is borrowed from Apostolidès to indicate the creation of objects that existed not to be consumed but to be interpreted during various aspects of court life, specifically at court banquets and feasts. Cf. *Le Roi-machine*, 105-113.

[38] In "Le siècle de Louis le Grand", *Parallèle des anciens et des modernes* (Imdahl and Jauss eds., Munich: Eidos, 1964), 165.

[39] Félibien, *Receuil des descriptions de peintures et d'autres ouvrages faits pour le Roy* (Paris: Sebastien Mabre-Cramoisy, 1689), qtd. Mousnier, *Institutions*, 1:522.

[40] Mousnier, *Institutions*, 1:89. The king thus partakes of the structure of the twinned self as constructed in Corneille's theatre.

[41] Chapelain, qtd. Apostolidès, *Le Roi-machine*, 31.

aims at occupying the throne at the centre. Perhaps this is why his fortunes failed to match those of his younger, more modest successors.[42]

## Mirroring:

The tautological tendency mentioned above in connection with the characters' self-revelation on Corneille's stage is also important as an indication of the doubling central to self-construction. To say "I am I" is to come into one's own by doubling oneself, to become oneself by standing to oneself as one stands to the other: "Le discours du héros cornélien ne retient pas seulement la formule *être soi* mais la formule auto-reflexive *être à soi*: revendication décisive de l'autonomie du sujet."[43] Corneille's idiom sets the stage for a discourse dealing with the interaction of self and other, and the formative properties of the reflexive relationship between the two entities.

There is ample precedent for the theme of social doubling in Corneille: not only are doubles and foils part and parcel of theatrical discourse but the topos infiltrates the discourse of Corneille's moralist predecessors as well. The Ciceronian topos of the friend as a second self ("Est enim quis est tanquam alter idem"), propagated through its Horatian and Montaignean variants, is de-metaphorised in Corneille's theatre to produce what has been aptly called a "dramaturgie du couple."[44] Corneille's accomplishment, however, is to give this second self, this double, the upper hand. In Corneille's theatre every character is determined by his or her double as well as the role that he or she plays.

The forms most frequently adopted by Corneille's doubles are those of the rival, the sibling and the lover. A given character may act in more than one of these capacities (usually the last two) before an other character. Nothing is single in Corneille's theatre; all of his protagonists are doubled by their siblings or their lovers. It is not insignificant that when Corneille

---

[42] See Alain Viala's *Naissance de l'écrivain. Sociologie de la littérature à l'âge classique* (Paris: Editions de Minuit, 1985), 217-238, for an account of Corneille's trend-setting tendencies and his boldness vis-à-vis the traditional channels of recognition at that point in time.

[43] Ann Ubersfeld "*Je suis* ou l'identité héroïque chez Corneille", 646.

[44] Fumaroli, *Héros*, 77. On the issue of the twinned self, Fumaroli quotes Jacques d'Autun's *La Conduite des illustres*, a text not without relevance here: "Je ne suis que la moitié de moy-mesme et mon amy en fait l'autre, s'il se veut trouver, il doit chercher dans moy mesme, et moy dans luy, lorsque la belle vie dans laquelle je vis s'achèvera, la moitié de moy mesme mourra avecque luy, et la moitié de luy mesme vivra dans ma personne." (*Héros*, 192)

decided to write *Oedipus Rex*, his changes moved in this very direction. Corneille's Oedipus has a sister, Dircé. Furthermore, the plot introduces Thésée as Dircé's lover. When the oracle is consulted, the fault for the plague assigned and the sacrifice of Dircé's brother announced, it is Thésée who steps forwards and tries to pose as the guilty party; "Je suis le frère, ou l'amant de Dircé." (*Oedipe*, 1487) Once Dircé finds out that Oedipus himself is her brother (rather than a mere political rival), her vitriolic speech is attenuated considerably; "Je n'ai point été jusques à vous haïr." (1800) The rival suitors that populate the early plays (Eraste and Tircis, Caliste and Dorise) constitute one another in a paroxysm of mediated desire.[45] Alidor's project of "vivre à soi" in *La Place royale* cannot be accomplished without his mediating Cléandre's desire for Angélique. Cléandre himself is doubled in the character of Phylis's brother Doraste. Horace takes up arms against a brother-in-law whom he considers a second self ("un autre soi-même.") The eponymous tragedy sees him turning every interlocutor into a double to be outdone, with Camille postulated as the test-case on which the ethical foundations of this procedure are shattered. *Rodogune* presents us with two close brothers, Antiochus and Séléucus, torn by their love for Rodogune and their filial love for Cléopâtre ("Nous n'avons eu qu'un seul sentiment" (117)), who, in their turn stand as rival manipulators of the men who would be king. Even though Corneille does not tell us that they are twins, the plot

---

[45] This phenomenon of doubling and formative mirroring stands in an isomorphic relationship with the notion of mediated desire as formulated by Réné Girard in *Mensonge romantique et vérité romanesque* (Paris: Grasset, 1961), *La Violence et le sacré* (Paris: Grasset, 1972) and *A Theater of Envy: William Shakespeare* (Oxford: Oxford University Press, 1991) where the link between mediated desire and role-playing is summarised thus:

> According to Aristotle, human beings love the theater because they love imitation. To act in a play seems more desirable than merely to attend one; it demands a more active involvement with mimesis... Why should imperson-ation be pleasurable? Aristotle never answers the question, but Shakespeare does: it is really a desire for the model's being. Acting owes its uncanny and ambivalent prestige to the mimetic *translations* that it mimics... The desire for *mimesis* has the same ontological goal as the mimetic desire of the lovers [in *A Midsummer Night's Dream*.]... Eros loves to display itself in front of as many admiring spectators as possible; it loves to be seen; it always gen-erates a *play within the play*. (59)

My use of the mechanism of doubling departs from Girard's insofar as desire becomes one among many manifestations of the mechanism of formative doubling, thus giving the ontological component of the process the upper hand.

implies it. Rodogune only barely makes the distinction between them: "Je voudrais être à lui si je n'aimais son frère." (368)[46]

The use of foils and doubles is more than a mere thematic or stylistic specialty of Corneille's. The formative power of these structures derives from the extent to which they teach the protagonists something about their formation qua subjects. Subjectivity or mastery are phases that are only attained once the mirror image has been reckoned with, once a given character is shaken out of his idiotic stupor and learns to see himself in the other. Octave's lost soul, which starts *Cinna* off in a state of desperate introspection, only attains its mastery of the universe through its realisation of Cinna as a mirror-image. It is only once Octave swaps places with Cinna and cedes his authority to him ("Fais ton arrêt toi-même, et choisis tes supplices" (1561)), once he sees himself reflected in his putative enemy's person that his new identity, Auguste, is formed. The rivalry that erupts between Rodrigue and Chimène only adds to their desire because it turns them into mirror images of one another:

> Tu n'as fait le devoir que d'un homme de bien,
> Mais aussi ce faisant tu m'as appris le mien. (911-912)[47]

Even Cléopâtre's death at the end of *Rodogune* attests to Antiochus' standing as an other through which she may, one day, live again: "Puisse naître de vous un fils qui me ressemble." (1825) In Corneille's theatre, the self can only be formed through its double.

The figure of the double is frequently developed in corporeal terms. The image-complex that equates Horace with "le bras de Rome" also serves to set up the synecdoches through which the various social orders are represented ("tous les gens de bien vous parlent par ma voix." (*Horace* 1482)) In *Cinna* the body of the subject under construction is identified with the body-politic as a whole. When Auguste speaks of "cet illustre rang,/ Qui

---

[46] The issue of doubling is exacerbated to an even greater extent in *Héraclius*, where the characters only become intelligible by virtue of their doubles and blindness to themselves. Indeed, from certain angles, *Héraclius*' complex format could be used to argue for its primacy as epitomising this very important aspect of Corneille's idiolect. For a discussion of Corneille's transformation of the tragedy of identity into a tragedy of aporia in *Héraclius*, *Dom Sanche d'Aragon* and *Oedipe* see Georges Forestier's *Esthétique de l'identité dans le théâtre français (1550-1680)* as well as John Lyons's *A Theatre of Disguise: Studies in French Baroque Drama (1630-1660)* (Columbia, S.C.: French Literature Publications Company, 1978).

[47] Cf. Doubrovsky's comment on this situation: "Alors commence le cauchemar du mâle: ce qu'Alidor découvre en Angélique, Rodrigue en Chimène, c'est moins l'*objet* que le *reflet* de leur désir," in *Autobiographiques. De Corneille à Sartre* (Paris: PUF, 1989), 34.

m'a jadis coûté tant de peine et de sang" (360-61) he is referring to the rank's having cost him so much of himself qua emperor. The use of blood as an irrefutable marker of identity also comes to the fore in plays centred on the question of disguise, such as *Héraclius* and *Don Sanche d'Aragon*, where Dona Léonor reminds us that,

> Le vrai sang des rois, sous le sort abbatu,
> Peut cacher sa naissance et non pas sa vertu. (1315-1316)

Much of *Horace*'s imagery deals with the flow of blood and tears as representations of those who shed them. *Horace* also provides a re-translation of the fissures that divide the Cornelian character internally onto the body politic: the central character of the play is civil war, Alba is Rome's other, and just as Cornelian characters cannot be singular entities, Cornelian landscapes must "twin" internally. As Corneille's career advances, this figure is projected onto the private space of the private body once again, culminating in *Polyeucte*, where the protagonist's dismemberment and martyrdom mirrors the idols and figurines whose statues he destroys.[48]

As the relationship of mirroring develops among Corneille's lovers, they also embark upon a relationship of the author-actor type mentioned above. In order to avenge her father's death, Chimène consistently tries to push Rodrigue into the other side of the vendetta, thus keeping the cycle of revenge alive. It is not for nothing that she repeats the phrase "mon père est mort" some seven times in the course of the play: the reminder helps to maintain the vindictive structure that binds her and Rodrigue to each other. If Cinna is to earn Emilie's love, he must accomplish what she cannot; "Je lui prescris la loi que mon devoir m'impose." (57)

At a certain point in time, the evolution of this mechanism brings with it an interesting twist, whereby a given identity will be reflected not so much in another subjectivity as in another situation, another scene. Alidor's project in *La Place royale* is to see his life unfold before him through the person of Cléandre, as it were:

> Je vais faire un ami possesseur de mon bien:
> Aussi dans son bonheur je rencontre le mien.
> C'est moins pour l'obliger que pour me satisfaire. (895-897)

In this respect his position combines those of Alcandre, Clindor and Pridamant of *L'Illusion comique*: he is both the author and spectator of the play that he is arranging and, through his identification with Cléandre, be-

---

[48] For an insightful reading of the helical forms that dominate *Polyeucte*, see Jean Rousset's *Forme et signification. Essais sur les structures littéraires de Corneille à Claudel* (Paris: Corti, 1962), 7-16.

comes an actor therein.[49] It is in this combination of the authorial preoccupation and the reflexive tendency that we come closest to the inscription of the playwright's situation in his own work.

## Le Cid:

The furious self-designation widespread in *Le Cid*,[50] the self-promotion and calls for blood, are all the product of Corneille's meditation on the distance, if any, between virtual self and real mask, between the hero's will and the manipulator's dramaturgy. As a theme revenge is eminently suited to Corneille's histrionics: no other social phenomenon involves such extensively formative doubling and role-playing. The shift in 1637 from a primarily comic to a darker timbre is paralleled by a sense of the inevitability of the role to which one is assigned: warriors are doomed to be warriors, emperors are doomed to be emperors and so on. In this context, much is made of the subject's wrestling with and within the confines imposed by birth and station in life. As we move from *L'Illusion comique* to *Le Cid*, Corneille continues all of the comedy's preoccupations with the playwright's "magic." In the world of historical tragedy, however, where magic is unlikely, what was once part of the plot is absorbed into the rhetoric of characterisation, whence Chimène's description of Le Cid as "l'auteur de mes malheurs." The accompanying focus on authority and authorship also affects the way in which the manipulative aspect of theatricality is thought through: in the virtual space of the stage, those by whose authority one acts and in whose name one speaks are contentions that turn friends into foes and bring civil wars into familial *foyers*.

Rodrigue's identity is the primary focus of the play. We are shown the making of Le Cid, in much the same way that *L'Illusion* shows us the making of Clindor. The most obvious difference between the two plays is in the duration of this process: Don Rodrigue becomes Le Cid in one day (more or less) whereas Clindor becomes Clindor after years of trials and

---

[49] Alidor thus joins the Erasmian tradition whereby the human condition is cured by the spectacle of its own alienation, and posits his own superiority as a master of the spectacle, *magister ludi*. Cf. Fumaroli's "Microcosme comique et macrocosme solaire," 95-102.

[50] In his *Descartes par lui-même* (Paris: Seuil, 1956) Silvestre de Sacy sums up this attitude thus:

> Si loin qu'il me mène et quoiqu'il doive m'en coûter, je sais trop bien pour me laisser abuser, ce que je dois à moi-même. Le *moi!* de Don Juan, le *moi!* de Medée, le *moi!* du Cid, le *moi!* de Port-Royal, le *moi!* de tous les prétendus étourdis de la Fronde, le *moi!* du siècle de Louis XIII. (17)

tribulations. In doing so, however, Don Rodrigue must pass through the many tests that make him the worthy possessor of that title. This affirmation is not as banal as it sounds: the tragedies of this period have far more to do with self-possession, with partaking of oneself as the immediate result of coinciding with the mask that one wears, than with tragic flaws pure and simple.

That *Le Cid* is a play about coming into oneself, a drama of self-possession and metempsychosis, is apparent at the outset. The earliest indication is the Infanta's choice of words in presenting her problem:

> Quand je vis que mon coeur ne se pouvait défendre,
> Moi-même je donnai ce que je n'osai prendre,
> Je mis, au lieu de moi, Chimène en ses liens,
> Et j'allumai leurs feux pour éteindre les miens. (100-104)

Now, it could be argued that the Infanta is speaking from a politically absolutist perspective, whereby she would own both Chimène and Rodrigue and giving one to the other would be her privilege and hers alone. When these lines are read alone, however, a different reading imposes itself; namely that the Infanta laments her lack of self-possession. If this second interpretation is accepted, the implication then becomes one of a self thrown into another, so that Chimène becomes a surrogate self for the Infanta, a puppet or representation through which she could become herself. The Infanta, qua royal personnage, is engaged in a quest for authority/authorship in the sense of wanting to construct a virtual space in which she would see herself mirrored and through which her identity would be confirmed. Her primary opponent in this endeavour will be Chimène, herself an "author" in the making, and one whose vindictive urge is merely a stepping-stone towards the construction of a world in which desire will live on in the distance that divides her from Don Rodrigue (especially if he were to die).[51] Thus the Infanta is herself part of the economy of selves under construction, participating therein in the same mode as that of Alidor and Alcandre, as an author mediated by a character.[52]

Rodrigue's identity is presented first and foremost as a double of the

---

[51] This rivalry also inaugurates another structure of conflict and doubling whereby two female protagonists hold the skipping-rope of tragedy between them, as witness Camille and Sabine in *Horace*, Emilie and Livie in *Cinna* etc. Cf. Georges Couton, *La Vieillesse de Corneille*, (Paris: Deshayes, 1949), 249-260.

[52] In this respect she inaugurates the tradition of Corneille's powerfully powerless queens who inhabit Corneille's theatre from *Rodogune* on. Cf. Anne Ubersfeld's "Corneille: Du roi au tyran, un itineraire" in *Actes de Wake Forest*, (Paris: PFSCL, "Biblio 17", 1987), 11-41.

man he kills, Don Gomès.[53] Seen as a revenge tragedy, *Le Cid* could very well pass for the tale of the return of the Count as he once was: young, feisty and capable. The first glimpse that we catch of this process is the one that shows him telling Rodrigue that, "Vous êtes aujourd'hui ce qu'autrefois je fus" (212) thus mapping the similarity between himself and Don Diègue onto the younger generation and anticipating the reflexive link between Rodrigue and Chimène. Another re-incarnation of the Count occurs after his death, when he is replaced during the Moorish attack by Don Rodrigue: "Viens, suis-moi, va combattre et montrer à ton roi / Que ce qu'il perd au comte il le recouvre en toi." (1099-1100) In other words, part of Don Rodrigue's transformation into Le Cid involves his transformation into Don Gomès. Finally, the Infanta reports the change to Chimène, calling on the testimony of the king to verify her account: "Le roi même est d'accord de cette vérité,/ Que ton père en lui seul se voit ressuscité." (1179-1180) The last transformation comes when the king pronounces that the Arabs, "A ce seul nom de Cid trembleront d'effroi" (1853) which echoes Rodrigue's words to the Count just before he kills him ("Au seul bruit de ton nom pourrait trembler d'effroi." (414)) Chimène's vindictive side is thus partially understandable: calling for the execution of Don Rodrigue is in effect calling for her father's death a second time, out of motives of authority rather than parricide. The demand for the death of Le Cid is merely an attempt on her part to maintain some sort of order within her tragic world; what she wants is a factual affirmation of the fact that her father is dead ("Enfin mon père est mort") and the avoidance of incest and chaos in a world where a father's spirit comes back to haunt his daughter in the form of her lover.

This scheme of metamorphoses, whereby Don Rodrigue becomes both Le Cid and Don Gomès raises some serious questions about his identity. From the outset the definitions of what and who he is are couched in very negative terms: he is only aware of himself differentially and only refers to himself as "Tout autre que moi." This is also something he views from a genetic viewpoint, so that when his father inquires about his courage, he responds with "Tout autre que mon père,/ L'éprouverait sur l'heure." (261-262) Rodrigue is only aware of what he is not; in fact, of his not being at all. The import of this differential self-designation (which is no less frenzied than that of most Cornelian heroes for all its negativity) is its invocation of alterity. Rodrigue knows very well that titles such as Le Cid are

---

[53] Or better yet, as a double who outdoes his mirror image, eventually surpassing all of Le Comte's past accomplishments. This pattern of outdoing a mirror-image will be made explicit as Horace's strategy on the battlefield and Octave's before his would-be assassin in *Cinna*.

culled from a number of places, rather than being monolithic labels attesting to his bravery; his perspicacity on this matter sets him apart from most other protagonists. His identity is literally manipulated throughout the course of the play. With every encounter he is "played" by his opponent or interlocutor and talked into showing what he is made of. Once he has told his father what he is (not), the latter issues his mandate: "Montre-toi digne fils d'un père tel que moi," (287) thus implying that if he is to be Don Rodrigue, he must behave in a manner commensurate with his familial background. In short he must live up to his name. This name, however, like the "je" it is supposed to construct, is a shifter that depends on the definition of the other before it can itself be defined. So Rodrigue proceeds to see his "negative self" wherever he goes, as witness his retort to Don Gomès:

> Oui, tout autre que moi
> Au seul bruit de ton nom pourrait trembler d'effroi,
> Les palmes dont je vois ta tête si couverte
> Semblent porter écrit le dessein de ma perte. (411-4)

Not only does the count become a mirror whereby Don Rodrigue sees the effects of the former's name, it is also a scene that animates his death-wish. (It should also be noted that the Count co-authors the procedure whereby Don Rodrigue becomes his father's son:"le fils dégenère/ Qui survit un moment à l'honneur de son père." (441-42)) Whether or not Rodrigue does prove a worthy successor to his father's name and a worthy possessor of the title Le Cid is an issue that can only be decided with any finality by Chimène, since Rodrigue plays to her at least as much as he does to his father and the king. Rodrigue's final plea to Chimène is very revealing in this respect; he finally puts matters in her hands (and hands are very significant in Corneille's idiom) and acknowledges both her authority and his role (together with the constraints it brings) as her lover:

> Vos mains seules ont droit de vaincre un invincible;
> Prenez une vengeance à tout autre impossible...
> Et dites quelquefois, en déplorant mon sort
> S'il ne m'avait aimée, il ne serait pas mort. (1793-99)

Here again Rodrigue sees an exception, but this time it is a projection onto Chimène's. The implications are clear enough: that because of the logic of formative mirroring, only Chimène can avenge herself against him, he who avenges everyone else in the play. Coupled with this combined mental and physical reflection is the sense that they were both singled out to play these parts before one another. The emphasis here is on love rather than valour; it is now Rodrigue's love for Chimène that provides the path of least resistance both to authenticity (his being himself in the fullest possible sense) and to annihilation (the only capacity in which he conceives of himself.) The words that he enjoins Chimène to use carry two connotations: not only the cliched implication of a desire that kills, but also of a desire and death that make him what he is: "Rodrigue-who-loved-Chimène." The corollary to the epitaph by which Rodrigue would sum himself up is that if he did not love Chimène, he would not live (and therefore not *be* at all.) Thus Rodrigue's being is very much in the hands of the figures around him; what he is depends on who exactly is doubling and evaluating him. The making of a Cornelian hero is very much a function of who is pulling his or her strings at that point in time.

Time, or lack thereof, is another important factor in the transformation of Rodrigue into Le Cid. From a certain viewpoint, the plot of *Le Cid* revolves around time: the conflict between Don Diègue and Don Gomès is one of seniority against merit, Don Diègue consistently lives through his son, Chimène frames her lamentation in temporal terms ("le passé me tourmente, et je crains l'avenir"), and Don Fernand invokes the passage of time as the universal panacea ("Laisse faire le temps.") The conflict central to *Le Cid* can be regarded as one between those who would recognise the flow of time (the king) and those who would not (all those who perpetuate the vendetta.) After Rodrigue has killed Don Gomès, his father praises him in terms of the collapse of temporality and asks that the king punish him instead of his son. It bears pointing out that Rodrigue hardly gets any time off between his exploits: he is sent off to kill the count, to do battle with the enemy, to a *duel à tout venant* by Chimène and so on. Once the hero's persona has been constructed, it must be re-enacted repeatedly in order for it to stand.[54] Hence the nefarious impact of the flow of time: history is what weathers the mask of identity and negates its operation. Don Fernand only manages to introduce the flow of time once it has turned into yet another exploit wherein Le Cid's persona will manifest itself (whence the apposition of "le temps" and "ta [Rodrigue's] vaillance" in the closing line).

The aforementioned emphasis on Rodrigue as a hired arm is reflected on a rhetorical level in the alienation that separates the warrior from his arm, thus providing yet another idiom into which the play's many schemes of manipulation are translated. The synecdoche that identifies Rodrigue with his arm is operative throughout the text of *Le Cid*. What sets him

---

[54] This will eventually turn into Horace returning from the battlefield to kill his sister. Pierre Malandain sums up the situation rather nicely;

> Il n'y a d'autre lendemain à la soirée du *Cid* que le jour du combat des Horaces, au pardon de Tulle que le péril d'Auguste, au sacre d'un empereur charismatique que le baptême du prince Polyeucte. ("Corneille ou la modification", *Revue des sciences humaines* 215 (1989), 22).

apart, however, is not so much his identification with his arm as his literal dissociation therefrom: Rodrigue's tragedy is that the separation between mind and limb means that he has no control over the effects of the latter. As is the case with his person, his arm is usually in someone else's employ.[55] Rodrigue is right to ask Chimène to kill him with the tainted sword and enact the end of the vendetta by mixing her father's blood with his. If she were to kill Rodrigue, she would at least bring the sum of all force vectors back full circle, and remain in control of the one element—Rodrigue's hand—that has run amock and set off a chain of tragic circumstances:

> Et pour venger un père emprunter d'autres bras,
> Ma Chimène, crois-moi, c'est n'y répondre pas,
> Ma main seule du mien a su venger l'offense,
> Ta main seule du tien doit prendre la vengeance. (946-950)

The demand is also significant in that it transforms synecdochic alienation into metaphorical doubling; the assonance of the second couplet indicates the mirroring with Chimène that Rodrigue is trying to effect (and thus, once again, become himself by playing someone else and vice versa). Sadly enough, he will never convince her to take up arms against him. Chimène, in Corneille's pantheon of characters, belongs to the category of those who act at a distance, much to Rodrigue's chagrin:

> Votre ressentiment choisit la main d'un autre
> Je ne méritais pas de mourir de la vôtre...
> Je vais lui présenter mon estomac ouvert
> Adorant en sa main *la vôtre qui me perd.* (1503-10; emphasis mine)

The last hemistich elegantly binds Rodrigue's desire and his self-representation through his annihilation, the scene of self-loss by which he defines himself and which he would (but never will) receive at Chimène's hand.

---

[55] Furthermore, the synecdochic scheme extends to the realm of the affects. Blood and tears generally, and the Count's blood and Chimène's tears in particular are very much in question. The tragedy, from Chimène's viewpoint, is that Rodrigue's bloodletting tends in the wrong direction: he kills the Moors, rivals and so on but none of the bloodshed replaces or makes up for the count's. Chimène's identity is marked by what she has to offer her father's memory: "Pleurez, pleurez mes yeux et fondez-vous en larmes." Her tears, however, do not extract Rodrigue's blood (through the mediation of the king). The attempt to do so is significant nonetheless: in the system of exchange within which *Le Cid* unfolds, synecdoches (hands, arms, blood, tears) and, by extension, selves, are swapped for the values (glory, race, *générosité*) that constitute individual identities. Cf. Jacques Ehrmann's seminal "Structures of Exchange in *Cinna*," *Yale French Studies* 1965, 169-199.

The reasons for the impossibility of Rodrigue's wish are straightforward: Rodrigue operates in a primarily physical register, while Chimène's register is verbal. Indeed, Rodrigue is not part of the universe of letters at all, as witness the fact that he does not speak before the king (Don Diègue and Chimène plead for and against him respectively). He even loses his native name for a title taken from another (conquered) language. Only a name that his arm has earned is good enough for Rodrigue, he cannot attach himself to a word (although once a label or appellation has been established, he does, in typical Cornelian fashion, adhere to the exigencies of his office). Chimène is, in fact, destined to speak in spite of herself, if only to give voice to what Rodrigue's actions mute, thus pitting her words against his sword and the attendant encomia:

> On le vante, on le loue, et mon coeur y consent!
> Mon honneur est muet, mon devoir impuissant!
> Silence, mon amour, laisse agir ma colère. (1136-39)

Her love's silence only gives way to her anger's words rather than action. From this point on, Chimène's case against Rodrigue and its pronouncement are linked very closely; to make that case is what she has destined herself to do. Even if the king were to display some ambivalence regarding her cause, her course of action is clear: "Il peut me refuser, mais je ne puis me taire." (1205) Eventually, Chimène renders herself into words (she authors herself) through her confession of love in the penultimate scene. Finally she becomes a Cornelian heroine (surrenders her authority, in a way) by living up to the words that Rodrigue's lie has extracted from her, as the almost remorseful tone of her last lines makes obvious: "Il faut l'avouer, sire/ Je vous en ai trop dit pour m'en pouvoir dédire." (1827-28) She is, in fact, owning up to having made herself Rodrigue's lover. Now the play can end.

Of related interest are the circumstances surrounding Chimène's avowal. It is no exaggeration to say that bringing her to own up to her love for Rodrigue is rather like pulling teeth, and with good reason, since it raises the question of whether or not the principle of authority and authorship should permit her playing along with, or being played by, the inhabitants of her microcosm. Hence the tortuous path taken with a view to evoking Chimène's admission: false words and play-acting, the tools of her trade. Chimène's secret is betrayed twice, once physically and once verbally. The first instance comes in IV.v., after Rodrigue has been dubbed "le Cid" by Don Fernand. Immediately after the king tells her that Rodrigue is dead, Chimène's pallour bespeaks her hidden passion ("et d'un amour parfait/ Dans cette pâmoison, sire, admirez l'effet." (1344-45)) The second is the scene following the duel with Don Sanche, where pallour is spoken and passion avowed. The second scenario is made even more intriguing through the ruse of the blood-smeared sword which makes Chimène come very close to repeating herself. *Le Cid*, in effect, recounts the tale of the substitution of "Rodrigue" for the name of the father between lines 858 ("Quoi! Du sang de mon père encor toute trempée?") and 1706 ("Quoi! Du sang de Rodrigue encor toute trempée?"). Apart from offering a different route to a conclusion we have seen before, this ruse also underlines the heritage of *L'Illusion comique* (not to mention nearly all the drama of the period) and the framed play; for what Rodrigue's stratagem and its outcome imply is that only a twice-told lie will bring out the truth, that the contrived is more real than the natural, that persuading Chimène to take off her mask will entail her donning another. In what amounts to a pre-figuration of Freud's theories of acting out, Corneille demonstrates that a positive truth is merely the falsification of a falsity.

### Horace:

With the publication of the Roman trilogy over the three consecutive seasons following *Le Cid*, the path to the self grows simpler as that self grows more complicated. The *mises en abyme* that supported Clindor's "biography" and the production of Chimène's declaration of love become part and parcel of Corneille's idiom. Self-fashioning, on the other hand, comes to the fore as theme and motive, although it is henceforth bound inextricably with its other, namely the emotional and physical fragmentation of the self. Chimène begets a number of followers, both male and female, who are torn between the sides that call for their allegiances (husbands and fathers, defenders and aggressors, and so on).

Perhaps the most obvious, not to say heavy-handed, figure for the body divided is that of civil war. *Horace* duly examines the consequences of a body politic turned against itself in a bloody struggle. This struggle is especially important as it results in the foundation of Rome as a separate political entity.[56] From the outset the predominant image is that of the circulation of selves and the corollary identification of that self with blood, so that the same (Roman) blood flows through the two camps and the similarity is mapped onto the individuals that circulate between them, the most important and problematic case being that of Camille (although both pairs of lov-

---

[56] See Jean-Marie Apostolidès's "Corneille, Tite-Live et la fondation de Rome" (*Poétique* 82 (1990) for an insightful reading of *Horace* against its historical sources (Livy, Denis of Halicarnassus) as well as Malandain, "Corneille ou la modification" on the way in which the substratum of Roman history informs the Cornelian text.

ers are caught in the tangle). Furthermore the use of marriage as an image of two social bodies in active confrontation maps onto a second level the political conflict between Rome and Alba. On this personal level, Camille's dilemma takes on a more fatalistic tone: her gift of herself to Curiace dictates that once he dies she—"la moitié de sa vie"—has to die as well.

Horace is the conformist, the automaton, the arm of the state. As an exemplar of the histrionic sensibility that motivates Corneille's characters, his case is striking. Once he has been chosen by Rome to be its representative warrior, Horace scripts the part that he intends to play:

> Mais vouloir au public immoler ce qu'on aime,
> S'attacher au combat contre un autre soi-même,
> Attaquer un parti qui prend pour défenseur
> Le frère d'une femme et l'Amant d'une soeur...
> Une telle vertu n'appartenait qu'à nous. (442-9)

The "nous" of the final verse refers, of course, to Rome's warrior class, men (presumably) virtous enough to put public before private interest. It bears pointing out, however, that this class does not exist at the beginning of the play, for the text of *Horace* narrates the creation of the Roman state—a state comprising king, aristocracy and commoners—in the aftermath of the civil war with Alba. In other words, the referent of Horace's "nous", namely his individual and social identity, will depend in no small part on his living up to the principles outlined above. Far from being a mere stylistic feature of the text, Horace's playing his part is literally a matter of life and death, all the more so in view of the surrounding political situation.

And so he does. He engages all of his "autre soi-mêmes" in mortal combat. These other selves come in two flavours: first, there are the warriors who are his equals or rivals, such as Curiace. Then there is Camille, whose murder after the war makes this play a tragedy. Horace, it will be remembered, does not kill his sister without provocation: the tears she sheds for Curiace (who, by virtue of his death, has become the enemy) are read by her brother as an act of treason. In itself, this is nowhere near as interesting as the fact that just before he kills his sister, he describes the murder as being reasonable; "C'est trop, ma patience à la raison fait place," (1319) he says. The reader may well wonder what sort of reason it is that allows a brother to kill his own sister. The answer lies in the logic that dictates Horace's behaviour: Horace is an actor, and as such would play the part of "le bras de Rome" on any stage that offers itself, including that of his own home. His killing Camille from this standpoint is perfectly "raisonnable": it is quite consistent with the identity that he forges for himself so theatrically.

Nor is killing the only theatrical act in *Horace*. The verse that Voltaire singled out as being incomparable, Horace Sr's "Qu'il mourût" (1021), hints at the fact that dying is the theatrical act par excellence. The verse, it will be remembered, is a retort to Julie's rhetorical question, "Que vouliez-vous qu'il fît contre trois?", referring to the fact that Horace ran after his two brothers were killed. Horace Sr's response pits "mourir" against "faire" and gives the act of dying an active sense that lends itself to theatrical display. The old man is not mocked. Death in Horace's idiom is a vector quantity, a performative utterance with a strong perlocutionary component, and Horace's deathwish proves quite clearly that he would only die for someone or something, that death per se to him is somehow inconceivable. It is a point made repeatedly in *Horace*, a play where no-one kills but everyone is sacrificed to the shades of the departed, and where the verb "tuer" is replaced by "s'immôler à." Horace invokes this principle just before he kills Curiace ("J'en viens d'immôler deux aux mânes de mes frères/ Rome aura le dernier de mes trois adversaires/ C'est à ses intérêts que je vais l'immôler"(1131-33)) and at the end of his defence ("Je m'immôle à ma gloire et non pas à ma soeur."(1594)) It is typical of him that both sacrifices are self-directed since they are both made to honour that which he will represent: Rome and his glory respectively.

Horace's self is, therefore, very much a function of his seeing and his being seen. It is only his assumption of the role that Rome imposes on him as its representative that allows his identity, his "je", to come about. The fact that he has nothing to oppose to Rome's demands ("J'accepte aveuglement cette gloire avec joie" (492)) implies that he is more of an actor than anything else; his sincerity, by modern standards, is very much open to question. In the context of the play, Corneille's intentions are quite clear: the shortest path to self-hood is also the most tortuous, the sincerest warriors are the ones with no self to put into their work. It is no exaggeration to say that Horace is nothing without a role and mirror-image to which he can refer.

As such the symmetries that divide the text of the play—between Horace and Curiace, Rome and Alba, self and other—are especially significant. From the moment that he is chosen, Horace decides that he will see nothing but mirror-images and other selves, as when he tells Curiace, "Albe vous a nommé, je ne vous connais plus." (502) Indeed, he sees the impending military confrontation and his subsequent glory as a re-naming, a doubling and simultaneous re-fashioning of the self: "Et peu d'hommes l'ont [la vertu] au coeur assez imprimée/ Pour oser aspirer à tant de renommée." (451-2) Curiace, for his part, has enough of an identity to resist these political histrionics, "Mais je vous connais encore, et c'est ce qui me tue;/ Mais cette âpre vertu ne m'était pas connue." (503-4) As the object of Horace's projecting, Curiace represents the other end of this particular ethical spectrum. Rather than see a reflection of himself on the other side of the battlefield, he sees nothing; he cannot even recognise his erstwhile friend, whose burst of anticipated reknown is too strong for Curiace's eyes ("l'obscurité vaut mieux que tant de renommée." (460)) Indeed, Curiace's gaze, though directed outwards and struck by Horace's rhodomontade, is really kept on himself all along; if he boasts of anything it is of his self-containment and self-possession ("Je rends grâces aux Dieux de n'être pas Romain,/ Pour conserver encor quelque chose d'humain."(481-2)) He is only too well aware of the price exacted by Horace's boasting, namely that he has already given himself over to the enemy whom he now sees as another version of himself. Curiace, though, treasures his identity and sees no need for role-playing.

In principle, Horace does find mirrors wherever he goes, ones that reflect a single, stable identity. When the three Curiaces try and meet his single-handed martial self with a triplicate *vertu*, he refuses and opts for a sequence of singularities instead.

Upon his return from the battlefield Horace sees himself reflected in all the eulogies hurled at him by father and admirers alike. All, that is, except Camille. What is interesting about her response to the death of Curiace is its similarity to everyone else's; she acknowledges Horace's identity and sees the conquering hero coming. Still, the Horatian self that she reflects is very different from the martial one. Her own self-incitation to this end is also worthy of note; "Dégénerons, mon coeur, d'un si vertueux père/ Soyons indigne soeur d'un si généreux frère," (1239-40) thus implying that her change will mirror his. Rather than speak of honour, she will speak of brutality, rather than applaud, she will condemn in an extended game of *jouer pour mieux ressentir*. Camille has to become someone else to tell her brother that he has become someone else, that she, in effect, will not recognise him (in the Hegelian sense.) And so when he does arrive, she offers him a portrait in words (re)presenting in no uncertain terms that aspect of Horace's character that he himself prefers not to acknowledge. Camille offers a double unworthy of Horace's hard-won nobility. In this light the epithet, "tigre alteré de sang qui me défend des larmes," takes on new meaning; it is a last desperate cry of authenticity and self-proclamation on the part of Camille occasioned by her having come into contact with Horace. Her awareness of this change shows in her reluctant mention of Horace's exploits; "Et que, jusques au ciel élevant tes exploits/ Moi-même je le tue une seconde fois!" (1289-1290) Thus Camille both does and does not reflect Horace; she reflects him but not in the mould in which he would have himself be cast. Thus caught between herself and his, Camille epitomises the duality so symptomatic of Corneille's characters. Her blatant mixing of identities, placing them side by side as opposed to masking one

with the other, earns her the title "monstre", which epithet allows Camille
to emerge as *Horace*'s most histrionic character, the monster who shows
and parades the duality in which she is caught and that she embodies. It is
ironic that the most cornelian character of this play is not Horace but
Camille.

Coupled with the logic of similarity and mirroring that dominates the
play is a calculus of self-worth: *Horace* presents an economy of identities
in the making. *Horace*'s characters are very liquid, they see themselves in
terms of blood and tears, with the men always melting into the former and
women into the latter. The blood that flows in both camps and the selves
that straddle the division between Rome and Alba are both eventually
translated into yet another circulatory metaphor; that of value. Soon the
space of *Horace* turns into one where selves, blood and characters all prove
eminently interchangeable as part of Corneille's meditation on value. Thus
we see Horace boast of having been chosen for the task of, "s'armer pour
sa patrie/ Contre un sang qu'on voudrait racheter de sa vie" (448) and pro-
posing the terms of the barter that he attempts to negotiate in Act V (his
blood for that of the Curiaces). The opposition between blood and tears
provokes the elder Horace's misogyny. To him, the two fluids are diamet-
rically opposed, and even the sight of tears threatens to inhibit the flow of
blood; "Prêts à verser du sang," he asks, "regardez-vous des pleurs?" (681)

Part of the conflict at the heart of this play is between a vindictive
economy, where only blood can repay blood, and a world designed by
Camille where exchange rates float and both blood and tears are negotiable
currency. Upon seeing Horace and the bloodsmeared swords, she declares,
"Recevez donc mes pleurs, c'est ce que je lui [à Curiace] dois," (1257) a
gesture that raises the value of the dead Curiace too high for Horace's lik-
ing. From his perspective, enough blood has been shed up to this point to
make bargaining fair:

> Et nos deux frères morts dans le malheur des armes
> Sont trop payés de sang pour exiger des larmes. (1260-1)

The two fluids are basically inseparable: a change in one will effect a
change in the other, so that despite Horace Sr's insistence to his daughter
on the ties that bind her to her brother ("qu'en un même flanc/ Le Ciel vous
a tous deux formés d'un même sang," (1193-94)) Camille can do little
more than proclaim the sort of change that has come about. In her eyes, it is
Horace who is the traitor, and his status as such is something to be emphasised with the corporeal idiom of tears rather than blood.

Horace's awareness of his histrionic status and the real costs it entails
are foregrounded during the scene of the trial in Act V and his candid ac

knowledgement of his contingency. Here he owns up to the theatricality of his existence—he *is* only insofar as he *shows* before the king;

> Et le plus innocent devient soudain coupable
> Quand aux yeux de son prince il paraît condamnable. (1539-40)

The royal panoptic eye is the final determinant not only of character, but of guilt and innocence and ultimately, being and not being. (In his complete submission to the will of Tullus, Horace also acts out, in typical Cornelian fashion, the banner of words and principles that he unfurls in Act II.) Without a public, even Horace is nothing. Moreover, Horace and his defenders blame circumstances for making his loyalty to himself and his principles look like inconsistency, calling the murder of Camille the result of an impulsive "premier mouvement". Horace, in effect, confronts his theatricality, his being as a quality entirely dependent on situation rather than being the embodiment of the essential(ist) *vertu* of which he boasts. Moreover, he phrases this contingency in visual terms that unmistakeably recall the situation of somebody on display before a public:

> Sire, c'est rarement qu'il s'offre une matière
> A montrer d'un grand coeur la vertu toute entière.
> Suivant l'occasion elle agit plus ou moins,
> Et paraît forte ou faible aux yeux de ses témoins.
> Le peuple, qui voit tout seulement par l'écorce,
> S'attache à son effet pour juger de sa force. (1555-1560)

Not uncharacteristically, Horace imputes to the audience the root causes of the changes that marked him. Even during his confession, his verbal self-portrait turns into a portrait of the audience, his collective self-projection.

If Horace's trial proves problematic, it is due in no small part to the fact that the audience lives up to its status as a mirror of Horace. Every speaker, including the king, repeats the litany that Horace is the founder of Rome and as such is above the law. In other words, everyone is taken in by his performance; the *éclat* of his performance is convincing enough to bring a royal pardon for the murder of Camille, as witness king Tulle:

> Sans lui j'obéirais où je donne la loi
> Et je serais sujet où je suis deux fois roi
> Assez de bons sujets dans toutes les provinces
> Par des voeux impuissants s'acquittent vers leurs princes.
> Tous les peuvent aimer, mais tous ne peuvent pas
> Par d'illustres efforts assurer leurs états...
> De pareils serviteurs sont les forces des Rois,
> Et de pareils aussi sont au-dessus des lois.

Qu'elles se taisent donc, que Rome dissimule
Ce que dès sa naissance elle vit en Romule
Elle peut bien souffrir en son libérateur
Ce qu'elle a bien souffert en son premier auteur. (1745-1758)

The king's pronouncement thus stands as an official royal wink—a dissimulation, a suspension of disbelief—before Horace's martial performance. The parallel drawn between Horace and Romulus, moreover, underlines the fact that all present owe something of themselves to Horace,
that they all identify with him (Sabine sums it up by saying, "Les noeuds de
l'hyménée et son amour extrême/ Font qu'il vit plus en moi qu'il ne vit en
lui-même," (1607-8)), and that, if he were to die, the Roman population
would die with him.

Horace, in other words, has succeeded in turning all of Rome into his
mirror image, and in establishing himself as its true representative to whom
even kings are grateful. He owes his success to his theatricality; to his un-
failingly consistent performance as "le bras de Rome". Despite the verbal
fireworks that argue in favour of royal absolutism in the fifth act of *Horace*, what Corneille seems to be showing, almost despite himself, is the
other side of the coin: the fact that a political order founded on theatricality
can survive only at tremendous human and social cost, and that those who
do not mirror the official order have no place therein.


### Cinna:

*Horace* sets up a number of paradigms that are taken up in *Cinna*, not
least among them the formation of an identity through self-projection in a
social community. The oscillation between duality and singularity as basic
formats for the histrionic self, as well as the uneasy projection of political
paradigms onto the space of private ethics all remain unresolved by Tullus'
grand gesture at the end of the play. *Cinna* continues the trend by examining the private self's intricacies. If *Le Cid* raised the issue of mastery and
representation in familial terms, *Horace* representation in political terms,
*Cinna* deals with ethical representation and self-mastery: here self-fashioning is investigated as a function of individual will.

*Cinna* treats self-mastery in terms of the consolidation of the selves that
have been built and all that has been built around them (and it is here that
Corneille's idiom is at its most ostentatious; the language and the plot are
as "exhibitionist" as the title character and the aesthetic that informs him.)
The earning of glory, the marking-out of territory and the winning of wars
have become foregone conclusions at this point; they now stand as part of a
chaotic and bloody past that threatens the order of Augustan Rome. In

*Cinna* the confrontation of two rival entities (the two families of *Le Cid*, the two states of *Horace*) is examined in direct relation to the problematic of violence as a mode fundamental to tragedy. The sense that this is a play dealing with its own violent background looms large in *Cinna*'s background, as witness the many references to the legacy of Brutus and Cassius and the assassination of Julius Caesar. The acid test of Octave's legitimacy is whether or not he is capable of inflicting violence on himself in order to become Auguste (vis-à-vis his subjects who must remain content with their status as passive recipients of violence.) In the context of Cinna's conspiracy, the question of manipulation translates into its less subtle variant: here the author/manipulator must choose between destroying the other or destroying himself. The solution that Octave opts for in *Cinna* is to destroy that part of himself that he sees in the other; and indeed it is only once this identification comes to pass between Octave and Cinna that Octave becomes Auguste.

Most of the stylistic and thematic idiosyncrasies that marked *Horace* recur in *Cinna*; the circulating self and the possible change in identity thus entailed, the image-complex equating blood and self-worth and so on. The foremost point of comparison (as well as contrast) would seem to be the image of the body politic divided against itself. Whereas *Horace*'s conquest was external (which is part of what makes it a tragedy: the spilling over of an external onto an internal domestic struggle), the war of *Cinna* is internal and hegemonic, more concerned with the sort of *reconquista* necessary to turning Auguste into his imperial self (and the play does make much of the difficult passage he negotiates from his first name, Octave, to the second). *Cinna*'s fascinating import derives from the solitary idiocy of its characters. As Anne Ubersfeld points out, "chacun dans *Cinna* se veut autonome, coupé des autres."[57] Such are the consequences of a world in which everyone has made a name for his- or herself and where rival self-affirmations enclose and imprison their producers. Hence Auguste's "heroic" stature: he manages to deviate from the trend and see himself reflected in Cinna. In this respect *Cinna* is more of a spiritual exercise, dealing more with remaining true to oneself and the self one is making than with the spilling of blood, which is not only left offstage but left out of the plot altogether.

*Cinna* is only tragic insofar as it involves the intrusion of a tragic history and ethics into an otherwise abstract and metaphysically convoluted scenario. The war-torn path that led to the situation of *Cinna* is invoked at every moment; it is a *Trauerspiel* to the extent that much is made of the past but not much is done about it. Another point of conformity with the

---

[57] "*Je suis* ou l'identité héroïque chez Corneille", 649.

canon is provided by the almost complete absorption of plot into character: whereas being and doing were only mutually constitutive in the case of the heroes of the earlier plays, here they seem to be part of what makes everyone function. Furthermore the intersection of being and doing is a function of perspectives: Auguste is the murderer of Caius Toranius (from Emilie's standpoint), Cinna and Maxime are generals who have served their leader well (from where Auguste views the situation), Emilie the dutiful daughter who masterminds the operation and lays down the law for Cinna to follow (from Cinna's perspective). The law is the other strand that wraps itself around the history to generate the text of *Cinna*: apart from the prevalence of the word, "loi" (coupled as it is with "foi") the image of the law acts as the direct translation in *Cinna* of the words (by) which the hero lives. Together with the tragic obligations created by history, this defines the roles that everyone is supposed to play. The conflict central to Cinna—both the play and the character—is one between the authority of the past, as represented by Emilie, and the future, as represented by Auguste. Between them, Cinna is played off, swapped alternately so that his status is reduced from eager assassin to obsequious lover to pointless puppet, moved and motivated entirely by the will of others. Cinna epitomises the sad plight of the *intrigant* in the tradition of the "weary prince" so common in the tragedy of the English Renaissance and the Spanish *siglo de oro*.

The obverse of Cinna in this as well as many other respects is of course Auguste, and many of the play's turning points are set by the establishment of parallels between them. Cinna plays the Other that mediates Auguste's self-mastery; Auguste, conversely, becomes the touchstone of Cinna's character—the assassination would earn the latter Emilie's hand and the title of the liberator of Rome. Face to face they embody the two strands outlined above, the historical vis-à-vis the ethical. Cinna is the grandson of Pompey. The laws of history, at least within the bounds of the play, dictate that there be some ill will between him and the emperor. But Cinna also fashions another lineage for himself, one he invokes every time he mentions himself. He operates under the weight of Brutus and Cassius' radical stoicism and sees his task as one of reviving their liberation of Rome (with the concomitant assassination of Caesar) under a contemporary guise. In this undertaking he is aided and abetted by Emilie, who never fails to remind him of his ideological background:

> Regarde le malheur de Brute et de Cassie…
> Sont-ils morts tous entiers avec leurs grands desseins?
> Ne les compte-t-on plus pour les derniers Romains? (265-268)

Cinna, in other words, can only become himself by playing Brutus to Auguste's Caesar. And Auguste, for his part, is burdened by hiw own historical legacy: the names of Sylla and Caesar are never far from his mind whenever he evaluates his situation and himself. Their conflict over the course of the play involves their coming to terms with the roles that have been imposed upon them, and their showing off their assumption of those roles to the best of their abilities: Cinna would play the most committed republican in Rome, Auguste its most august, magnanimous ruler.

Auguste and Cinna do not emerge unscathed from their confrontation, as there is a great deal of mirroring between emperor and would-be assassin. As is the case with *Horace*, *Cinna* narrates a series of identifications, only whereas Auguste sees himself everywhere except in himself, Cinna sees himself nowhere except in himself. The plot is resolved when each one can identify himself in and with the other.

Auguste's two confrontational speeches, in II.i. and V.i. are very revealing in this respect. Auguste's overture to the issue at hand concerns what mirrors he effectively has available. First, he points out that he should, in principle, see himself reflected in his past deeds; "Cette grandeur sans borne et cet illustre rang/ Qui m'a jadis coûté tant de peine et de sang." (360-61) Having established that "sang" is a condensed version of the self, the second verse might translate as that, "which once cost me so much of myself," the self whose image in the mirror of history is not forthcoming. Second, Auguste remarks that even if such reflection were attainable, the mediation of another human being, namely a courtier (Cinna, Maxime), would still be required; "Enfin tout ce qu'adore en ma haute fortune/ D'un courtisan flatteur la présence importune" (362-63). Since neither his past deeds nor his present courtiers provide Auguste with a decent representation of himself, introversion is the next logical step: "Et comme notre esprit, jusqu'au dernier soupir,/ Toujours vers quelque objet pousse quelque désir/ Il se ramène en soi, n'ayant plus où se prendre." (366-69) It is only at this point (having found that something inside him is missing) that he turns outwards, first to history and then to his advisors, Cinna and Maxime, for a self-portrait or a definition of what he should be.

From here on and until he outdoes himself on the issue of clemency in the final act, Auguste gradually shifts away from himself and nearer Cinna. This is seen on two levels, plot and character. The effective betrayal of the imperial Auguste is mirrored by the effective betrayal of the messianic Cinna at the hand of Maxime. Furthermore, Emilie's influence is mirrored by Livie's, each urging her beloved to play his part, to be himself to the very end. Although their counsels are substantially different, what they try to effect on a formal level is a hierarchical *rapprochement* between Cinna and Auguste. Livie tells Auguste that he will only prove himself and attain Sylla's peace of mind by treating Cinna as an equal without at the same time abdicating (thus urging him to both be and not be himself, or to bridge the gap he sets up between punishment and resignation; "Donc il faut qu'il la venge, ou cesse d'être prince." (1254)) Emilie, through an unwittingly analogous gesture does her best to induce a situation wherein Cinna would negotiate the being and not being himself, by urging him to assassinate Auguste and replace him qua vindicator of Pompeii rather than a latter-day Brutus.

Cinna himself sees the process through the same quasi-hallucinatory procedure by which Camille saw herself in a world of Curiaces. He dwells incessantly on the scenario in preparation, but rather than see himself becoming himself through his planned assassination, he sees his other self, Auguste, at the moment that defines *him* (Auguste playing the magnanimous ruler over and over):

Il me semble surtout incessament le voir
Déposer en nos mains son absolu pouvoir,
Ecouter nos avis, m'applaudir et me dire:
Cinna, par vos conseils je retiendrai l'empire,
Mais je le retiendrai pour vous en faire part. (807-11)

Moreover, when he does embark upon his assigned endeavour, his identification with his putative victim is all too clear, as witness his parting words to Emilie:

Et ma main, aussitôt contre mon sein tournée
Aux mânes d'un tel prince immolant votre amant
A mon crime forcé joindra mon châtiment,
Et pour cette action dans l'autre confondue,
Recouvrera ma gloire aussitôt que perdue. (1062-1066)

This passage leaves us in no doubt regarding the simultaneity of the killings: by the end of the third act, Cinna is convinced that killing Auguste would be tantamount to (literal and figurative, metaphysical and political) suicide.

The famous confrontation with which the final act opens brings the mirror-effect around full circle: Auguste effects the final mutation by playing Octave to death and by mirroring Cinna. In his soliloquy of IV.ii. he calls himself Octave and accounts for his Octavian self to himself, clearly perceiving himself in his war crimes. Having accomplished this task, self-appropriation is not too difficult;

Remets dans ton esprit, après tant de courages,
De tes proscriptions [i.e. de toi-même] les sanglantes images. (1137-8)

And once the rather unattractive version of the self represented by these proscriptions (violent, conspiratorial, criminal, Cinna-esque) has been interiorised and acknowledged as such, the representation of the part that is missing is all that is needed to complete the process of the forging of a new entity; "Fais un tourment pour lui de son propre trépas,/ En faisant qu'il [Cinna] le voie et n'en jouisse pas." (1183-84) Octave will literally project (and therefore eject) that part of himself that is Cinna, thus becoming Auguste the emperor. Hence the change in the pronoun that dominates this soliloquy from "toi" to "nous", as in "Jouissons plutôt nous-mêmes de sa peine." (1185)

So when the two antagonists do meet, Auguste offers Cinna what Cinna had failed to offer Auguste in act II: a portrait and an interpretation, both historical ("Tu fus mon ennemi avant même que de naître" (1441)) and ethical, prescribing the same aims as the ones he himself had taken in the previous act, self-knowledge through self-representation; "Apprends à te connaître, et descends en toi-même." (1517) Just in case Cinna should fail at this undertaking, Auguste reminds him that he is, all told, little more than a mask or a figure for imperial power, "C'est elle qu'on adore, et non pas ta personne." (1529) Finally, he dares Cinna, if he were to carry out his intended assassination, to oppose himself to the patricians of Rome, who literally coincide with their self-representation (their mask) and therefore do not face the same disadvantage as Cinna (or Auguste for that matter); "tant d'autres enfin de qui les grands courages/ Des héros de leur sang sont les vives images?" (1537-38) To top it all off, he swaps places with Cinna, granting the latter his authority just to show him what it would be like: "Fais ton arrêt toi-même, et choisis tes supplices." (1561)

Once Auguste's self-portrait has been completed through his sketch of the other, and a measure of self-mastery thus attained, there is little left for him to do other than repeat the process with all that he sees around him, and extend his (now whole, now complete) identity to include all of creation. Exemplarity and universality lie on the other side of the chiasmus that circumscribes him and Cinna, who retorts after his inquisition that, "Vous devez un exemple à la posterité" (1555) thus hinting that he himself or his annihilation should serve as an example and function in the same way as the images of Sylla and Caesar in Auguste's mind. To this Auguste can only respond with, "Tu me braves, Cinna," (1557) that his now expanded self-image will not allow of any reflection or doubling on such a minor level as Cinna's. Auguste's universality and its recognition as such is announced by Livie; "la clémence est la plus belle marque/ Qui fasse à l'univers connaître un vrai monarque" (1265-66) which is tantamount to saying, "qui fasse à lui-même connaître un vrai monarque." Moreover, Octave's clemency is worthy of note as a gesture that Cinna, the double, cannot counter, since clemency and mercy were the privileges of kings alone. In doubling Cinna, Octave turns the ordinarily bi-directional flow of

doubling into a vector pointing away from the one true monarch and towards his subjects, thus anticipating the optics of the court of the sun
king.[58]

Ultimately, everyone in the play finds a mirror. Especially significant
here is the indictment of Maxime, who emerges as the optical scapegoat
and thus the reverse image of Auguste. The fallen general mirrors everyone
through his betrayal; "Il nous a trahis tous, mais ce qu'il a commis/ Vous
conserve innocents et me rend mes amis," (1735-36) thus uniting, by his
marginality, Cinna, Auguste and Emilie. Once Auguste pardons Cinna, thus
proving that he can out-perform his rival, he proceeds to project his imperial image not only on those he rules, but through all of history:

> Je suis maître de moi comme de l'univers,
> Je le suis, je veux l'être. O siècles, ô mémoire
> Conservez à jamais ma dernière victoire! (1696-98)

Things have now reached a point where all doubling and mirroring are
out of the question due to the infinity of the man's self-conception; "O
vertu *sans exemple*." (1731) Indeed, if Auguste is accessible at all to human
perception, it is only by way of a *via negativa*, through what he is not. He
has effectively become a God; ineffable, irrepresentable, made available
only through his reverse mirrorings:

> "O clémence qui rend
> Votre pouvoir plus juste et mon crime plus grand." (1731-2)

Auguste's deliberate assumption of his role ("Je le suis, je veux l'être")
stands in stark contrast to the waverings of Cinna and Maxime over his assassination. Furthermore, his pardon is pronounced with such *éclat* as to
mark a very important point: Cinna's trial is a show trial, designed to display the emperor's moral victory over his enemies, past, present and future.
Auguste's clemency is theatrically enacted with a view to confirming the
emperor's identity as Augustus Caesar, a man who forgives his enemies
and guides the state with a steady hand (rather than the bloodthirsty warrior, Octave, who came to the throne after a bloody coup d'état). In the
contest over which Roman has the most *vertu*, Auguste's tactic proves that
the gentler gamester is the soonest winner, that the path of political efficacy
leads through theatre, that any gesture that does not lend itself to spectacular theatrical display is meaningless.

Thus *Cinna* develops the implications of *Horace* and *Le Cid* in an inter-

---

[58] One of the more interesting consequences of Corneille's use and illustration of
clemency as a theme is Racine's *Britannicus*, which can be read as a counter to *Cinna*.
Cf. Alain Viala, *Racine. La Stratégie du caméléon*, 130-135.

esting fashion. Whereas the royal identities of Don Fernand and Tulle were confirmed by their chosen warriors (Rodrigue and Horace respectively), Auguste's is confirmed ironically, by the hand of a warrior turned assassin. Nevertheless, as the scene of Auguste's pardon shows, the identification between king and warrior stands firm. The politics of masking and mirroring as developed by *Cinna* also underline the fact that the ruler's identity can only be created as a result of his forgiving his subjects and taking on the full cost of absolutism in human terms.[59] Once again, though, Corneille shows us the other side of the coin: the royal pardon becomes a favour through which the king is assured of his subjects' support in any circumstance, thus effectively wiping out the possibility of opposition or impartial justice. This was, in fact, the tactic that Louis XIV employed to consolidate his power after the Fronde. It is to Corneille's credit that he thought out the full implications—political and social as well as literary—of an order founded on theatricality decades before the Sun King's installation at Versailles.

### Postscript: The Author and His Doubles:

All of the internal playwrights in *Le Cid* and elsewhere (the king, Chimène, the Infanta, Alidor, Alcandre) reflect the situation of Corneille, the bold writer that lives through his creations rather than taking his cue from the powers that be. Granted, he does take stock of his situation in his dedications (the one for *Horace* starts, "C'est de votre éminence [Richelieu] que je tiens tout ce que je suis") but his gratitude to his patrons does not significantly alter the direction of the lines of force running through his work, as witness the *Excuse à Ariste* and his refusal to eulogise Louis XIII.

Equally significant is Corneille's attitude towards the nobility. The connotations of the pastoral coating that covers *Mélite*, *La Suivante* and *La Place royale* and the aristocratic status of their characters is fairly obvious: these are the trappings of the *beau monde* to which Corneille aspires.[60] Its enclosure within a contained stage bears out his standing as an outsider looking in, acting out the phantasm of (social, textual) authority in this social echelon. Even more important is his self-sufficiency: the only other to which he seeks recourse in this operation is himself. There is an important isomorphic relationship between his situation and that of his protagonists, especially of those plays that investigate the issue of royalty: Oedipe and

---

[59] Cf. Apostolidès, *Le Prince sacrifié*, 14-26.

[60] Cf Fumaroli, *Héros*, 36-61 for a development of the pastoral underpinnings of Corneille's protagonists.

Don Sanche d'Aragon are kings more out of merit than birth alone. When Oedipe turns to his counselor, Iphicrate, for a definition of his identity, the response is quite simply, "Un enfant exposé dont le mérite éclate." (1705) Similarly, Don Sanche's situation is summed up by Carlos as someone who "Quoique fils d'un pêcheur, a passé pour un prince." (1700) Corneille's self-fashioning "par la bouche d'autrui" and his ennoblement,[61] gained entirely though his writing, attest to the parallels between the textual current running through Corneille's real life and the social current running through his texts. Indeed, Corneille was exceptional in devoting himself entirely to writing plays, as well as his assiduous insistence on equating dramatic production with heroic exploits in the service of the king.[62] His poem *Au roi, sur Cinna, Pompée, Horace, Sertorius, Oedipe, Rodogune qu'il a fait représenter de suite devant lui à Versailles, en octobre 1676* bears this out explicitly. Corneille puts on equal footing his dramatic output and his childrens' military service:

> Compte mes bons désirs comme autant de services.
> Je sers depuis douze ans, mais c'est par d'autres bras
> Que je verse pour toi du sang dans nos combats:
> J'en pleure encore un fils, et tremblerai pour l'autre
> Tant que Mars troublera ton repos et le nôtre. (3:1313-14)

Like Rodrigue and Horace, Corneille identifies himself, his "service" and that of his two sons (his second selves) with his arm. By bridging the gap between the empirical and the textual, Corneille succeeds in establishing a firm foothold in both worlds and re-casting himself qua noble playwright. By acting out the paradigms of his own work—de-metaphorising the figurative link between rank and role and assimilating the "bovaryste" tendency of his characters—he adds a set of quotation marks to his name. The upstart lawyer from Rouen and the nobleman in the new Republic of (French) Letters are synthesised in the verbal mask "Corneille."

Thus Corneille founds an institution whose legacy would extend far beyond his time, namely the construction of a self through writing and the preoccupation with the theatre as a locus that lends itself to that sort of writing. The literary and social framework that he constructs defines the rules of literary strategy for writers of several generations after his own. In the immediate context of the seventeenth century, however, there is a bi-

---

[61] It is not insignificant that it was Corneille *père* who received the title, thus re-creating Pierre Corneille at the age of thirty-two as someone who would never have occupied a common rank.

[62] For more on Corneille's attitude vis-à-vis the literary establishment and his readers, see Alain Viala's very informative essay, "Corneille et les institutions littéraires de son temps" in *Pierre Corneille. Actes du colloque tenu à Rouen.*

furcation of the paradigm leading to two parallel, independent tracks, each of which is treated in one of the following chapters. The first deals with Thomas Corneille's *romanesque* theatre as a response and reaction to Corneille's histrionics, using pastoral devices to call the model's viability into question. The second covers Molière's social citicism as a way of uncovering the antinomies of a theatrically-generated world. Both lead to the eighteenth centuries assimilation and modification of this profoundly influential issue.

# Chapter Two

# Molière: Imagination and Its Discontents, or, When Is a Self Not a Self?

No sooner has Corneille established a systematic version of the histrionic foundations of identity than Molière reacts with his own, anti-histrionic brand of theatre, calling all of his predecessor's grandiose claims into question. The equivalence that Corneille proposes between mask and self was not lost on Molière, who was an experienced actor. Molière's choice of profession may account for his decidedly sceptical temperament: unlike Corneille, for whom the fusion of self and mask was a consummation deterred by a speech impediment, Molière was well aware of what it means to lose oneself in a role and of the consequences of such a loss.

As against the theatrical worlds of Corneille, where much depends on a tragic consistency of character and on living up to a name that one has made for oneself, Molière's is a world where consistency is staged that it might be called into question: names and identities prove slippery and the excesses of reason and ritual create a universe brought to the brink of folly. Corneille's primary concern was with the possibility of remaining true to the "loi" or the role that regulates one's character. Molière, on the other hand, deals with the ridiculous consequences of being too true to oneself.[1] Corneille's theatre pits identities against one another as a means of examining their construction; Molière examines the consequences of such resemblances in order to call into question the possibility of distinguishing between true and false selves. Corneille's theatre presents us with scenarios that establish identities through the staging of a self and the discovery of an

---

[1] For an account of the changes in characterisation that accompany the shift from Corneille to Molière, see Karolyn Waterson's "Du héros guerrier au fourbe héroïque: La transmutation des valeurs héroïques cornéliennes dans le théâtre de Molière" in *Dix-Septième siècle* 113 (1976). In addition to studies already mentioned—notably Forestier's—my reading of Molière follows in the footsteps of Gérard Defaux's *Molière ou les metamorphoses du comique* (Lexington, KY: French Forum, 1980); J.D. Hubert, *Molière and the Comedy of Intellect* (Berkeley: U of California P, 1962); James F. Gaines, *Social Structures in Molière's Theater* (Columbus, OH: Ohio State UP, 1984); Lionel Gossman, *Men and Masks* (Baltimore: Johns Hopkins UP, 1963); Jacques Guicharnaud, *Molière. Une aventure théâtrale* (Paris: Gallimard, 1963); Robert McBride, *The Sceptical Vision of Molière* (New York: Barnes & Noble, 1977) and Marcel Gutwirth, *Molière ou l'invention comique* (Paris: Minard, 1966). Page numbers to these works will only be given in cases where I quote them directly.

other, while Molière takes such scenarios one step beyond to show how
self-fashioning can only occur by reference to that other.

The transition from one paradigm to the next comes across with particular clarity in *Tartuffe*. Tartuffe uses his performances to corroborate his image as a *dévot*, and vice versa. And so he spends a great deal of time per-
fecting this image, first at the church where he caught Orgon's eye (and
everyone else's: "Il attirait les yeux de l'assemblée entière" (285)) and then
chez Orgon. Furthermore, the many *jeux de miroirs* that allowed the identity of the Cornelian hero to be thought through and stabilised take some
disturbing turns with Molière. Orgon and Tartuffe refer to each other as
"frère" repeatedly, only to have the similarity lead to Tartuffe kicking Orgon out of the house and declaring, "C'est à vous d'en sortir, vous qui parlez en maître / La maison m'appartient, je le ferai connaître" (1557-8). The
notion of *éclat* which once acted as the criterion for the glory of the Cornelian hero leads rather less gloriously to Tartuffe's justifying his own at-
tempted exploits with Elmire: "Le mal n'est jamais que dans l'*éclat* qu'on
en fait." (my emphasis) And whereas Corneille's political drama postulates
self-sacrifice for the state as the most virtuous deed possible, Tartuffe sacrifices his adopted family to the king for personal reasons:

> Mais l'interêt du Prince est mon premier devoir;
> De ce devoir sacré la juste violence
> Etouffe dans mon cœur toute reconnaissance,
> Et je sacrifierais, à de si puissants nœuds
> Amis, femme, parents, et moi-même avec eux. (1880-5)

This is, of course, a declamation worthy of Corneille. Molière's strategy, therefore, seems to consist of putting verses of typically Cornelian
bombast in the mouths of really despicable characters.

*Tartuffe* also highlights Molière's focus on the family as a court in
miniature, as a small-scale model and nuclear matrix of the court society.
In Molière's idiom the family is examined as a hierarchy in and of itself,
with the paterfamilias sitting at its head and with the identities of its members defined by their rank therein.[2] In this respect it serves as a very useful
model for the posing and answering certain questions. What, after all, is to
be made of identity in a world where bodies are substituted for one another
with the same ease and impunity as names, as in *Amphitryon*? What is to be

---

[2] For an account of the structure and operation of the home in seventeenth-century
France, especially with regard to the near omnipotence of the father, see Mousnier, *In-
stitutions*, 1:89-95. For a treatment of the subject with specific reference to Molière, see
Apostolidès, *Prince*, 132-177 and Fumaroli, "Aveuglement et désabusement dans *Le
Malade imaginaire*" in M-T. Jones-Davies, ed., *Vérité et illusion dans le théâtre au
temps de la Renaissance* (Paris: Jean Touzot, 1983).

made of a space where Tartuffe's, "C'est à vous d'en sortir, vous qui parlez en maître" is possible? What is to become of identities articulated in a holistic manner (that is, as a function of the rank one holds in a given hierarchy)[3] if any one place is occupied by someone other than its rightful owner, and how, moreover is the validity of such ownership to be determined, given the ease with which displacements and usurpations occur?

Molière's point seems to be that if theatricality is in fact the way of the world, then the world is in a very sorry state indeed. The axiomatic status of the world as stage comes across with particular clarity in the *Lettre sur la comédie de l'imposteur* which closes on the following note:

> [N]'étant pas assez fort pour résister aux mauvais exemples du siècle, je m'acoutume insensiblement, Dieu merci, à rire de tout comme les autres, et à ne regarder toutes les choses qui se passent dans le monde que comme les diverses scènes de la grande comédie qui se joue sur la terre entre les hommes.[4]

Initially, he pokes fun at the world's theatricality, ostensibly "correcting" a given situation by ridiculing the unreasonable excesses of human behaviour; *castigat ridendo mores*. As his career progresses, however, Molière makes manifest his complicity with the histrionic universe in which he has found himself. His earlier plays cast the errors and hangups of the world's Sganarelles and Arnolphes in a truly laughable and, perforce, reprehensible light. But over the course of his subsequent plays, Molière manages to undo even this distinction between reasonable and unreasonable behaviour, showing that reason depends on its other, and that one can only be reasonable by giving unreason its due.[5] Finally, in his last comedy-ballets, Molière uses theatre to modify and treat his protagonists' theatrical idiosyncrasies. The imaginary invalid's homeopathic cure signifies Molière's coming down squarely on the side of the histrionic extravagance that was the object of his earlier vitriolic critiques.

As he works through the theatrical construction and presentation of the self, Molière foregrounds systematically the gaps separating self from other

---

[3] The term is borrowed from Louis Dumont, who defines holism (as against individualism) thus: "On désigne comme holiste une idéologie qui valorise la totalité sociale et néglige ou subordonne l'individu humain... On désigne par individualiste, par opposition au holisme, une idéologie qui valorise l'individu... et néglige ou subordonne la totalité sociale." (Dumont, *Essais sur l'individualisme* (Paris: Seuil, 1983), 263-264). Molière's plays deal with the problems incurred by individual perturbations of holistic social systems.

[4] In his *Œuvres complètes* (Paris: Gallimard, 1971), 1:1180.

[5] Cf. Fumaroli, "Microcosme comique et macrocosme solaire", 95-97.

and mask from player. This spectacle of alterity is a staple of his theatre. Rather than being presented with the opposition between the Horaces and the Curiaces, we witness the tensions that arise between real and false authority figures, be they aristocrats (*Dom Juan, Le Bourgeois gentilhomme*), gods (*Amphitryon*), fathers (*Tartuffe*), or doctors (*Le Malade imaginaire*). Nor is this all. In what follows, we shall see that the identity and operation of the real authority figure depends in no small part on the false one, or rather with falsity in general, if by falsity we mean play-acting, toying with masks, pretending to be other than what one "is". The aim of Molière's comedy seems to be to use this incorporation of alterity as the most important aspect of his characters' self-fashioning. Jupiter needs Amphitryon's identity to accomplish his erotic adventure, the king's perspicacity in *Tartuffe* is nothing without the impostor's "patriotism", Dom Juan's identity as *grand seigneur* is nothing without his rendition of himself as an anti-nobleman or *méchant homme*, and Jourdain would be remarkably uninteresting without the noble class that both includes and excludes him. Finally, at the end of his life, the pattern culminates in *Le Malade imaginaire*, a play that proves eloquently that the theatrical formation of the self depends in no small part on the incorporation of an anti-self, a specular other.

In what follows I should like to trace Molière's uses of alterity as part and parcel of the construction of the self, paying particular attention as I do so to the ways in which the identities of Molière's characters are invented and re-invented as a function of the procedures that regulate the theatrical worlds they inhabit.

## I. Amphitryon:

*Amphitryon* translates the aforementioned tension between real and false authority figures into the physical doubling between Jupiter and Amphitryon. Jupiter is tired of the social onus that his position of authority places upon him, and decides to engage in theatrical exercises in search of relief from his responsibilities.

Jupiter is and is not himself, just as he is, and is not Amphitryon. The same argument applies, mutatis mutandis, to Amphitryon. In other words, Jupiter's impersonation deprives the Theban general of his identity, which identity was itself defined as a role in a hierarchy of roles: one role displaces another. Both Jupiter and Amphitryon see themselves as actors; the only difference between them derives from Jupiter's awareness of the fact that one can play a number of parts, both military and erotic, while Amphitryon sees everything in terms of soldiering alone. Consider the pompously Cornelian tone he sounds upon returning from the battlefields:

Fasse le Ciel qu'Amphitryon vainqueur
Avec plaisir soit revu de sa femme
Et que ce jour favorable à ma flamme
Vous redonne à mes yeux avec le même cœur
Que j'y retrouve autant d'ardeur
Que vous en rapporte mon âme! (856-60)

Jupiter, on the other hand, presents an explicit case to Alcmène: before her, he wants to play the part of the lover and have his performance erotically applauded.

En moi, belle et charmante Alcmène,
Vous voyez un mari, vous voyez un amant,
Mais l'amant seul me touche, à parler franchement,
Et je sens, près de vous, que le mari le gêne.
Cet amant...
Souhaite qu'à lui seul votre cœur s'abandonne... (589-596)

The fact that rank and role are the sole determinants of identity means that identity can be ascertained by the external signs that are their correlates. When Sganarelle sides with Jupiter against Amphitryon in the third act, his reasoning is consistent with this reality. Sganarelle argues that it is Amphitryon, not Jupiter, who is the impostor because, "C'est un enchanteur qui porte un caractère/ Pour ressembler aux maîtres des maisons." (1636-7) The situation is hilarious, of course, but the spectator doesn't laugh without afterthought: the parallels between this situation and Tartuffe kicking Orgon out of house and home are obvious. Molière is quite clear on this point: predicating a social system on the theatrical representation of identity is a recipe for instability, notwithstanding the rigid hierarchies that obtained under absolutism (and the similarities between the social backdrop to *Amphitryon* and seventeenth-century France are explicit). If gods (or noblemen, or kings) establish themselves by playing their parts, then there is nothing to stop the fraying of the social fabric, starting with the "nuclear" family and the dissolution of identities both individual and communal (Sganarelle puts it best when he says to his master: "L'on me des-Sosie enfin/ Comme on vous des-Amphitryonne" (1860-1)). Molière's critique, tempered as it was by the obligatory statements at the end of the play ("Un partage avec Jupiter/ N'a rien du tout qui déshonore" (1902-3)), was not lost on the many members of the audience whose beds were shared by the king.

The question of why an absolute god would impersonate one of his subjects in order to mount such a theatrical seduction should also be addressed. As a strategy it is suspect, especially in the hands of one who wields so much power. Jupiter, I think, plays the part of Amphitryon for the same reason that the sadist identifies with the masochist: in order to ascertain the full extent of his power. Jupiter cannot "measure" his status as omnipotent god unless he steps outside himself and becomes another, seeing how this other sees himself and sees him. Of course, like Jupiter, this other—namely Amphitryon—sees himself through the eyes of those under *his* command, namely Alcmène and Sosie. Both Jupiter and Amphitryon depend on their underlings for a sense of their identity, which, like that of Pascal's found king, is the performative effect of a theatrical ritual. Jupiter and Amphitryon derive their identities from the fact they are addressed as a god and a general respectively. The text of *Amphitryon* shows how easily these identities change once the god is addressed as a (henpecked) husband and the general as an impostor. Jupiter the god can only confirm his status at the top of the hierarchy by swapping places with a mortal, by experiencing alterity, and by taking that alterity with him.

The game of impersonation and mimicry in *Amphitryon* effectively blurs the distinctions between true and false, actors and spectators, and hints at a world where all roles are equivalent. Furthermore, this world is one where power increases in direct proportion to one's ability to act and collect roles, which is what places Jupiter several notches above Amphitryon. This marks a rapprochement between Molière's thought and the rigid equivalence between self and mask that we see in Corneille's theatre. Far from looking askance at the theatrical basis of identity, Molière seems to accept it fully, asserting acting as a first step towards entry and integration in the social order. In what follows, we shall see how Argan is "socialised" by learning how to act.

## II. Le Malade imaginaire:[6]

For the maker of comedies the comédie-ballet provides a very eloquent source of metatheatrical emphasis;in the idiom of the theatre it is a translation of the act of pointing to the mask, of presenting pure theatre, pure vocality and corporeality, of re-stating the basic truism that underlies the process of creation, namely that people are mediated by theatre and theatricality. *Le Bourgeois gentilhome* stages the consequences of this mediation in

---

6 The recent explosion of studies devoted to the comedy-ballets has been useful in preparing this section, notably Claude Abraham's *On the Structure of Molière's Comédie-Ballets* (Paris: PFSCL, 1984), Charles Mazouer, *Molière et ses comédies-ballets* (Paris: Klinksieck, 1994), Stephen Fleck, *Music, Dance and Laughter: Comic Creation in Molière's Comedy-Ballets* (Paris: PFSCL, 1995) as well as the essays collected in *Littératures classiques*, 21 (1994) and Volker Kapp, ed., *Le Bourgeois gentilhomme. Problèmes de la comédie-ballet* (Paris: PFSCL, 1991).

the person of M. Jourdain, for whom being noble consists of playing at being a nobleman, in taking part in the rituals of the nobility, all with a view—he hopes—to reaching the point where the mask of the nobility stays on and permanently replaces the *bourgeois* face underneath. So taken is he with this idea—that the performance creates the rank and the identity—that he plays at belonging to any noble caste, even Turkey's. He undergoes a *cérémonie turque* and becomes a Turkish "nobleman", Mammammouchi. This ceremony starts with a review and erasure of every possible identity of Jourdain's ("Anabatista? Zuinglista? Bramina?"), before the Frenchman has his new title foisted upon and beaten into him by the "Mufti" and his entourage. Interestingly enough, Jourdain is commanded to avoid being ashamed of his new incarnation as he was of his old one ("Non tener honta/Questa star l'ultima affronta.") Jourdain's metamorphosis is complete at this point. As far as he is concerned, if the French nobility and the title M. *de* Jourdain is unattainable, a new identity as a Turkish nobleman with the (fake, nonsense) title of *Mammammouchi* will do handsomely.

M. Jourdain's case is equally interesting from another perspective. At the end of the play we are left wondering what Jourdain's status really is, if he is a true nobleman or an imaginary nobleman, whether his obsession with class and status has been cured or merely appeased. One cannot deny that the musical *intermède* and the *cérémonie turque* have taken place, and that Jourdain's status has been altered, however slightly. The problem, from his perspective, would seem to be finding someone who can validate his new status, his new identity, which only seems to exist inside him. Until he does, he will simply be regarded as a madman, someone who is alien to himself, someone who claims to be other than what he is. At the end of *Le Bourgeois gentilhomme* we are left with the spectacle of someone who both is and is not himself, someone who doubles himself in a very problematic way, with the spectacle of alterity.[7]

M. Jourdain is a self-consciously theatrical adaptation of Dom Juan. *Le Bourgeois gentilhomme* repeats the articles made in *Dom Juan* about the hollowness of the aristocracy's claims to an ethical basis for their power. It also re-iterates the very subversive arguments that noblemen are made, not born, and that they are made by participating in the theatrical practices of the court society.[8] The send-up of courtly ceremonies and rituals (by which

---

[7] Cf.Marie-Claude Canova-Green's indispensable "Le jeu des images et des rôles" in *Littératures classiques* 21 (1994): 79-90.

[8] For a reading of the extent to which the court ballet reflected and re-confirmed the world view of the court and its inhabitants, see Claudia Jeschke, "Vom *Ballet de cour*

titles and their consequences are established) in the Turkish ceremony stands as a double-edged sword, simultaneously affirming and lampooning the theatrical bases of society and the desperate need that they create for performance as a sign of social distinction.[9] The similarities between court ritual and its farcical other leave the spectator wondering not only whether Jourdain will ever be "cured", but whether he needs to be cured. The content of M. Jourdain's particular class obsession is particular to him, but it does, of course bear affinities with Arnolphe's jealousy, Harpagon's avarice, Orgon's religious devotion, and, of course, Argan's hypochondria. All of these characters have hangups and all are stuck, in one way or another, trapped in the realm of the *imaginaire*. As such their "treatment" by various theatrical endeavours operates by convincing them of the actual fusion of mask and identity, of *être* and *paraître*. As Georges Forestier puts it:

> Au cinquième acte du *Bourgeois gentilhomme*, à la dernière scène du *Malade imaginaire*, Jourdain et Argan font plus qu'être dupes des apparences agitées devant leurs yeux par les personnages intéressés (les Maîtres et les médecins, le gentilhomme intéressé et l'hypocrite Béline) ou par les auxiliaires des jeunes premiers (déguisement de Covielle, travestissement de Toinette): ils se persuadent *sur eux-mêmes* que l'acceptation du paraître vaut transformation de l'être. (*Esthétique*, 560)

Molière has his obsessions, too. Not least among them is the preoccupation with doctors and medical practice, as witness the long string of plays that foreground them thematically: *Le Médecin malgré lui*, *Le Médecin volant*, *L'Amour médecin*, *M. de Porceaugnac* and, of course, *Le Malade imaginaire*. In all of these cases, the medical profession is presented as being an eminently theatrical one. Molière's medical obsession reflects a view that doctors are authority figures and, as such, invite comparison with the other authority figures—*dévots*, *grands seigneurs*, gods and so on—dealt with in his plays. Not for nothing is the claim made in *Le Malade imaginaire* that everyone considers them gods, with the powers that surpass those of the royalty. As the *praeses* of Argan's graduation ceremony puts it,

> Totus mundus, currens ad nostros remedios
> Nos regardat sicut Deos;

---

zum *Ballet d'action*. Über den Wandel des Tanzverständnisses im ausgehenden 17. und beginnenden 18. Jahrhundert", in Kapp, ed. 188-190.

[9] Cf. Volker Kapp, "Langage verbal et langage non-verbal dans *Le Bourgeois gentilhomme*" in Kapp ed., 108-113.

Et nostros ordonnanciis
Principes et reges soumissos videtis.

Typically, Molière displays the actor underneath the doctor's mask. *Le Malade imaginaire* makes the point that to be a doctor one has merely to take on the appearance of a doctor, as witness the scene of Argan's conversion:

> **Beralde**: Mais, mon frère, il me vient une pensée: faites-vous médecin vous-même...
> **Argan**: Mais il faut savoir bien parler latin, connaître les maladies, et les remèdes qu'il y faut faire.
> **Beralde**: En recevant la robe et le bonnet de médecin, vous apprendrez tout cela, et vous serez après plus habile que vous ne voudrez.
> **Argan**: Quoi? l'on sait discourir sur les maladies quand on a cet habit-là?
> **Beralde**: Oui. L'on n'a qu'à parler avec une robe et un bonnet, tous galimatias devient savant, toute sottise devient raison. (III.xiv.)

Clothes make the man, in other words, l'habit fait le moine. Est médecin qui parle en médecin: to be a doctor one need only speak like one, and to speak like one, one need only change one's appearance to the point where one's being changes accordingly. Beralde says, in the 1675 version of *Le Malade imaginaire* that medicine is one of the things "dont l'apparence nous charme", so mastering medicine depends on mastering these charming appearances, which is, needless to say, a very theatrical enterprise.

Through the idiom of medecine, *Le Malade imaginaire* looks into the realm of the imaginary and its attendant structures. It is in these terms that Argan's "malady" is best defined. Argan suffers from extreme idiocy, in the etymological sense of the term. He is lost in himself, in his particularity. So much so that he has no self to speak of, just a body. His every act centres on his body: he communicates in strictly corporeal terms, the time he spends working out his medical bills involves a re-evaluation of his body in financial terms. His relationships are divided into those that ostensibly preserve his body (the doctors, Béline) and those that allegedly destroy it (Toinette). His relationship with his daughter needs the mediation of a son-in-law who, of course, has to be a doctor. He quarrels with Toinette because "elle a eu l'effronterie de me dire que je ne suis point malade." (I.vi.) This altercation underlines his cogito: "I have a body, therefore I am". Or more simply "I am a body". His illness is the only mirror that allows his coming into contact and gauging (literally, numerically, financially) his corporeal (and only) self.

Trapped as he is in the too, too solid flesh, Argan has no conception of the other, of alterity, of the possibility of being outside himself. No is he open to the possibility of other people differing from themselves, which explains why he is so easily duped. He is completely taken in by his doctors' performances, he is convinced that they know whereof they speak, that their *être* corresponds to their *paraître*, that they embody the knowledge with which they ostensibly cure him. The possibility that they have simply donned masks with a view to tricking him is entirely foreign to his way of thinking. All that the quack Purgon has to do to make him believe that he will fall terminally ill is to utter a series of performatives—passing through one imaginary state after another—that Argan mistakes for the real thing:

> **Purgon**: Je veux qu'avant qu'il soit quatre jours vous deveniez dans un état incurable... que vous tombiez dans la bradypépsie... De la bradypépsie dans la dyspépsie... De l'apepsie dans la lienterie... Et de l'hydropisie dans la privation de la vie...
> **Argan**: Ah, mon Dieu! je suis mort.                    (III.v-vi)

Similarly, the possibility that Béline has married him just for his money is not intuitively obvious from his perspective. Argan's idiocy, in short, marks him as a foreigner in the very theatrical universe of Molière's plays, where role-playing is the norm.

What ensues in *Le Malade imaginaire* is a series of lessons in theatricality, in alterity, undertaken with a view to introducing Argan to the reality of the histrionic universe around him and the possibility of differing from himself. All the world's a stage, and Argan's body is not necessarily at its centre. The dialogue is shot through with self-reflexive pronouncements that refer to the metacomic framework. Béralde, to cite one instance, offers the plays of Molière to his hypochondriac brother as well as the many ballets as a mirror and homeopathic drug. Angélique's suitors make their cases in and through the language of the theatre: Diafoirus the younger invokes the example of the singing statue of Memnon, an emblem of the actor as marionette, and his rival counters with an impromptu comédie-ballet as the only accurate representation of the passions that move him. Argan's investment in his corporeal self is mediated by what, in Molière's idiom, is the most ceremonious, decorous and ritualistic of all professions. At the end of the play Argan is no more cured than Monsieur Jourdain's bourgeois origins finally erased: what counts is what intervenes between the beginning and end of the play and thus between Argan's old and new selves, namely the ritual of medical (theatrical) praxis that Argan undergoes. In watching *Le Malade imaginaire* we see Argan the day he be comes someone, the day he attains the sort of mock heroic self-mastery that could on a formal level, easily rival Auguste's or Rodrigue's.

One of the more significant lessons is the one staged by Angélique's suitors, Diafoirus and Cléante. In both of their performances, theatricality abounds. Thomas Diafoirus, the ostensibly brilliant, up-and-coming doctor and Argan's candidate, is an orator, first and foremost. He pleases Argan because he speaks well rather than by the brilliance of his diagnostic insight. He has a number of prepared speeches, all of which make use of some familiar tropes and oppositions, and all of which have been rehearsed like parts. To Argan he says:

> Monsieur, je viens saluer... en vous un second père; mais un second père auquel j'ose dire que je me trouve plus redevable qu'au premier. Le premier m'a engendré; mais vous m'avez choisi... Ce que je tiens de lui est un ouvrage de son corps, mais ce que je tiens de vous est un ouvrage de votre volonté; et d'autant plus que les facultés spirituelles sont au dessus des corporelles, d'autant plus je vous dois, et d'autant plus je tiens précieuse cette future filiation. (II.v.)

In other words, his own father gave him a body, but Argan will give him a mind, a spirit, and in so doing a new identity (une nouvelle filiation). The speech he delivers to Angélique is even more telling: "Madame, ne plus ne moins que la statue de Memnon rendait un son harmonieux lorsqu'elle venait à être éclairée des rayons du soleil: tout de même me sens-je animé d'un doux transport à l'apparition du soleil de vos beautés." (II.v.) So Diafoirus presents himself, or rather re-presents himself (since he is performing) as a body (une statue) or a puppet brought to life by the spectacle of Angélique's beautés. Equally remarkable is Diafoirus's invitation to Angélique:

> **Thomas Diafoirus**: [J]e vous invite à venir voir, l'un de ces jours, pour vous divertir, la dissection d'une femme, sur quoi je dois raisonner.
> **Toinette**: Le divertissement sera agréable. Il y en a qui donnent la comédie à leurs maîtresses; mais donner une dissection est quelque chose de plus galant. (II.v.)

Toinette's sardonic rejoinder emphasises the very real continuity between medecine and theatre.

Cléante, on the other hand, improvises, on the spot, a pastoral *comédie-ballet* that stages his star-crossed affair with Angélique. "Un berger," he tells us, "était attentif aux beautés d'un spectacle qui ne faisait que commencer [i.e. love happens only at the theatre] lorsqu'il fut tiré de son attention par un bruit qu'il entendit à ses côtés. Il se retourne, et voit un brutal qui de paroles insolentes maltraitait une bergère." (II.v.) We go from there to a climax where Angélique and Cléante vow, in song, to die rather than leave each other for anyone else. Thus everything preceding this scene is re-translated into a theatrical idiom: Angélique is the bergère Philis, Cléante is the berger Tircis, Tircis's rival (the "brutal") has been chosen by Angélique's father and so on. Not only is all the world a stage, but the "facts" as it were have to be presented theatrically in order to be valid. The point is not lost on Argan, who catches the hint and puts an end to the performance immediately.

The third act of *Le Malade imaginaire* is full of contained plays and improvised performances. In order to change Argan's views on the many doctors in his life, Toinette "plays" a doctor for him, imitating and outdoing her rivals with prescriptions and Latin insults, and, in what amounts to an ingenious *coup de théâtre*, interrupting her performance to enter the room as Toinette. Argan is not blind to the resemblance between Toinette in disguise and Toinette as herself; "Si je ne les voyais tous deux," he says, "je croirais que ce n'est qu'un". (III.ix.) He strongly suspects that he is watching someone play a part, watching a spectacle of alterity. It is this oscillation between herself and her character, her wavering between the assertion of the trappings of medical authority and conforming to what Argan wants to hear ("je voudrais... que vous eussiez toutes les maladies que je viens de dire, que vous fussiez abandonné de tous les mèdecins, desesperé, à l'agonie, pour vous montrer l'excellence de mes remèdes, et l'envie que j'aurais de vous rendre service" (III.x.)), in short, her foregrounding of herself as a divided entity that provides the final twist to Argan's conversion to a different conception of alterity and his adherence thereto. Until he sees such an alterity staged before him, until he sees the mask and its bearer and the dialectic that allows the one to fuel the other, Argan remains the idiot caught in the hall of mirrors that is his body. So in addition to enlightening Argan on the nature of health care in seventeenth-century France, Toinette's play shows Argan, in no uncertain terms, the possibility of an *être* and a *paraître* that do not coincide, the possibility of one person being two people.

Argan is a quick learner and his discovery of falsity is immediately put to good use. He can now engage with the rest of the characters as an actor rather than as a spectator.[10] Under Toinette's directorial auspices, Argan plays at being dead, and his feigned death brings out Béline's hypocrisy and Angélique's filial piety. Once again, the facts have to be staged theatrically to be valid. Thus Argan takes his first faltering steps towards inclusion in a histrionic universe where nothing is real unless it is staged: Toinette's *coup de théâtre* cures Argan of his idiocy, at least as far as his

---

10 Cf. Fumaroli, "Aveuglement et désabusement..."

family is concerned (so one might argue that by playing a doctor Toinette actually becomes a doctor).

One spectacle of otherness engenders another, and all of these plays make a seasoned performer out of Argan, who has, by this point, learned enough to know how to act. Rather than being "into himself" he can get caught up in what surrounds him, and he goes from being someone who suffers from a "culte de ses entrailles" to someone who can don a mask (or a doctor's outfit) and become someone else, someone who can transform his *être* by changing his *paraître*, ready to take part in the show before which he had hitherto been a bewildered spectator. Now that he can differ from himself, now that he can "be" two people in one (just like Toinette), he is ready to be received as an actor/doctor by the faculty of medicine.

The final *intermède* is the most theatrical of all in *Le Malade imaginaire*. The scene corresponds very roughly to the *cérémonie turque* that transforms Jourdain into *Mammamouchi*, but here it is taken a step further. The central feature of this scene is repetition, or rather *une répétition*, a rehearsal, and what we see staged before us is a rehearsal of what Argan will do as a doctor, which is to play the same part over and over again. Whenever he is asked about a new disease, he always offers the same formula: "clysterum donare, postea seignare, ensuitta purgare." What matters here, for all medical intents and purposes, is the speech act, what matters is that Argan speak in macaronic Latin through the mask that designates him as a doctor (read: actor) rather than the details of the actual prescription. Past this stage, if he *is* at all, it is only insofar as he is on display, a creature of ritual and ceremony.

At the end comes the equally ceremonious reception of Argan into the learned body, the body of learning, the "docto corpore" of medical practitioners, and here again Argan shows his gratitude in meaningful terms:

> Vobis, vobis debeo,
> Bien plus qu'à naturae et qu'a patri meo:
> Natura et pater meus
> Hominem me habent factum;
> Mais vos me, ce qui est bien plus,
> Avetis factum medicum.

Argan has been fashioned anew, he has acquired a new identity (nay, "ce qui est bien plus", a super-identity) under the theatrical patronage of the medical corps. With this new identity he can both separate from and control his body.

Thus an imaginary cure heals an imaginary invalid. Argan is cured by being brought face to face with that which is lacking in him, namely lack itself, alterity, difference, otherness. Furthermore, the cure reflects on its own conditions of possibility, so that Argan is presented with the spectacle of (self-conscious) imitation in the hope that he will imitate imitation self-consciously, a path that leads to self and other simultaneously. The many plays-within-the-play and spectacles of theatricality engender a similar sensitivity to theatricality in Argan himself. Unlike the cures which preceded the final act, nearly all of which entailed an "emptying out" of Argan's body—his *être*—through bleedings, purging agents and so on, theatre and the histrionic sensibility provide a cure based on the exterior, based on appearances, on the *paraître* that Argan must learn to understand for his cure to be effective.

Molière's œuvre thus presents us with the obverse of Corneille's: a world in which the theatre is used as the foremost tool not only for the investigation of the self but for calling it into question, where glory is defined just as much by lack as by possession (of names, histories, arms, money or whatever), as much by honour as by dishonour ("Un partage avec Jupiter n'a rien du tout qui deshonore." (*Amphitryon* 1902-3)). Here the point of such textual constructs as the self or an identity is their immediate mutation; the more a self is predicated on what it is not the truer to itself it will seem to be. And such Cornelian virtues as stageworthy *éclat* and a radically stoic submission to fate are shown for what they are: hilariously impractical in a world of flesh and blood where the body is just as real as the mask.

The invention(s) of the other as presented by Molière bring him closer to the spectre of modernity (by now looming large on the horizon of literary history) than Corneille's emphasis on eternities and ostensibly timeless glory. Perhaps the most important difference between the two playwrights lies in the use that they make of alterity. The Cornelian hero, as we have seen, tries to duplicate himself incessantly by creating doubles everywhere: thus Auguste at the end of *Cinna*, thus Horace on the battlefield, thus Rodrigue at Chimène's. There is, however, a fundamental bias in the mechanisms of reflection: Horace looks for his reflection in Camille only to find that her allegiance lies elsewhere. Similarly, Rodrigue turns to Chimène for some sign of approval only to hear her unending lament, "Enfin, mon père est mort." In both these cases, the hero's foil (Chimène, Camille) sends the mirror-image to a different destination. As they search for themselves in their lovers, Rodrigue and Horace only discover the other (le Comte and Curiace, the "autre soi-même"). There is, therefore, an instability inherent in these identities as they stand.

Molière recognises this problem and works it out by ridiculing the possibility of a self being played out incessantly without its losing something in the process. But at the same time Moliere is clever enough to construct plots and situations to help him out of the impasse: with Argan we have someone who is both self and not-self fused into one. At Toinette and Beralde's urging, he is persuaded to look for the other in the other (through the theatrical representation of himself, as opposed to the narcissistic representation of himself) and, because of the bias of the mechanism of doubling, winds up finding himself in the theatrical image that he produces of himself. Now he is both actor and spectator vis-à-vis himself and his self is stable. Corneille's characters look for the self in the other, while Molière's incorporate the other and manage to create a stable, albeit limited (Jourdain is only a "Turkish" nobleman, Argan can only ever be his own doctor), identity.

Molière thus provides a very elegant answer to the question at the head of this chapter. When is a self not a self? When it is a self, when it is itself. For Molière reminds us that every self, every identity, depends on the incorporation of an other, of a non-self, for its constitution. Selfhood depends on alterity for its creation, an alterity without which the self is likely to break down, and no longer be. Only when it is not itself—once it incorporates that which it is not—can a self properly be said to "cohere" and be a self.

Molière, as is well known, put a lot of himself into Argan. He was ill when he wrote *Le Malade imaginaire*, and he died shortly after he first played Argan in 1673. It is, I think, a point not to be missed that an ailing man tried to outwit death not—as is so often claimed—by laughing at death onstage, but rather by constructing a space where the mask is the only reality, where the dying body is completely inconsequential, and where Argan the mask outlives those whose bodies it adorns.

### III. Acting and/as Social Critique:

The situations presented in *Amphitryon* and *Le Malade imaginaire* are of a piece with Molière's other, more "canonical" comedies such as *Tartuffe*, *Dom Juan* and *Le Misanthrope*, as well as the farces. All are plays where the protagonists use disruptive behaviour in order to make a point about the theatrical worlds that they inhabit. They illustrate Molière's use of his theatre as vehicle for the critique of the court society and the limitations of its inner logic. In what follows, we shall attempt a reading of some of these texts in light of the framework established above, paying particular attention to *Le Misanthrope* and *Dom Juan* with a view to making manifest the prevailing themes of Molière's critical project, centred as it is on the histrionic bases of individual and social identity, and, on the social instability that results from histrionic self-fashioning.

Molière's early farces, for example, parody the tone of high tragedy: J.D. Hubert has already underlined the Cornelian overtones of Mascarille's bombastic, "Plus l'obstacle est puissant, plus on reçoit de gloire." (*Molière*, 3) This parody of Corneille is not gratuitous: the implication is that if identity is indeed dependent on a part being played, then all that one needs to do to establish an identity is to say certain things in a certain way, i.e. effectively, rhetorically, theatrically. In other words, a servant as clever as Mascarille could conceivably climb the social hierarchy and truly become an *imperator* of sorts, simply by acting like one while the crowds proclaim,"*Vivat Mascarillus, fourbum imperator*" (794).

The subversion of social hierarchies and playful manipulation of identities are, of course, part of the comedian's stock-in-trade. The comic element derives from the vacillation of identity between the possible and the actual: Mascarille, in principle, is the servant, he who gets beaten; Mascarille, in effect, is the master dramatist who rearranges the world he lives in and beats his master. Amphitryon, in principle, is he who shares Alcmène's bed; Amphitryon, in effect, is he who is kept waiting outside the doors of his own mansion. Monsieur Jourdain, in principle, is the upstart desperately trying to join the French nobility; Monsieur Jourdain, in effect, becomes a Turkish "Mammammouchi". In all of these cases, play-acting aids and abets the subversion process: Jupiter pretends to be Amphitryon, and Jourdain's many lessons in music, dancing, and philosophy subtend his imaginary social ascent. At a certain point, however, the substitutions and displacements take on a darker tone, as when Tartuffe turns Orgon out of house and home and usurps his place as its putative "maître". And it is here that the viewer (or the reader) is left wondering whether anything can be done to safeguard Orgon's identity as *paterfamilias* against the intrusions of an impostor who knows how to turn lies into truths by acting appropriately, and whether there is any possibility of distinguishing sincere from hypocritical behaviour. For *Tartuffe* foregrounds explicitly the disturbing possibility that the impostor's play actually determines reality, and founds a social hierarchy of its own, one founded on theatricality and acting rather than the traditional familial pieties. Similarly, Jourdain's many antics imply that the *noblesse* of 1670 is defined by its singing and dancing skills rather than its right to bear arms and pay the *impôt de sang*. Indeed, the entire social order seems to have taken to heart the music teacher's claims that, "Sans la musique, un Etat ne peut subsister." (I.ii.) And the fact that Molière takes the trouble to stage the making of the impostor and his eventual success puts him a step or two ahead of Corneille; here we have a text that demystifies the illusion of authority by revealing it to be a theatrical act, and iconoclastically destroys the figure of authority by showing him to be no better than the actors that the French church fought so vehemently. It also bears pointing out that this demystification depends on the staging of the gap between self and mask, as opposed to the celebration of their coincidence, as was the case chez Corneille. Rather than proclaiming, "I am the part I play", Molière's characters seem to say, "'I' is just a part I play."

The consequences of this implication—that even the least "deserving" elements of society can make their way to the top and do so with impunity because they play their part well—comes to the fore in the comedies written between 1665 and 1669. Like Mascarille, Tartuffe, Alceste and Dom Juan are concerned with their *gloire*, a most cornelian undertaking. All three are disturbed by nothing so much as they are by not having an audience to applaud their constant improvisations of devotion, sincerity or charm respectively. Their being "found out" does not disturb any of them in the least, any more than being condemned as a liar would disturb an actor on a stage. To them the only real threat is that of not being in a position to play a part, create an identity and have that identity be validated by a spectator. All three are good actors, and all three prove socially subversive by virtue of their histrionic skills: Tartuffe drives Orgon out of house and home, Alceste issues one rude, *malséant* threat after another to the court society that surrounds him, and Dom Juan keeps marrying women and abandoning them, subverting the ritual of marriage and undoing as he does so the institution that (supposedly) holds society together. The social consequences of their behaviour mean nothing to them. Here, as elsewhere, the play's the thing.


### IV. Le Misanthrope:

In conceptual terms (as opposed to chronological ones) Alceste mediates Tartuffe and Dom Juan: he synthesises the theatrical self-awareness of the former with the social arrogance of the latter. Alceste's sincerity depends on its being performed, promoted and applauded as something heroic. As his fan, Eliante, points out, "Et la sincérité dont son âme se pique/ A quelque chose en soi de noble et d'héroïque." (1165-66) This "quelque chose", far from being limited to the nobility that she attributes to it, inheres in the spectacular character of Alceste's behaviour, which is underhandedly applauded by Oronte: "L'état n'a rien qui ne soit au-dessous/ Du mérite éclatant que l'on découvre en vous." (266-7) Indeed, Alceste's frantically anti-social display of his preference for principles over people—little more than a desperate ploy in a search for their admiration and esteem—recalls Horace's sociopathic claim to preferring bonds of violence to bonds of kinship. (Perhaps a more sympathetic comparison would compare Alceste to Rotrou's Saint Genest, the actor who becomes himself with every performance: *Saint Alceste, comédien et martyr.*)

Alceste's only real desire is the display of his emotions, as witness his early retort to Philinte: "Moi, je veux me fâcher, et ne veux point entendre." (5) Indeed, the only thing that Alceste is interested in hearing is the sound of his own voice as it enacts and is inflected by every emotion he can conjure up. Without this perpetual staging of outraged emotional virtue, Alceste cannot exist.

Clearly, in pre-Romantic times, such behaviour incurs serious charges, nay the most serious charge, namely that of ridicule. And yet the logic behind Alceste's "ridiculous" patterns of behaviour is especially significant. It has been argued, for instance, that Alceste, "is ridiculous because he is part of the picture,"[11] meaning that Alceste's insight into the shortcomings of his companions is counterbalanced by his blindness to his own. From a different perspective, however, Alceste would seem to be only too well aware of his being part of the picture; what he really wants to do is to prove his superiority by stepping outside it. This casts the end of the play in a different light: Alceste's abandonment of the court society in favour of an unworldly *désert* is a geographic expression of his imaginary superiority, the exalted place from which he would presumably be able to look down upon the society that has failed to live up to his expectations. His parting shots to Eliante and Philinte—"Puissiez-vous, pour goûter de vrais contentements/ L'un pour l'autre à jamais garder ces sentiments" (1801-2)—bear this out, the implication being that they might be good enough for each other but certainly not for him. Furthermore, Alceste's final explosion is of a piece with this tendency:

> Trahi de toutes parts, accablé d'injustices,
> Je vais sortir d'un gouffre où triomphent les vices,
> Et chercher sur la terre un endroit écarté
> Où d'être homme d'honneur on ait la liberté.          (1803-6)[12]

Far from being pushed to this expedient by the successive rejections of Célimène, Alceste has, in fact, been preparing for it from the start of the play (and, one is tempted to imagine, the start of his life; for in the opening scene he says, "Et parfois il me prend des mouvements soudains/ De fuir dans un désert l'approche des humains." (144-5)) In fact, Alceste will do

---

[11] W.G. Moore, *Molière: A New Criticism* (London: Oxford, 1949), 124; qtd. Hubert, 144.

[12] It is ironic that Alceste's exit verses pre-figure the ones that would furnish the Troupe Royale with its smash hit the following year, namely Pyrrhus's outburst in *Andromaque*: "Haï de tous les Grecs, pressé de tous côtés,/ Me faudra-t-il combattre encor vos cruautés?" (291-2) Clearly, Molière was capable of striking a genuinely tragic note, even in a comedy.

anything in order to be seen performing this defiant rejection of and spectacular withdrawal from Parisian society. Others engage in theatrical displays of false affection, while Alceste engages in theatrical displays of false hatred. Ironically enough, this hatred has to be seen by the very people Alceste claims to detest in order to be valid. Alceste lives to see and be seen, and be heard, and be applauded, to a far greater extent than those whose behaviour he condemns.

Alceste's is the dilemma of denunciation: he can only describe and denounce a society as being a society of actors by being an actor himself. The objectivity to which he pretends only exists insofar as it is represented theatrically. His ethics are, therefore, ethics of a most theatrical sort: were it not for his many spectators, they would not exist (at least not in such intense form). But their very theatricality undermines them. *Le Misanthrope* is a play about the antinomies of "serious" social criticism in the seventeenth century. The valourisation of exteriority as a locus from which one's individuality and moral superiority can be proclaimed is undone by the inconvenient fact that this proclamation has to be displayed and witnessed *within* society in order for it to operate effectively. Otherwise the status of this proclamation would be reduced to that of a voice clamouring in the extra-Parisian *désert*. Alceste constantly menaces his peers with the threat of abandoning them, and eventually he does. But the moral value of this act of abandonment can only be established once it has been witnessed and "authenticated" by those present (those being abandoned, those about to be left behind) as an act performed in a fit of virtuous indignation. If, on the other hand, one were to step back and consider Alceste as a socially alienated individual—which is to say, by seventeenth-century French standards, not an individual at all, not even a human being—then one can only read it as a pure performance and laugh, much as twentieth-century audiences laugh at stand-up comics who "insult" them. Alceste is in a double bind: the full flavour of his bursts of moral outrage can only be appreciated if these paroxysms are read as performances. And yet reading them as performances effectively cancels out their moral content. The lesson of *Le Misanthrope* is clear: in the court society that absolutism engenders, the only effective means of social criticism is laughter, not indignation.[13] Moreover, those who, like Alceste, insist on speaking for themselves, and refuse to represent, or be represented by, their surrounding social order, are the ones most vulnerable to this sort of criticism, as well as its inevitable

---

[13] It bears pointing out that this double bind is itself part of Molière's critique of Corneille's histrionics; for how can one claim that all the world's a stage without being oneself an actor upon that stage, and ipso facto subject to the criticism that one's statements—including the one about all the world being a stage—are theatrical and false?

consequence, namely social alienation and effective exile from the court, the only world worth inhabiting.[14]


## V. Dom Juan:

To be an aristocrat is to represent the aristocracy, to play the social role of an aristocrat. As such, the representative of the aristocracy is in a precarious, almost subversive position. This is the case for two reasons: first, this game of representation is played out on the borders between the aristocracy and other orders, a place where one runs the risk of being "corrupted" by their mores. Second, and more significantly perhaps, because the aristocracy is identified by its representatives, and said representatives can modify the rules of social representation ("manners") to their advantage, with potentially devastating results. This is the case with Dom Juan. Like Alceste, he is an anti-social actor, and, like Alceste, he takes pains to show that his social niche is not good enough for him by stepping outside it. His chosen role of *grand seigneur méchant homme* underlines the fact that, under absolutism, aristocrats could do as they pleased, provided that whatever pleased them did not destabilise the social hierarchy of roles that defined society. Unfortunately, the impunity with which the aristocracy did as it pleased ensured nothing less than such a destabilisation. Dom Juan's behaviour brings out the *méchant homme* in the *grand seigneur:* he combines, in the spectacular fashion typical of Molière's characters, the display of his privileges with the degeneration that inevitably results therefrom. In doing so he effectively shatters the hollow myth that the aristocracy, by virtue of its being the most excellent (in the ethical sense) social order, is the one that holds society together and leads it on. Dom Juan is a *gentilhomme bourgeois* of sorts, delighting in his downward mobility, and performing a paradoxical role in order to show up the nobility to be no better than the rest of the population.

Dom Juan's revolt at the sheer facticity of way in which society is organised comes across in his troubled relationship with his father: "J'enrage de voir des pères qui vivent autant que leurs fils." (IV.v.) Dom Juan's utopia is a world where he would have appeared parthenogenetically in his early twenties, ready to seduce women unencumbered by the oedipal weight of father, family and class obligation. The contrast with the world of

---

[14] In this respect, Alceste is an avatar of the "modern" individual who perpetually asserts the fact that he is simply too good for this world. Cf. Louis Dumont's use of the concept of the "individu-hors-du-monde" in *Essais sur l'individualisme*, 33-114, as well as our readings of Rousseau and Sartre.

*Le Cid* could not be greater: it will be remembered that Le Comte reminds Rodrigue that "le fils dégénère/ Qui survit un moment à l'honneur de son père" (*Le Cid*, 443-4), while Dom Juan is only happy to de-generate from his lineage. Responsibility frightens him, due to its links with his detested communal self. Indeed, the entire plot of *Dom Juan* takes the form of a farcical series of spectacular escapes from responsibility: Dom Juan has no sooner run away from one trap than he risks getting caught in another, and every escape provides him with an opportunity to show off his privilege and how he refuses to pay the price for it (in terms of ethical, noble behaviour). He borrows on the strength of his good name, but does not pay his creditors; he marries, but abandons his wives (without even taking the time to enjoy a sexual relationship with them); he gives to the poor, but does so in a spectacularly un-charitable manner, and so on. His entire existence (if one can call it that) is a quixotic alternation between illusion and disappointment: he produces all the simulacra of nobility and then proceeds to declare them to be just that; simulacra, totally lacking in material (or, for that matter, ideological) backing. Ironically enough, this auto-deconstructive routine, whereby the image of the nobility is created and undone simultaneously, must, in order to be effective, be performed with Dom Juan's particular *éclat* and be witnessed by those spectators—women, peasants, bourgeois—who are only happy to be duped by the spectacle of the aristocratic male in all his glory.

Dom Juan's supplementing the role of *grand seigneur* with *méchant homme* is part of a one-man critical project aimed at a social order so corrupt that it can no longer claim his allegiance. This is the project of seduction, taken in the etymological sense of leading away or separating.[15] Dom Juan's is the part that explicitly states the separation of signs and referents (which separation is the sign of a lack of social stability; Dom Juan seems intent on re-creating the very conditions that drive him away from his social caste). His seductive praxis also underlines the separation of being and appearance that marks him: as his discourse separates words and things, so his theatrical "routine" separates him from the weight of the role he was

---

15 For an extensive reading of this issue see Claude Reichler's *La Diabolie. La séduction, la renardie, l'écriture* (Paris: Minuit, 1979), 23-75. Reichler attaches full etymological weight to the term *diabolie* (*dia-ballein*: to separate) in his reading of Dom Juan's diabolically seductive discourse. Pierre Chabert is more direct, seeing in Dom Juan's discourse a theory of his conduct: "Il ne séduit que dans le sens particulier et restrictif de tromper par l'intermédiaire de fallacieuses promesses de mariage (avec les paysannes) ou par le biais du déguisement (avec les dames du haut rang). Pour un séducteur, on pourrait rêver mieux. Les techniques de séduction pourront s'affiner, et de beaucoup. Mais surtout dans la théorie. Ainsi le Don Juan ne paraît un si habile séducteur que parce qu'il discourt—que parce que Don Juan s'est transformé entre-temps en théorie du Donjuanisme." ("Dom Juan, le théâtre" in *Obliques* 1:4 (1974), 87).

born into. One sort of separating involves telling everyone what they want to hear: he mimics the discourse of the good creditor for M. Dimanche, the discourse of virtue when religious virtue is in question, and the discourse of love with the women that he encounters. Dom Juan marries Elvire and then abandons her: he performs a gesture that founds a social order in miniature followed by a negation of that order and the society consequent upon it.[16] He separates himself from the parts that he plays with the same ease with which he separates Charlotte from Pierrot. Dom Juan, in other words, is actively engaged in not being what he seems, in representing falsity, in systematically stressing the gap that separates his being from his appearance.

The definition of a *grand seigneur* was someone who was *fiable*, someone who was trustworthy. Dom Juan's mission aims at the destruction of an entire social hierarchy based on these principles of fidelity and trustworthiness by showing them up to be principles that inhere in performances and performative moments and, as such, principles unsuited to the foundation and regulation of society. The Don's many broken promises call into question the social contract—secular or divine—that validates performatives like "I do", institutions like marriage and social orders like the nobility. A society is only as solid as the performatives on which it is based, and Dom Juan, by making empty promises, produces worthless performatives that are the mark of an equally worthless society. His behaviour turns his ambient social space into one that is not good enough for him.

None of this is gratuitous, of course, and Dom Juan is no reformer: his point is the *demonstration* of his standing above the rules. Hence his perpetual need for an audience and his sheer willingness to start performing the minute he sees a potential spectator present, turning on a show of charm for the ladies, valour for the gentlemen (Carlos and Alonse), devotion—both religious and secular—for Elvire, extreme courtesy and deference for his father, and generosity for the dead. He obeys to the point of absurdity the rules of proper social conduct: rather than hit his father or react with insults (as he does in most of the *Dom Juan*s that precede Molière's) he simply offers his enraged father a seat. Similarly, in the following scene where we see Elvire make her final attempt at converting the

---

[16] For an incisive reading of the uses and abuses of performative language in *Dom Juan* see Shoshana Felman's *Scandale du corps parlant. Don Juan avec Austin ou la séduction en deux langues* (Paris: Seuil, 1980). The question of language generally in *Dom Juan* has received extensive treatment elsewhere. Studies by Defaux, Forestier and Reichler have already been mentioned, but also helpful were Marie-Rose Carré's "Mots en échange, mots en liberté: Molière devant les théories linguistiques de son temps" (in *Dix-Septième siècle* 104, 1974) and Sylvie Romanowski's "Le Rôle du langage dans le *Dom Juan* de Molière" in *Neophilologus* 59 (1975).

trickster once and for all, his response is limited to a lukewarm but polite invitation that she spend the night. Finally, when the commander's statue comes to dinner, Dom Juan makes a point of seeming level-headed enough to ask for "une chaise et un couvert", to toast the commander's health and accept the latter's dinner invitation. As is his wont, Dom Juan plays the received idea of the unshakeable, nonchalant aristocrat, "que rien ne saurait ébranler" (IV. viii.) to an extreme with a view to showing its emptiness. Eventually, even Dom Juan's death is integrated into his theatrical routine of unobliging behaviour, as is summed up by Sganarelle's closing statement: "mes gages, mes gages." At this point, Dom Juan has repaid all his ethical and financial debts through his death, except for the debts incurred against Sganarelle's corporeal labour. In other words, the structure of bad debts continues past the end of the play, and Dom Juan continues to play the "grand seigneur méchant homme" from beyond the grave.

*

*    *

The hollow nature of Tartuffe's religious fervour, Alceste's sincerity and Dom Juan's nobility is a direct consequence of Molière's sceptical reading of Corneille's histrionics. For all their exaggeration, however, the three actors play their parts well: Tartuffe manages to dupe Orgon and Mme Pernelle, Alceste manages to touch Philinte (who remains a fast friend to the bitter end), to charm Célimène (who is otherwise easily bored) and to offend Oronte (who would have laughed off the entire affair were Alceste not so convincing), and Dom Juan's seduction works on everyone and everything, including inanimate objects like statues. Those in their company believe them, and the spectator oscillates between the two positions, the one suspending disbelief before these skilled performances, and the other preferring to dismiss their effects as the inevitable result of human vanity and stupidity. These two vantage-points combine in a synthetic focus whereby each character seems simultaneously to be and not to be what he represents: Tartuffe is and is not religious duty incarnate, Alceste is and is not the epitome of heartfelt sincerity, Dom Juan is and is not a *grand seigneur*, all three stand as simulacra of otherness within the self, or rather of a self that is not a self, signs of an identity that is not one (*une identité qui n'en est pas une*).

As such their status bears a striking resemblance to the figure of the found king in Pascal's *Premier discours sur la condition des grands*.[17] Like the shipwrecked man whom the island's natives take to be a lost king,

[17] In Pascal, *Œuvres complètes*, (Lafuma ed., Paris: Seuil, 1963) 366.

the spectators (and victims) of Molière's characters make them what they are: the performative effect of a theatrical process.[18] One might say of them what Louis Marin said of Pascal's actor-king, namely that he is trapped by his role as his spectators are trapped by theirs:

> L'homme—en simulant le simulacre royal—piège les habitants de l'île dans l'obéissance et le respect que légitimiment ils doivent à leur maître. Mais ceux-ci, inversement, en le saluant comme leur vrai roi, le piègent dans cet être-roi qu'il n'est pas. (*Récit* 142)

The theatrical facticity that Marin applies to royal power also applies to the social identities of Tartuffe, Alceste and Dom Juan. Like the found king, their identities are the arbitrary result of their performances.

One last feature that binds these metaphysical comedies is the moral *basso continuo* running through them. Dom Juan's debts to Sganarelle notwithstanding, gods (represented by kings, kings' envoys, moving statues, spectres, and so on) manage to jump out of the machine at the end of the play, allowing glory to go bang and displaying the punishment of the hypocrite, the sociopath, the *méchant*. With time, however, Molière's sceptical tendencies take over and morality is muffled, as the playwright takes pains to demonstrate the spectator's (and, for that matter, his own) complicity in his characters' questionable behaviour.

All of which underlines the antinomies of the court society and the limitations of its inner logic. Molière's critical scepticism turns histrionic reasoning against itself, showing effectively that things are not what they seem but that one has no choice but to go along and pretend that they are (otherwise, one runs the risk of turning into Alceste). He thus demonstrates the extent to which role-playing traps both player and audience in a rigid dialectic of performance and counter-performance. The arrest of Tartuffe seemed to imply that the touchstone by which identities were evaluated and reality established was the king. But in a world where "found" kings are indistinguishable from real ones, and where the procedures used to construct an identity also subvert that identity, no recourse to an external vantage-point (such as Alceste's *désert*) providing an "objective" view of society is possible. Consequently, no denunciation of the theatricality of everyday life is possible, as the case of Alceste makes abundantly clear. In a world where identity depends on acting, the only legitimate course of action in any given situation is more acting.

Having reached this point, the internal pressures of the society of the absolutist court undergo a number of modifications. Rather than lead to a

---

[18] For an interesting psychoanalytic reading of this situation, see Slavoj Zizek's *Looking Awry* (Cambridge: MIT P, 1991), 32-34 and 73-76.

breakdown of the histrionic model of self-construction, they bring about its expansion: the rest of France, as well as the rest of Europe, starts actively mimicking the Sun King and the court of Versailles. And rather than making people stop playing parts, they add to the parts that people play: henceforth an identity will be defined both as a part and as a historical narrative, which narrative becomes a means of evaluating the "honesty" of the player and as a means of drawing distinctions between true and false. It is to these modifications that we turn in the next chapter.

# Chapter Three

# The Impostor and the King:
# Thomas Corneille and the Ruses of the Romanesque

Unlike his older brother, Thomas Corneille has not merited much attention from modern critics. What few there have been (most notably Reynier,
Lancaster and Collins) have tended to divide his literary output into
*tragédies romanesques, tragédies corneliennes, tragédies raciniennes* and
the comedies.[1] This system betrays the preoccupations of its proponents,
(nearly all of whom, admittedly, openly avow its inadequacies). Chief
among them is the desire to assimilate every literary text composed between 1600 and 1699 to one or the other of the paradigms created by
Corneille and Racine, to the detriment of the *romanesque* plays of Thomas
Corneille.

Such is not our aim here. Indeed, it would be rather difficult to under-
value the romanesque identity plays any more than they have been so far.
Despite their routine denigration, one uncomfortable fact remains: Thomas
Corneille's most successful play, and *the* smash hit of the century, *Timocrate*, is one of these romanesque plays.[2] So what we shall attempt is a
demonstration of the importance of those plays by tracing certain modes of
operation that are common to both the romanesque plays as well as Thomas
Corneille's other, more acceptable because more mainstream, works,
proving as we do so that the romanesque is, in fact, bound inextricably with
the operation of what has come to be called "classicism" as exemplified by
Pierre Corneille.

From Pierre Corneille, Thomas inherited a sense of the sorts of things
that worked onstage. His early adaptations of Rojas, Lope and Calderon
bear witness to a real sensitivity to popular tastes that often surpasses his
older brother's scholarly concerns. He also developed a sense of how the
theatre could be used as a locus for the investigation of identities and a
taste for those devices that indicated a genre coming to grips with itself: the
stage-within-a-stage, the use of disguise as a catalyst in the genesis of an

---

[1] Collins uses the term "tragedy of feeling" to counter Reynier's "tragédies raciniennes". Collins lists *Timocrate, Bérénice, Darius, Pyrrhus* and *Antiochus* as romanesque identity plays. Reynier adds *Persée et Démétrius, Théodat* and *Bradamante* to
the list.

[2] According to Reynier, 126. Lancaster calls this judgement into question in his
*History,* 3:184-185.

identity and a set of low-tech special effects designed to display a characters' courage and valour.

Foremost among the variations on the theme of disguise are the theme of the king and the impostor or the disguised king whose identity is gradually revealed. This is, of course, a theme that occurs with great frequency in romanesque literature. More significant for our purposes is the skill with which both Corneilles manipulated it for their ends. If in *L'Illusion comique* Pierre Corneille showed Clindor's identity crystallizing into that of an actor, and in *Horace* showed an image of the self that identifies itself with and against "un autre soi-même", thereby enacting the definition of identity as a synthesis of masked self and mirrored other, he becomes haunted towards the middle of his life (the period during which Thomas Corneille writes his first plays) by the possibility of the monarch being subject to these same laws of histrionic self-articulation. If all the world's a stage, and all the men and women merely players, does the king fall into this category? What if, rather than being the superhuman peg from which the court society was hung, the king were just as much of a histrionic invention as its many inhabitants? How, if at all, is it possible to distinguish between a king and an actor, an impostor?

This concern turns into a sub-genre among Pierre Corneille's many plays, reaching its pinnacle in *Héraclius* and *Don Sanche d'Aragon*. In both of these plays a stranger proves himself to be a king by emitting all the signs common to his royalty, leaving no doubt as to his royal status. *Héraclius* turns on a series of substitutions whereby the eponymous heir to the imperial throne is kept hidden long enough to ensure his safety from a bloodthirsty usurper, Phocas, until the latter is overthrown in a timely conspiracy and Héraclius is crowned. *Don Sanche*, cleaner and better written, shows us a "lost" king. Carlos, supposedly a fisherman's son, shows up in the Aragonese army and dazzles everyone with his courage. After a whole series (five acts' worth) of noble deeds and heroic acts, he is revealed to be the rightful heir to the throne of Aragon. What is really at stake here is less the irony of history than the fact that a displaced nobleman has been restituted. What really matters is the ostentatious display of virtue and *générosité*, qualities that shine through Carlos's destiny despite his nominally humble station in life. Any member of the audience watching *Don Sanche* would have been disturbed not so much by the lack of *vraisemblance* (which is what, anachronistically, gets to the modern reader) but by the fact that he or she sees, onstage, a character whose essence and appearance do not coincide: here is a common, ignoble character emitting all the proper signs of nobility, namely courage, honesty, and a taste for violence. The spectator, in other words, would be disturbed by the fact that a character playing a part that is not really his own, that all of these noble traits only belong with someone sporting a noble title or rank. The lesson of the play, of course, is that things in general, and people in particular, rarely are what they seem, even to themselves;

> …combien a-t-on vu de Princes déguisés
> Signaler leur vertu sous des noms supposés,
> Dompter des Nations, gagner des Diadèmes,
> Sans qu'aucun les connût, sans se connaître eux-mêmes? (51-54)

Hence the epithet that Corneille attaches to his play, *comédie héroïque*: all's well that ends well, and the spectator leaves the theatre having discovered that this commoner is indeed a nobleman, since no-one with such noble virtues could possibly be anything else.

Of course, the appeal of this sort of plot is easily understood, and Thomas Corneille was smart enough to capitalise on it when he did, in the way that he did. The typical Parisian audience on any presentation-night was composed largely of the upper bourgeoisie and the nobility. The nobility, in an age of diminishing returns and ever-decreasing power, enjoyed being told that no matter what happened, only the truly virtuous element in society would attain a noble rank; that no matter what happens,

> Le vrai sang des rois, sous le sort abbatu,
> Peut cacher sa naissance et non pas sa vertu.
> (*Don Sanche d'Aragon*, 1315-1316).

The "middle classes", for their part, liked hearing that perhaps if they displayed enough virtue, in just the right way, perhaps they too might be allowed into the circles of the nobility or possibly even the court.

As a result, Thomas Corneille's fills his plays with " romanesque" situations reminiscent of those in *Héraclius* and *Don Sanche d'Aragon*, odd scenarios that take their obsession with disguise and identity to a surreal extreme. The examples are not lacking: a man is asked who he is and cannot answer the question because, as he puts it, he has not prepared an answer (*Le Geôlier de soi-même*). A woman tells her son to kill himself (*Laodice*). A man takes another man aside to reveal an important state secret, namely that he is his interlocutor (*Darius*). A man is taken prisoner by the leader of his enemy's army, and fails to recognise him later at his own court (*Timocrate*).

As he does so, Thomas Corneille employs techniques that one would associate with modern thrillers and detective novels rather than seventeenth-century drama. The question that underlies his plots is always *who*: In his *Ariane*, the heroine is haunted by the question of who took Theseus away from her (the answer, interestingly enough, is her sister, Phèdre). In the prologue to his *Circé*, Mars comes onstage in a winged chariot and full military attire (and Thomas Corneille's description is not insignificant: he is "orné de tout ce qui peut le faire connoître pour le dieu qui préside aux combats"[3]; like the shows of virtue that we saw before, he emits every possible sign to confirm his identity) to ask about his own displacement; who, he asks, is this new God of war that he keeps hearing about? Who is this *usurpateur*, and is it fair that he usurp all the glory that was once attached to Mars himself? (The answer is Louis XIV). In *Antiochus*, we ask with whom is the young protagonist preoccupied? In *Darius*, who is the person who is rumored to be the rightful heir to the Persian throne but is supposedly tucked away somewhere, either at the court or in the city? In *L'Inconnu*, who is this secret admirer who keeps sending the countess all these amazing gifts?

In other words, even though only a handful of Thomas' plays are characterised as being romanesque identity plays, they all deal with the issue in one way or another. Moreover, the answer to the question, "who?" always has something to do with the person asking it, and this is where Thomas Corneille introduces the theme of the double: the answer to Ariane's question is her sister, Phèdre; the answer to the question of *Darius* is Darius himself, Antiochus is enamoured of Stratonice, his father's fiancée; the conspiracy against the emperor Honorius is masterminded by his tutor and most insistent interrogator, Stilicon; and so on. Two voices are endlessly at play in Thomas Corneille's spectacles; the one asking "who?" and the other answering "I".

Nor is this all. Thomas Corneille's interest in the fabulous, the magical and the romanesque derives from a profound understanding of the force of theatrical illusion, capitalizing as it does on the spectators' desire. There is no better example of this than *La Devineresse*, where a fortune teller so dominates (and domineers) her clients' imaginations with theatrical tricks and rigged machinery that she ends up controlling the polity. Elsewhere similar tricks are turned: people that clamour for kings like audiences for their favourite performers (*Darius*, *Laodice*), suitors in disguise whose entire seduction depends on their victims' narcissism (*Le Baron d'Albikrac*, *La Comtesse d'Orgeuil*) and women who control their lovers by keeping their identities secret (*Les Engagements du hasard*). In all of these cases, power derives from the carefully controlled staging of individual identities. The act of naming, or declaring, an identity becomes a performative statement that founds a social order by producing and circulating spectacular fictions of authority—masks, doubles, simulacra produced with the beholder's desires in mind—the very sight of which secures the onlooker's obedience.

---

[3] Prologue to *Circé*. References to the plays will be by act and scene number, following the 1758 edition of Thomas Corneille's *Théâtre complet*.

As Thomas imitates Pierre he takes things one step further. Pierre, it seemed, was content to investigate the construction of identities. Thomas, on the other hand, looks at their operation in the social context of the very rigid hierarchies of seventeenth-century French society where every rank corresponds to a role to be played to death. Like the characters of his older brother, Thomas Corneille's characters live in worlds where the shortest distance between two points is not necessarily a straight line, where in order to become themselves they have to play a part, but that part is usually fictitious (unlike Pierre's characters who just played themselves).

Consider *Timocrate*, which centers on the eponymous king of Crete who falls in love with a princess of Argos. Her mother, however, has sworn vengeance on her father's murderer and has offered her daughter's hand in marriage to whoever will deliver him to her. So Timocrate disguises himself as a mercenary adventurer named Cléomène (probably the world's most polite mercenary), and goes off to fight with the Argives, distinguishing himself in the process. When the war between Crete and Argos picks up again, he seems to fight his own army to protect the kingdom of Argos, and fights the Argives under his own banner. When the play opens, Timocrate has made a name for himself in Argos as Cléomène the swashbuckler (so he has donned this disguise a number of times in order to impress the princess and her mother). Now, in the middle of the third act, a certain Nicandre, a prince of Argos, is taken prisoner by the Cretan army under Timocrate, treated like a king and then released (which, of course, is meant to be a *spectacular* show of virtue on the part of king Timocrate, so that the audience knows he deserves to be a king and to get what he wants). A few scenes later Timocrate, alias Cléomène, greets him at the court of the queen of Argos, and this time Nicandre does not recognise him. One possible interpretation, suggested by one critic, is that Nicandre has at this point already decided to betray Argos to the Cretans, although that would be out of character.[4] There is, however, an even stronger supplementary explanation. The same sort of histrionic logic operative in Pierre Corneille's tragedies is at work here; the *invraisemblable* and the *romanesque* have a logic that parallels that of the *vraisemblable*. Timocrate is whatever his role at any given point declares him to be, namely Timocrate in Crete and Cléomène in Argos. Such is the fervour with which the younger Corneille creates a world in which things are what they seem because they have to be.

*Laodice*, to take another example, shows us the queen of Cappadocia who has killed all her sons (all the male heirs to the throne). Her youngest, Ariarate, was taken hostage by the Romans, so that they might put him on

---

4 The suggestion is made by David Collins, 63.

the throne of Cappadocia once he is old enough to assume power. Unbeknownst to Laodice, Ariarate has been living in the Cappadocian court under an alias, namely Oronte, her most trusted courtier. The play opens on a tense note: the people of Cappadocia are tired of Laodice's reign and clamour for their king. A Roman ambassador, Aquilius, announces that he is bringing Ariarate home to install him on the throne. We find out soon enough that this "Ariarate" is an impostor being brought to Cappadocia to meet his death at the hands of Laodice, but none of the characters (except the real Ariarate) knows this. So when Laodice tells Oronte to kill her son Ariarate, he pleads for his own life as though it were the life of another. Interestingly enough, the show of virtue in this instance is fake rather than real, since there is nothing especially lofty about begging for one's own life. So we have Oronte pleading for Ariarate's life, or rather Ariarate pleading for his own life, but the only effective way of doing that is by playing the part of Oronte, using prosopopeia to articulate what he dares not:

> Croyez, en m'écoutant, que c'est lui qui vous prie,
> Qu'en regardant sa mere il la cherche attendrie,
> Et qu'enfin à vos pieds il vous dit par ma voix,
> *Accordez-moi la vie une seconde fois,*
> *Je vous suis odieux. Mais, quoi? Qui vous anime?*
> *Etre né votre fils n'est pas un si grand crime.*
> *Daignez lui faire grace en faveur d'un respect*
> *Que jamais rien de moi ne vous rendra suspect,*
> *Prenez-en pour garant la foi sincere et pure*
> *Qu'à la faveur du Ciel ma tendresse vous jure,*
> *Cette foi que jamais les plus durs changements...*     (III.iii.)[5]

Laodice interrupts what she takes to be an exercise in rhetoric. She cannot believe what she hears because as far as she is concerned she is listening to Oronte pretending to be someone else, or that he is just trying to show off his very noble qualities, which, in fact, she finds attractive. Being a consummate politician, on the other hand, she is so moved by what she hears that she interrupts him for fear of seeming weak. Ironically enough it would be a good thing for her to feel just a little weak, since she is his mother after all.

Thus to get to where they want, to the only place that they can occupy in life, Thomas Corneille's characters have to play a part, and assume a false identity in order to exist long enough that they might one day be able to assume their own.

---

[5] Cf. Forestier, *Esthétique* 280-281.

This playing of fictitious parts is accompanied by devices that figure the player's involvement in the part, such as the mirror of fiction. *Le Feint astrologue* shows us a protagonist whose fictitious predictions of his social circle always come true, a situation not unlike that of *La Devineresse*. In *Don Bertrand de Cigarral* a young man, Alvar, is invited by his cousin Bertrand to tell the latter's fiancée, Isabelle, a story with a view to entertaining her. Alvar, who also likes Isabelle, turns the situation to his advantage and tells the tale of his own encounter and infatuation with Isabelle, culminating in the moment of narration itself; "Il soupire, il lui parle, et devant son rival/Sans qu'il s'en aperçoive, il lui conte son mal." (II,iv) The declaration works very well, and Isabelle duly projects herself into the story, informing Alvar that the feeling is mutual in terms of the story's "protagonists": "Je plains fort l'un et l'autre, et doute qui des deux/En ce triste rencontre est le plus malheureux." Alvar and Isabelle communicate by adopting autobiographical "roles" borrowed from the idiom of narrative "fiction", doubles that make it easier for them to manage their lives.[6] Through the mirror of fiction, the fictitious role engenders the self-as-other.

This device leads to situations where the double scripts the role that defines the self and vice versa. This is the predicament of Jodelet and Frédéric in *Le Geôlier de soi-même*, a play that combines the theme of royal imposture with that of the mirror of fiction in modified form. Frédéric, a Sicilian prince, having killed Rodolfe, prince of Salerno, in a tournament, discards his armour and takes refuge in the country château of the king of Naples. Jodelet comes across the armour, puts it on, and assumes the role that comes with the change of costume. Jodelet sees his accidental stumbling upon the armour as the accomplishemt of a "destiny", the realisation of a tale foretold;

> Je me fis l'autre jour encor horoscoper
> Et j'ai appris que bien-tost, si l'effet suit la cause
> Le marquisat pour moi sera fort peu de chose. (I.v.)

He rehearses the role, brushing up on his rather rusty command of the courtly idiom in order to prepare for the many amorous conquests he intends to make (things like, "Je viens ici rendre et la cape et l'épée,/Car mon ame d'amour est toute constipée." (I.v.)) Still, his rehearsals do not eliminate the problem of his new identity, and when the king's guards ask him, "qui va là?" his response is telling; "La vilaine enquête que voilà!/ J'avois réponse à tout hormis à qui va-la." (I.viii.) Here Jodelet speaks for the many characters in Thomas Corneille's theatre who adopt fictitious roles without paying due attention to the historical details involved, a situation

---

6 This situation has its parallels in *Le Malade imaginaire*. Cf. Collins, 49.

that repeats itself in many of the tragedies and announces a shift away from
theatre and towards narrative as the determinants of identity.

The comic import of *Le Geôlier de soi-même* derives from Jodelet's
inability to master history, by which I mean both the many shifts in his
social standing and the details of the history attributed to him. Frédéric, on
the other hand, becomes the handsome stranger à la Don Sanche, whose
incessant displays of virtue earn him a great deal of social power. In a
manner typical of the romanesque idiom, the mere appearance of this
unhappy stranger earns him the heart of Isabelle, Rodolfe's sister, and the
task of governing her country estate ("Que n'obtiendrez-vous avec tant de
merite?" she rhetorically asks, even before this stranger has had a chance to
prove himself). By coincidence, it is to this very castle that Jodelet is
delivered, so that the unknown prince is the keeper of an impostor who has
assumed his identity. In captivity Jodelet assumes the identity attributed to
him, aided and abetted by his "audience":

> Mais pourquoi m'obstiner à ne point me connoître?
> Puisque chacun ici d'une commune voix
> Soutient que je suis prince, il faut que je le sois.
> On est plus grand seigneur quelquefois qu'on ne pense...(II.vi.)[7]

Needless to say, the trick fails, thanks in no small part to Jodelet's inability to grasp the skills essential to his social survival (and which, not
coincidentally, are aristocratic trademarks): history and language. Jodelet's
relationship with history is quixotic, arising, as we have seen, from the
sense that his social transformation is an inescapable destiny. Early on in
his captivity, Octave, Frédéric's stable-boy, tries to inform his "master" of
certain passages in his history:

> Seigneur, il vous souvient qu'un jours sans mon secours
> Un cruel Sanglier eust terminé vos jours,
> Il vous souvient de plus que le Roy vostre pere...       (II.vi.)

To which Jodelet responds with a characteristic interruption; "Ma foy,
s'il m'en souvient, il ne m'en souvient guere/ Ay-je autrefois aimé la
chasse au sanglier?" Nevertheless, Jodelet is quick to master those parts of
his new history to which he has been introduced, and later on when Laure
alludes to his putative military adventures ("Tant de rares exploits dont
l'honneur fut la cause/ Tant de périls passés..." (III.viii.)), he can only assume that she is referring to the misadventure with the wild boar mentioned
by Octave;

---

7. Jodelet's situation as "found nobleman" parallels in a comic mode the situation
of the "found king" in Pascal's first *Discours sur la condition des grands*. We will
return to this issue at the end of the following chapter.

Oui, j'en sai quelque chose;
Je suis fort périlleux. On dit qu'un sanglier...
Mais ce n'est pas à moi de m'en glorifier,
*L'histoire en parlera*; puis telles vanteries
Parmi nous autres grands sont des forfanteries. (III.viii; emphasis mine)

Frédéric, being a prince, is of course resourceful enough to convince Jodelet that he was the one who killed Rodolfe by capitalising on a mechanism already in place: accusation through flattery. In a very well composed comic scene, there is an insidious tragic murmur as an aristocrat's guilt is transferred to a peasant's. Frédéric pleads his own cause as though it were Jodelet's, building on the latter's penchant for a braggadocio reminiscent of Pierre Corneille's Matamore, and on the confusion between the aesthetic displeasure Jodelet has caused with his rough manner and the political displeasure he himself has caused by killing Rodolfe. The scene illustrates the ease with which Jodelet is tricked into playing a part other than his own:

**Jodelet**
Qui l'a tué [i.e. Rodolfe]?
   **Frédéric**
Vous-même.
   **Jodelet**
Ai-je d'un assassin l'envisagement blême?
Vous perdez le respect!
   **Frédéric**
Apaisez ce courroux,
Il méritoit la mort, combattant contre vous.
C'est dans un champ d'honneur, c'est par une victoire
Que son sang répandu redouble votre gloire;
Ne craignez point d'en voir l'éclat diminué.
   **Jodelet**
Ah! Puisqu'il est bien mort, c'est moi qui l'ai tué.
J'y fais réflexion, oui, c'est moi...          (III.ix)

The same pattern and mode of flattery that was used to convince Jodelet of the wild boar incident now brings him closer to the noose. Jodelet's deliberate self-obliteration for the sake of the part he has to play adds a serious dimension to his quip that, "Quand on meurt pour le Prince, on vit dans l'Histoire." (II.vi.) On one level, he is simply announcing his prerogative ("Un Prince n'a-t-il pas pouvoir de pendaison?") On another, he speaks for himself as someone who sacrifices his real self—Jodelet—in order to substitute for a prince who is in trouble, all in a desperate bid to assure himself of a place in a "noble" history.

Places in history are not easy to come by, though, and Jodelet's eludes him. At the end of the play, Frédéric is pardoned and Jodelet is "défédériqué" in due course, his transformation of a name into a verb marking and delimiting his activity as theatrical performance.[8] Jodelet's failure to imitate Frédéric's rhetorical acrobatics and substitute for him necessarily follows from the premise on which the play is predicated, namely that the only way in which such a substitution would prove effective is one where issues of class and social order are not ignored (which is, in effect, the situation in Molière's *Amphitryon*): only a prince of Frédéric's rank could possibly substitute for him, and play the seductive stranger to both Isabelle and Laure. According to the expectations of the seventeenth-century audience, it is imperative that Jodelet cut a ridiculous figure in this context; he is, after all, grafted onto a history that is not his own and, Thomas Corneille assures his spectators, never can be.[9]

The relationship in which Frédéric and Jodelet stand as masked self to false double is emblematic of a structure that recurs with some frequency in Thomas Corneille's theatre. This takes us to another area where Thomas Corneille goes beyond his brother's endeavours. Whereas Pierre Corneille was content to posit an associative link between simple and double, Thomas makes it causal. The importance of this causality, as well as the impact of the display of a false identity is at the centre of *Darius*. The real Darius is the rightful heir to the Persian throne, but he is living at the court under an assumed name (Codoman) while the throne is occupied by another man, Ochus, who thought that he had killed every member of the royal family. During the course of the play, Darius displays a lot of virtue, protecting the throne from a plot concocted by the prime minister Mégabise, one of whose tricks, ironically enough, is trying to convince Darius (alias Codoman) that he is, in fact, the long lost Darius. In any case, by the end of the play, Megabise is jailed, Ochus is displaced, and Darius gets the throne, all, we are led to believe, by being his good, honest, virtuous self. Thus the real Darius plays the part of another not only to become himself, in a way, but to establish himself within a social hierarchy over which he will preside (and like all foreign courts of the period Thomas Corneille's

---

[8] Jodelet uses the verb in his confrontation with Edouard, Frédéric's brother, who of course denies Jodelet's claim to being Frédéric;

Si vous étes le seul qui me défédérique,
J'incague vos raisons prêtes à m'alléguer
Autant de fois qu'il faut pour les bien incaguer. (V.viii.)

This is also a remarkable prefiguration of Sosie's pithy statement, "Et l'on me des-Sosie enfin/ Comme on vous des-Amphitryonne" in Molière's *Amphitryon* (1860-1).

[9] Such insinuations of lower-class individuals into aristocratic circles will only succeed with the advent of the mechanisms that Marivaux will introduce. Jacob, *le paysan parvenu*, represents Jodelet's success, even though his success is marred by the visibility of his social origins on his *hétéroclite figure*. Cf. *infra* chapter 5.

Persian court has nothing to do with Persia and everything to do with France). Sitting on the throne, moreover, is the only appropriate place for him in this hierarchy, the only one commensurate with the very noble qualities to which he has treated the audience hitherto. Not only is justice served, not only does the nobility recover its rank, in this instance, it also recovers its true role, the one that it was meant to play.

The plot of *Darius* is punctuated by instances of revelation: the secret swapped in confidence between Mégabise and Darius is exchanged with a number of other characters in the play. The antagonism between king and impostor is further exacerbated by the identical nature of their discourses. Unlike *Le geôlier de soi-même*, where the differences between king and impostor were blatantly obvious, the drawing of distinctions between true and false claims to royal stature in *Darius* is impossible. Both Mégabise and Codoman claim to be Darius, but the only mark of legitimacy—a letter from Tiribase—has been lost. It is therefore up to each claimant to prove that he is the real Darius. During their second confrontation, Darius alias Codoman asks Mégabise to substantiate his claim to being Darius. The latter demurs, daring his interlocutor to contradict him. Now, from the viewpoint of the omniscient spectator, the difference between Darius and Mégabise rests on the ostensible virtue of the former and the mendacity of the latter. Nevertheless, the dramatic tension inherent in their confrontation hinges on the fact that both have something to hide, and in a plot so full of peripeteias as *Darius*, one never quite knows what to expect. Like the odd circumstances that united Frédéric and Jodelet, the facticity of the disguise common to both renders them suspect and mutually interdependent. Darius-Codoman's position corresponds to Frédéric's, who hides his real identity due to political danger, and whose nobility shows through the disguise nevertheless, and who makes his interlocutors say things like, "Ces nobles sentiments me le font trop paroître/Ou Darius n'est plus, ou Codoman doit l'être." (II.ii.) Mégabise's situation, on the other hand, is that of Jodelet, who adopts an assumed (in every sense of the word) identity and cannot cope with the consequences. His assumption of his chosen part echoes Jodelet's:

> Mon cœur du péril vainement combattu
> Prenant le nom d'un prince, en prendra la vertu
> Avecque tant d'éclat je le ferai paroître
> Que je démentirai le sang qui me fit naître. (III.vi.)

Like Jodelet, Mégabise assumes that if he plays the part well enough, seconded by his audience, the mask will stay and he will "become" Darius.

The opposition between prince and impostor deepens with every twist and turn of the plot. Mégabise's plan backfires when king Ochus hears

about his assumed identity and has him arrested for treason, but Mégabise
refuses to stop pretending to be Darius. In an almost comic exchange of
threats and counter-threats, the king's accusations serve only to increase
Mégabise's conviction that he is in fact Darius. When the real Darius steps
in and tries to clear up the misunderstanding, Mégabise is quick to retort,
"Oui, lâche, on me connoît, et tu n'as point la gloire/ De trahir seul un
prince imprudent à te croire." (IV.vi.) Finally, in a scene that parallels the
Charlotte-Mathurine altercation in *Dom Juan*, Mégabise and Darius face
off in a *dépit vertueux* that turns on each of them calling the other a liar.
With the people clamouring for the real Darius and threatening revolution
without him, Mégabise repeatedly raises the stakes in his game of liar's
poker, insulting the king with his dares ("Doute, j'y consens, doute, et
perds-moi si tu l'oses,/ Quelle que soit ta rage, au moins ai-je ce bien/
Qu'en répandant mon sang tu hazardes le tien" (V.iii.)) and, since being
Darius entails facing the threat of execution, competing with Darius on the
issue of who is to die first ("Va, quitte ce faux zéle. Offrir pour moi ta vie,/
C'est joindre l'imprudence à l'amitié trahie.") Finally, when Amestris produces Tiribase's letter in support of Darius's claim, Mégabise is genuinely
shocked, like a sleepwalker awakened; "Par quel fatal revers vois-je tout
découvert?/ J'espére en Tiribase et c'est lui qui me perd." (V.iii.)) The
mask has been on for so long that Mégabise is incapable of identifying
himself as anyone other than Darius.

The many juxtapositions of single and double, or prince and impostor,
in Thomas Corneille's theatre are not without their uses insofar as they
make manifest a rather uncomfortable fact: the impostor may not know
whether he is or is not a liar, and will have to wait until he is shown up by
his real, "authentic" counterpart, whose authenticity depends in no small
part on a confrontation and, to certain extent, an identification with his
false double. In a world where identities depend on their display, facing
one's double becomes an essential formative step since it is the only one
that separates the object from its image. The well-known technique of using one character as a foil to another is thus incorporated onto the level of
plot by Thomas Corneille: Frédéric's identity depends on Jodelet's gaffes
as its negative pole, and Darius carefully engineered political victory depends on displays of virtue that depend as much on a receptive audience as
they do on having an enemy of the right sort.

The active management of one's self by the manipulation and circulation of proper doubles soon leads to situations where the double is created
deliberately. Early on in *Timocrate*, the queen of Argos receives the Cretan
ambassador who issues an ultimatum on behalf of his king, Timocrate: either Timocrate be allowed to marry Eriphile, of whom he is enamoured, or
the war continues as before. The queen duly asks her generals and princes

their opinion. In the event, they are Léontidas, Nicandre and Timocrate *alias* Cléomène. In other words we have, onstage, the queen, her princes, and Timocrate posing as the illustrious Cléomène before his own ambassador. Once again, in accordance with the logic of the *romanesque*, Timocrate *is* as Timocrate *plays*, and at this point, he plays Cléomène and is not, we assume, recognised by Cresphonte. Furthermore, when the queen asks him his opinion, he argues in favour of peace rather than war, much to the surprise of those present who see him as Cléomène and not Timocrate. In other words Timocrate needs his double, his mask, "Cléomène" in order to speak for him and protect his political interests. Without him he stands a very good chance of losing the war.

The romanesque flourish does not end there: in the following scene, Cléomène and Nicandre discuss their inclination for Eriphile, the princess. Cléomène-Timocrate makes use of a subtle ruse in the process: when Nicandre tells him that he loves the princess and fears losing her to whoever kills Timocrate (in accordance with the queen's wishes), Cléomène surprises him by confiding that he, too, loves the princess, and because he is not a prince, and therefore unworthy of her hand, he would rather lose her to an enemy king in whom she has no interest, from whom she would "reservera le cœur en lui donnant la main" (I.iv.) than lose her to a putatively worthy rival. All of which allows yet another spectacular quantity of virtue to burst forth onstage, but also increases Timocrate's chances of getting what he wants without "doing battle" with Nicandre. As a double, Cléomène is well-nigh indispensable to Timocrate's emotional well-being.

Similarly, in *Laodice*, it is Ariarate himself who stages his return and revelation. His many doubles are an integral part of his self-construction. This self-construction is played out on two fronts, against himself, and against the false Ariarate brought in from Rome. Like Mégabise in *Darius*, the appearance of this false double teases out everybody's "real self": Laodice's infanticidal tendencies stage a strong comeback, and Ariarate's virtue is foregrounded. His constant referrals to himself in the third person, while made inevitable by his disguised situation, also allow him to treat his real identity as a double. When he confides his autobiography to Phradate, he speaks of his infanticidal mother so kindly that his interlocutor is moved to recognition:

> Ah! Souffrez que pour moi tout le secret éclate
> Ce que vous m'apprenez me montre Ariarate,
> Puisque sous un faux nom il nous abuse tous,
> A vos rares vertus je le dois croire en vous. (I.iii.)

Here again, Ariarate can only say "I am Ariarate" from the place where he is identified as Oronte, the "virtuous" courtier. Only as his own double can he display the "rares vertus" that establish and legitimate the (fiction of) his authentic authority.

That Ariarate is the most powerful figure in the play cannot be disputed. From the very start of the play, his curious powers as the queen's legislator and counselor are noted by all and sundry; "C'est être plus que roi que maintenir les rois" (I.i.) Ariarate's power depends in no small part on the degree to which he controls people's imaginations (especially his mother's) with his fictions, revelations, secrets and spectacles:

> Rome a donné ce temps à ma juste priere,
> Pour me laisser fléchir la haine de ma mere...
> J'aime à le taire [mon secret] exprès jusqu'à ce qu'elle apprenne
> Qu'Ariarate vit, et vient la faire reine,
> Et que j'ai éprouvé si, dans ce doux appas,
> Oronte abandonné ne la touchera pas... (I.iii.)

Despite his precarious position, Ariarate wields far more power than he would have without the mask of Oronte. When Phradate informs him of the false Ariarate's arrival, his calm response ("N'en soyez point surpris/Par un avis secret j'ai déjà tout appris" (II.iv.)) indicates greater access to more information than anyone else in Cappadocia. Ariarate is omniscient, omnipotent, and in full control of what those around him think and feel. Everything depends on what he shows and what he hides, to whom he reveals his identity and before whom he stands as king. Indeed, in his idiom a monarch's power consists entirely in its visibility, in its being shown: "Qu'on montre Ariarate, Oronte n'est plus." (II.iv.) In his discussion with Laodice, he tries to calm her down by reassuring her that nobody, not even the legitimate king, can outshine her or interfere with her display of power:

> Que peut-on espérer contre un roi légitime?
> Qui saura, malgré vous, malgré tous nos projets,
> Gagner, *en se montrant*, le cœur de ses sujets? (III.iii.; emphasis mine)

Typically, Ariarate's discourse hints at his own legitimacy; on the theatre of Cappadocian politics everything has a second meaning.

Thus he puts all of his stage management skills at the service of the process of the revelation and display of his identity. The arrival and assassination of the false Ariarate are part of this undertaking of the staging of the spectacle of the real Ariarate. The false Ariarate episode is nowhere to be found in the source that Thomas Corneille specifies in his introduction to *Laodice*, but is perfectly in keeping with the aesthetics of real double versus false double.[10] In view of Ariarate-Oronte's secret commerce with

---

[10] Justin makes no mention of the false Ariarate episode in his *Epitome*, where he narrates the fact that Laodice killed all but one of her children. What one does find,

Rome, and in view of the fact that we are never told that the false Ariarate is an impostor until his death, the whole affair looks like a spectacle of inauthentic authority set up by Ariarate as a background against which to set his own apotheosis as the real, right king. The account of the assassination (IV.iii.) is dominated by visual terms and shows Ariarate to be both a clever politician who erases his tracks and a "good" king who will not tolerate dishonesty. Every participant is an actor concerned with his glory, playing to the multitude who clamours for its "king". As "Oronte", Ariarate fabricates a violent dispute with Aquilius over the custody of the false "Ariarate", who is "accidentally" killed in the resulting fracas.

The assassination is basically a spectacle produced by Oronte and Aquilius for the viewing benefit of the public. Aquilius himself admits as much to queen Laodice; "Il [Ariarate] est vivant, Madame, et le bruit de sa perte/Fut une illusion heureusment offerte" (IV.vii.) This spectacle is effective: it results in a proliferation of other political spectacles in the Cappadocian palace. Laodice proceeds to send the falsely accused prince Anaxandre to a spectacular death as an exercise in riot control:

> ...Le peuple animé de rage et de douleur,
> Dans son emportement ne cherchant qu'où se prendre,
> Quoiqu'ait fait Théodot, s'est saisi d'Anaxandre;
> Et sans souffrir qu'on le menât au fort,
> *Du prince Ariarate il faut venger la mort,*
> A-t-il dit; et soudain, comme sûr de son crime,
> Sans rien examiner, il l'a pris pour victime. (V.i.)

In other words, Ariarate's sham assassination of the false Ariarate leads to the removal from his path of yet another member of the opposing camp, Anaxandre.

Ariarate's most spectacular display comes at the end of the play when Laodice plays Jocasta to his Oedipus, informing him that she has abandoned her political ambitions in favour of "Oronte's" hand in marriage, and consenting as she does so to let her son rule; "Et ce fils si long-temps par ma haine opprimé/Seroit encor haï si vous n'étiez aimé." (V.ii.)[11]

---

however, is a proliferation of histories centred on the theme of the double, such as the tale of Mithridates V Eupator (Racine's *Mithridate*), who protects himself against all poisons by taking poison, fathers and sons with the same names (Laodice names her youngest Ariarate after his father), kings who marry their sisters and rule with them, and so on. All in all, it makes for a series of very *romanesque* episodes in ancient history.

11 It bears pointing out that the threat of incest is always there in the identity plays: Cf. *Héraclius*, *Pyrrhus*, *Bérénice*. Clearly the routine classification of *Laodice* in a separate category from the *romanesque* identity plays takes no account of the modalities that they have in common.

Faced with this horrifying prospect, Ariarate drops the mask and reveals his identity, adding yet another burst of filial piety to his show:

> Mais, quand d'amour pour moi votre cœur est surpris;
> Comment vous avouer que je suis votre fils?
> … … …
> Quoi que puisse arriver, vous régnerez, Madame.
> Si mes vœux n'avoient eu qu'un trône pour objet,
> Je n'aurois pas deux ans paru comme sujet:
> Je n'aurois pas deux ans par un respect sincere,
> Tâché de mériter les bontés de ma mere,
> Les armes à la main, sans craindre son courroux,
> J'aurois osé paroître… (V.ii.)

Ariarate's use of the verb "paraître" as a synonym for "être" is not accidental, implying as it does a perfect fusion between intention and action, being and appearance: rather than say "Je n'aurais pas été sujet" he says "je n'aurais pas paru comme sujet." When he says "J'aurais osé paraître": the reader can easily fill in the lacuna with "tel que je suis." Laodice interrupts him before he can detail his matricidal fantasm, but what Ariarate makes clear is part of the intention behind his charade, namely to "re-naturalise" a "de-natured" mother who kills her children, or, in more realistic terms, to use sentiment as a shield against the violence of the political sphere and as a way of hiding his intention to displace his mother. He claims that he loved his mother more than the throne, but the claim itself is belied by the carefully engineered coup d'état on which the plot of this play is centred. Knowing that, in order to rule, he must play to the gallery and the populace, Ariarate cloaks his post-Oedipal, matricidal will in the costume of filial piety, all with a view to fusing the metaphors of authority and desire and assuring himself of the love of the crowd when he appears before them. Soon enough, Ariarate's "horror" at his mother's incestuous advances, which parallels his own horror at both her and his violent intentions, explodes in a scene where it is realised through its display before the crowd:

> Ayant sû que le peuple au palais amassé,
> Pour voir son nouveau maître avoit déjà pressé,
> Sur l'appui d'un balcon obstinée à paroître,
> La reine aux factieux se fait d'abord conoître…
> *Va*, dit-elle, *sans toi je sai ce qui m'est dû,*
> *Peuple lâche, et de qui les timides maximes*
> *T'ont fait jusques ici dissimuler mes crimes,*
> *Sans toi, qui contre moi te veux prêter mon bras,*
> *Tu tremblerois toujours et ne punirois pas.*
> Là, tirant un poignard dont elle étoit saisie,
> Avant qu'on l'ait pû voir elle a tombé sans vie,
> Un seul coup, malgré nous, a terminé son sort.(V.vi.)

The Cappadocian masses, who by now have been treated to and partici-pated in a series of spectacles (the appearance of "king" Ariarate, his as-sassination, the "punishment" of Anaxandre), finds itself unable to with-stand the sight of the phallic Laodice any longer (and there is no mistaking the connotations of her "bras"). Their horror at the mere sight of this woman is not insignificant, indicating their total sympathy with Ariarate's feelings towards this horrifying, incestuous maternal monster and their lack of identification from her person (hence their "dissimulation of her crimes"). Thomas Corneille shows, in this *récit*, the degree to which this illegitimate monarch is separate from the body politic, which according to the political theology of absolutist France, could not be led by anyone other than a male monarch. Her suicide marks a fairy-tale ending to a spectacle that refuses to show Ariarate in any light other than one of complete inno-cence and legitimacy. The crowd identifies with its figurehead, the male king Ariarate. Having seen the phallic mother disappear in a burst of obsti-nate violence, they are now ready for the happy end to the turbulent spec-tacle of Cappadocian politics, the appearance of the king. The play ends with Aquilius saying, "Allons lui [au peuple] faire voir et sa reine et son roi."

Ariarate's predicament, like Darius' and Timocrate's, is that of the prince whose identity, whose entire being, must be displayed and forged through its spectacular 'paraître" and who must use disguise as a political tool aimed at keeping social chaos—in the forms of incest and revolution—at bay.

The modalities underlying *Timocrate, Darius* and *Laodice* are also at work in a play traditionally considered to be one of Thomas Corneille's most "Racinian", the immensely popular and much anthologised *Le Comte d'Essex*.[12] The plot revolves around a misunderstanding and a chain of frustrated desire: queen Elisabeth loves Essex who loves Henriette who is married to the Duc d'Irton. When Essex first heard of Henriette's marriage, he tried to prevent it by mounting a small-scale coup and surrounding the royal palace with a group of his followers. The count's political enemies capitalise on the suspicious parallels between the count's behaviour and regicide, accuse him of treason and persuade the queen to order his execu-tion.

---

12 Comparisons with Racine tend to focus on the disposition of the text: "The tem-perament of Corneille's play is Racinian in the usual sense of this epithet, that is, by its structural simplicity, the psychological development of situations issuing directly and almost exclusively from the emotions, and the featured treatment of love and jealousy. Yet [Thomas] Corneille did not imitate Racine in any specific details." (Collins, 163)

Elizabeth's unrequited love for Essex is, of course, nothing new in Thomas Corneille's theatre, nor is the fact that she does not know who her "rival" is, which recalls Thomas Corneille's other racinian tragedy, *Ariane*.[13] What is worthy of note is the count's stubborn refusal to defend himself against the charge of sedition, adducing only the argument that his innocence should be plain for all to see. His narcissism, which critics like Reynier have tended to see as the play's biggest flaw, is, however, what makes *Le Comte d'Essex* a typical product of Thomas Corneille's idiom.

Essex is an actor. David Collins is right to say of him "This disenchanted hero is really no different from Horace and Nicomède." (170) He is as much, if not more of, an actor than Pierre Corneille's heroes, wearing his disenchantment like a mask. Essex's endless braggadocio brings him closer to *miles gloriosus* or the Matamore of *L'Illusion comique* than the sympathetic hero of a tragedy. Darius played to the court, Ariarate played to the population of Cappadocia, and Essex plays to the entire universe. He is convinced of the fact that the universe is watching him, and describes himself as someone "Qui vit de son bonheur tout l'univers jaloux." (IV.iii.) He knows (as does everyone else) how much the state needs him;

> L'intérêt de l'Etat rend ma grâce certaine,
> Et l'on ne sait que trop par ce qu'à fait mon bras
> Que qui perd mes pareils ne les retrouve pas. (I.i.)

Why, then, should he bother to ask for a pardon? His resolute refusal to beg forgiveness hinges on his unwillingness to state the obvious: his innocence is conspicuous, on display, witnessed by the entire universe, so why should he make excuses to those who pretend not to see it? Why should he play a part other than his own saintly, perfectly innocent one?

> Quoi, quand leur imposture indignement m'accable;
> Pour les justifier je me rendrai coupable,
> Et par mon lâche aveu, l'univers étonné
> Apprendra qu'ils m'auront justement condamné? (IV.iii.)

As far as Essex is concerned his enemies have brainwashed the queen with their "imposture" that takes advantage of her weaknesses. (Let us mention, in passing, that there is no mistaking the rather heavy-handed sloganeering at work here and elsewhere in Thomas Corneille's theatre: women (Laodice, Elisabeth) cannot rule properly because they fall on the

---

[13] The *Liebeskette* is something of a constant in Thomas Corneille's theatre: in *Ariane*, Oenarus loves Ariane who loves Thésée who loves Phèdre; in *Circé* Circé loves Glaucus who loves Sylla who loves Mélicerte; in *Maximian*, Constantin loves Fauste, who loves Sévère, who is married to Constance, who loves Licine; in *Antiochus*, Antiochus loves Stratonice who is engaged to Séléucus, and so on.

wrong side of the division between authority and desire; both fall in love with their subjects. Clearly there is a great deal of anxiety expressed here regarding the king's amorous relations with the women at court and the necessary bonds of desire tying monarch to subject). So much so that Essex sees his arrest as an act of emotional and political suicide:

> Vous avez dans vos mains ce que toute la terre
> A vu plus d'une fois utile à l'Angleterre.
> Marchons: quelque douleur que j'en puisse sentir,
> La reine veut sa perte, il faut y consentir. (II.vii.)

Essex's logic is megalomaniacal, to say the least. If he goes, the state must go with him. If he dies, the queen will die as well. Essex does not hesitate to multiply the points of comparison between himself and the sovereign: "J'ai regret qu'aveuglée elle attire sur soi/ La honte qu'elle croit faire tomber sur moi." (IV.i.) (Elisabeth, for her part, is just as vain as Essex, as witness her self-conscious lament; "O vous, Rois que pour lui ma flamme a négligés/ Jetez les yeux sur moi: vous êtes bien vengés." (II.v.)) So real is the possibility of his displacing the monarch that, from certain points of view, it is impossible not to see Essex as a pretender to the throne, and the conflict between him and the state as one between an impostor and a king. Yet the only person who is blind to this resemblance is Essex himself, the man who would be king. Hence his surprise at his arrest, which is reminiscent of nothing if not Mégabise's "Par quel fatal revers vois-je tout découvert?" Essex's fatuity is nothing more than the desperately histrionic tone of one who does not know whether he is king or impostor, loyal subject or traitor, guilty or innocent. His endless attempts at effecting his innocence by proclaiming it evince a theatrical mode of operation, based on the principle that there is nothing in the world either good or bad but that Essex makes it so. Only an endless iteration of the fact that his innocence speaks for itself can cover up the very suspicious circumstances surrounding his arrest. He knows that the queen loves him and disavows it, knows that surrounding the palace with his "followers" looks bad and disavows it, attempts to pass off a coup d'état for an act of love and an act of insurgency for the foundation of a *Liebeskette*: his revolt against authority becomes a revolt against the authority figure's desire ("Le crime n'est pas grand de n'avoir pû l'aimer", he says (IV.i.)). Consequently, it is difficult to take all of his fatuous claims to innocence seriously. When we hear him accuse Raleigh and Cecil of counterfeiting his writing, the claim sounds rather specious, and the reader wonders whether Essex might not be guilty after all:

> Souffrir que contre moi des écrits contrefaits...
> Non, la postérité ne le croira jamais.
> Jamais on ne pourra se mettre en la pensée,

> Que de ce qu'on me doit la mémoire effacée,
> Ait laissé l'imposture en pouvoir d'accabler...
> Mais la reine le voit, et le voit sans trembler.          (IV.i.)

Rather than offer convincing counterclaims, Essex simply vaunts his past accomplishments, reassuring himself that no-one would believe that a state hero would sink so low.

Essex's guilt or innocence is, of course, neither here nor there, guided (and cursed) as he is by the fact that in the realm of human affairs, there can be no separating intention from action. His rank in the political hierarchy has been undermined for reasons that may or may not be of his own making. The invisibility of his innocence to all but himself (Can the queen not see that the accusations are false? Can she not see that I am innocent?) reflects the anxieties of a world in which the political order has been turned upside down, all because of a perversion in the link of desire that links monarch to subject: Elisabeth loves Essex who does not love her back. Essex's constant self-doubt attests to the fact that legitimacy is an illusion, but a necessary one. In a properly-constructed state, the illusion of legitimacy "works" (as it did with king Ariarate before his people); in an improperly-constructed one—like a state ruled by a woman—it does not. Everything depends on the eye of the monarch, before whom "Le plus innocent devient soudain coupable." Like *Horace*, *Le Comte d'Essex* examines the vicissitudes of a political system where everything is what it seems and nothing is what it seems because it all exists insofar as it is on display for the observing eye of the monarch, who may or may not be on display, who may or may not be one of the many actors that he or she observes. As Essex plays his innocence to the entire universe, he cannot know whether he is guilty or innocent, in much the same way that Mégabise did not know whether he was Mégabise or Darius, until the instance of his death.

*<br>*   *

Thus Thomas Corneille uses the aesthetics of *éclat* to great effect, mapping the totalitarian terrain of absolutism. The topoi of the necessary disguise that allows a better self to emerge in relief, and the double that overtakes the simple, come together in a very effective way in *L'Inconnu*.

At the start of *L'Inconnu* we are presented with a quartet of lovers: a marquis, a countess, a knight (le chevalier) and a woman named Olympe. The fact that the characters have stock names is not insignificant, for this play is, in many ways, Thomas' *summa* on dramatic praxis.[14] The four lovers are arranged in two straight lines, the marquis loves the countess, and the knight loves Olympe, and that would seem to be that, except for the fact that the countess keeps getting messages from a stranger, an *inconnu*, and that these messages are very elaborate displays of love and affection. The stranger does not just send her letters; he sends actors and actresses, hires whole troupes to come to her castle, stage song and dance routines (usually ones involving allegories of youth and love), give her a lot of gifts and, in the middle of the routine, designate one of their number to jump out and give the countess a message of love entreating her to reciprocate the love of the stranger.

We of course know that the stranger is none other than the marquis himself. He takes the trouble to tell us early on that he is testing the countess's love for him, although what he seems to be testing is his place in the hierarchy, the place that identifies him as *l'amant de la comtesse*. He actually points out that without performing this test, he risks losing the woman he loves. In order to be himself in the best possible manner, he has to be someone else, or posit someone else as a double.

All of the marquis' tricks have an interesting effect on our quartet, not least among which is the morphological transformation from scattered group to the *Liebeskette* typical of pastorals. Not unexpectedly, much of the plot centres on the characters playing detective and trying to find out who the marquis actually is. His gifts and interludes are the start of much lively speculation. The countess becomes increasingly taken with this very gallant invisible stranger. At a certain point the marquis enlists the help of Olympe to try and convince the countess to succumb to the stranger's charms. She does, and the countess follows suit, but along the way Olympe herself is so taken with the marquis' display of gallantry, generosity and pretended indifference that she falls in love with him. So the introduction of the stranger allows us to move to a different structure, where we have the knight who loves Olympe who loves the marquis who loves the countess who loves the stranger, who, of course, is unattainable and therefore eminently desirable; his invisibility makes him perfect and allows him to top the hierarchy because people are never as desirable as they are when they are unattainable.

We in the audience of course see all of this with a relatively omniscient gaze; *L'Inconnu* is not a surprise à la *Timocrate*. From this vantage-point the marquis seems to be going to extraordinary lengths to prove his love for

---

14 In this respect it is very difficult to agree with Reynier's dismissive comment, that "De *L'Inconnu*, il n'y a pas grand'chose à dire: à proprement parler, ce n'est pas une pièce, ce n'est guére qu'un prétexte à divertissements." (282)

the countess and keep her interested. These lengths have to be extraordinary, though, for if *L'Inconnu* proves anything it is that the best way to say anything is to say it with theatre. Theatre is not simply the locus of the revelation of the truth, it now furnishes the code of social interaction. The play ends on an interesting note, too: when the marquis reveals himself, he returns to the countess something that she had given to one of the actors (in one of the gifts) to give to his master, *L'Inconnu*. In other words we have here a system of social exchange, a mechanism of self-presentation, indeed a language centered on theatre. Theatre is now negotiable currency, and the best way to present oneself is to mask oneself. The marquis' antics mark the final stage in the development in the theme of the double as threat: the best way to seduce someone is to create a rival, and success is never so certain as when that rival is oneself.

At this point all the strands that we have been talking about come to a head: we have in *L'Inconnu* the identity play par excellence, using the device of the stage within a stage to reflect on the nature of theatre, the rules of pastoral and the laws of social interaction. Theatre proliferates at the countess's castle; the borders separating the theatricality of the musical interludes from the theatricality of everyday life as exemplified by the members of the quartet are difficult to discern. Indeed when the marquis does reveal himself he does so by allegorically masking himself: he does not say "I am the *inconnu*" but rather has a cupid come on-stage and give the countess a portrait of the marquis. The use of the well-known *précieux* motif of the exchange of portraits is not accidental: in the histrionic world created by Thomas Corneille, every utterance, including declarations love and revelations of identity have to pass through this filter, this medium of theatricality. At the end of the play, the marquis' place as the countess's lover is confirmed, and because of the detours that he took his place at the top of this hierarchy of lovers is confirmed as well.

*L'Inconnu* is by many measures Thomas Corneille's answer to Pierre's *Illusion*, acting as Thomas' apology for his particular brand of theatre. In both cases we have a playwright and actors turning to each other to attain their aims (and there is no mistaking the parallels between the marquis and the directorial figure suggested by Alcandre), but whereas in the first we have a progressive construction of an identity, in the second we have a steady unveiling of an identity, a revelation, an *aletheia* that arranges an entire social order. We see similar phenomena elsewhere: Darius becomes king, Ariarate becomes king, Timocrate gets his girl, and all rule happily ever after. Ironically enough, this unveiling depends entirely on masking in order to operate effectively.

The *romanesque* literary space created by Thomas Corneille, like the physical space of *la cour et la ville*, is one where roles and masks matter because they are, to borrow a phrase, *bonne à penser;* they are good to think with. They allow manipulation and experimentation, not of abstract concepts but of identities, names and titles and all that is consequent upon them. Such experimentation, theatrical though it might be, lead to important results and conclusions: added support to the peg of absolutism from which the society of the seventeenth century was hung, explanations of the many comings and goings at the court documented assiduously by the likes of Saint-Simon, advice to those who so ardently desired a position therein, and so on. Finally, they offered a strong confirmation of the *Weltanschauungen* held by the privileged inhabitants of the courts whose structure mirrored the *romanesque* worlds staged by the writers in their employ, worlds where the truth was much stranger than fiction.

*
*   *

The texts covered in this chapter carry a certain prognostic value: not only does the relationship between the king and the impostor announce the hard-nosed critique of the monarchy evinced in Montesquieu's *Lettres persanes* ("Ce grand roi est un magicien"), but the swapping of roles and histories between singles and doubles (Alvar and Isabelle, Frédéric and Jodelet, Mégabise and Darius) announce the use of narrative fiction as a role during the eighteenth century, from Marivaux's *Ile de la raison* to Rousseau's *Confessions*. The closed social circle of *L'Inconnu*, spanned by desire and intrigue, pre-figures *le monde* in no uncertain terms. The intervention of the *romanesque* as both theatrical framework and mode of operation allows a displacement from role-playing to storytelling as the dominant mode of producing illusions and identities. This change is accompanied by other evolutions: the impostor's dilemma translates into the tales told by and about upstarts (Marivaux), seducers (Crébillon) and self-made saints (Rousseau).[15] The seemingly timeless confrontations of the Horaces and the Cids of French classical theatre give way to personalities produced by the act of narration itself. Rather than argue "I play a part therefore I am" they proclaim "I enact my history therefore I am."

---

[15] The term is borrowed from Huizinga, *Rousseau, the Self-Made Saint* (New York: Grossman, 1976).

# Chapter Four

# The Eighteenth Century

Crébillon's preface to *Les Egarements du cœur et de l'esprit* contains the following prescriptive observation:

> Le Roman, si méprisé des personnes sensées, et souvent avec justice, serait peut-être celui de tous les genres qu'on pourrait rendre le plus utile, s'il était bien manié, si... on le rendait, comme la Comédie, le tableau de la vie humaine, et qu'on y censurât les vices et les ridicules. (41)[1]

The suggestion is remarkable for the economy with which it sums up the concerns of the age that follows one where comedy as a genre was not quite as respectable as its author would have us believe. By 1736, some seventy years after Molière's death, the "étrange entreprise que celle de faire rire les honnêtes gens" has become something of a paradigm in its own right, respectable enough to provide sufficient exemplarity for Crébillon's purposes. Which exemplarity is now to be transferred to the space of fiction, a genre perfected in the eighteenth century, taking on guises that it would keep for a while to come. Crébillon is concerned with the utility of the novel, with its ability to instruct and the risk it runs of lapsing into a pure frivolity that might catch the reader's eye but would in the last analysis teach him or her nothing.

Crébillon also re-iterates the commonplace description of the theatre holding the mirror up to (human) nature, thus implicitly assigning a content to the novel's instruction: fiction will tell the reader something about his or herself. This applies to the narrator as well. Crébillon is, in this respect, indebted to one of his immediate predecessors, Marivaux, whose literary output was motivated and enabled by the text's oscillation between the twin foci of creator and creation, narrator and narrated entity, author and actor. Marivaux's *Spectateur français* sums up rather nicely a situation that also applies to Marianne, Jacob or Silvia: "Dans tout le cours de mes aventures, j'ai été mon propre spectateur comme celui des autres."[2] The process of histrionic self-fashioning in the eighteenth century aims at the transmission of this lucid stance through the involvement of self and other.

---

[1] In *Les Egarements du coeur et de l'esprit* (Paris: Gallimard, 1977). The novel itself will henceforth be referred to as *Les Egarements*.

[2] Qtd. Rousset, *Forme et signification*, 64.

The situation of the writer under the regency is of some relevance to our analysis. The regency effected a relativisation of the values that had hardened into absolutes at Versailles. Orders became classes; the rigid social hierarchies whose legitimacy was not open to question in 1661 gave way after 1715 to planar configurations driven by the dynamics of exchange that linked them to each other. Everything, including the crown and its coffers, acquired a price under the new arrangement. The abolition of economic and financial certainties under John Law's (eventually disastrous) experiments bear out this tendency. The royal function was no longer operative as a direct link to the divine and coming under increasing attack from aristocratic institutions as they recovered from Louis XIV's totalitarian grip. One of the more telling instances is the change in the ritual following Louis XV's coronation on October 29, 1722. When the king "cured" the victims of scrofula, the formula that he uttered changed from "Le roi te touche, Dieu te guérit" to "Le roi te touche, Dieu te guérisse."[3] Thus in the space of seven years, the symbolic order of absolutism lost its meaning, affirmative statement became prayer and divine myth became secular history.

The legacy of seventeenth-century theatre was to influence very heavily many of the names most commonly associated with this period, among them Marivaux, Crébillon *fils* and Rousseau. To the very end of the century, the theatre was to remain the fastest way to establish oneself as a writer in Paris.[4] At the same time, there is an overall shift of interest towards the novel as a new and influential space of literary production, one which remains aware of its debt to the theatrical paradigms established during the seventeenth century. In 1713, Lenglet-DuFresnoy described the study of history and the novel using terms that recall the learning process at work in *Le Malade imaginaire*: "en un mot, c'est apprendre à se connaître dans les autres."[5] Diderot's *Eloge de Richardson* makes explicit the novel's takeover of the processes of the theatre, turning the reader into one of the players on the scene:

> O Richardson! on prend, malgré qu'on en ait, un rôle dans tes ou-
> vrages, on se mêle à la conversation, on approuve, on blâme, on

---

[3] Cf. Roland Mousnier, Institutions, 1:523. Mousnier also mentions instances of the gathering of evidence by the king's intendants of successful cures as proof of the king's divine favour in order to shore up the infrastructure of royal mythology against its continuing erosion: "On n'en était plus à dédaigner les preuves expérimentales du miracle."

[4] Cf. Lough, *An Introduction to Eighteenth Century France* (London: Longmans, 1960), 231-276.

[5] In his *De l'usage des romans* (Paris, 1734), 75.

admire, on s'irrite, on s'indigne. Combien de fois ne me suis-je pas surpris, comme il est arrivé à des enfants qu'on avait menés au spectacle pour la première fois, criant: *Ne le croyez pas, il vous trompe... Si vous allez là vous êtes perdu.* Mon âme était tenue dans une agitation perpétuelle. Combien j'étais bon! combien j'étais juste! que j'étais satisfait de moi![6]

Thus the modus operandi that marks this century is no less theatrical than its forebears, no less maniacal regarding its relation to alterity. The tools and tricks of the trade, however, differ significantly: whereas Corneille and Molière created characters whose sole aim in life is to play themselves, Marivaux and Crébillon create ones who aim at narrating themselves. Similarly, the relationship between self and other changes: if the seventeenth century saw the establishment of the individual, the eighteenth century creates the sect. The atmosphere that engenders *l'homme sensible moyen* expands the definition of theatrical space by turning the gap between audience and orchestral pit through a full ninety degrees, so that the audience is always onstage, to and for itself. The ever-critical Rousseau laments the fact that Molière "corrigea la cour en infectant la ville."[7] When people go to the theatre, it is to see and be seen rather than to watch the show: "Personne ne va au spectacle pour le plaisir du spectacle, mais pour voir l'assemblée, pour en être vu, pour ramasser dequoui fournir au caquet après la pièce, et l'on ne songe à ce qu'on voit que pour savoir ce qu'on en dira."[8] Similarly, the scene at the opera in *Les Egarements* serves primarily as a point of encounter between Meilcour and Hortense. As a result the stage is no longer the sole privileged locus of self-discovery; if the souls of the eighteenth century had a smithy it was to be found in other places, other contexts, ones that also functioned as stages where human behaviour was no less ostentatious (in Rousset's sense of the word) but where the gap between player and spectator is to be gauged in radically different terms. Even a critic as misanthropic as Rousseau partakes of this expansion of theatrical space when he prescribes, in his *Lettre à d'Alembert*, festivals for

---

[6] *Œuvres* (Paris: Gallimard, 1951) 1090.

[7] Rousseau, *Œuvres complètes* (Paris: Gallimard, 1959-1995; henceforth *OC*), 2:253.

[8] Rousseau, *OC*, 2:254. Louis-Sébastien Mercier adds a gendered twist to his summing-up of the situation: "Il faut donc, quand on est femme, avoir dans une petite loge son épagneul, son coussin, sa chaufferette, mais surtout un petit fat à lorgnette, qui vous instruit de tout ce qui entre et de tout ce qui sort, et qui vous nomme les acteurs. Cependant la dame a dans son éventail une petite ouverture, où est enchâssé un verre, de sorte qu'elle voie sans être vue." ("Petites loges" in *Tableau de Paris*, (Amsterdam 1783-1789) 2:320.)

his republic that turn every inhabitant into an actor: "Ne faut-il donc aucun spectacle dans une republique? Au contraire, il en faut beaucoup... Mais quels seront enfin les objets de ces spectacles? qu'y montrera-t-on? Rien, si l'on veut; donnez les spectateurs en spectacle; rendez les acteurs eux-mêmes." (*OC*, 5:114) Theatricality is now the social god whose centre is everywhere and whose circumference nowhere.[9]

The ubiquity of the theatrical is nowhere more apparent than in the use made of space during the eighteenth century. The change between the seventeenth and eighteenth centuries can be described as a shift from symbolic space to virtual (mimetic) space. Louis XIV's court was a spectacle aimed at involving the court's inhabitants. The multiplication of courts and palaces during the following century aimed at the separation of the court inhabitants from the setting that surrounded them. If anything, the outsider looking in is reminded not so much of the glory of the monarch and of the cohesion of society as of his or her irrevocable exclusion from the charmed circle framed by the palatial walls. Hence the importance of the facade in the architecture of the period, which, as described by Starobinski, acts as an interface between real and virtual space:

> Le rôle de la façade développe ici toute sa signification. Côté cour, sur le dehors, face aux autres, la façade marque la limite d'un univers privilégié, en déployant élégamment les signes qui imposent *l'illusion d'une autorité*. A l'intérieur, côté jardin, ou derrière les portes refermées pour celui qui loge dans le domaine, les lambris et les glaces établissent en revanche *l'autorité de l'illusion*. (*Invention*, 74)

The uniformity of architectural style that stretches from Versailles to Berlin and beyond re-creates the stage setting of the Parisian *salon* in a manner that all too often outdoes the original.[10] Within the palace there was a similar proliferation of the entire semiophoric system associated with the French court and culture, all aimed at mapping out the terrain of imitative duplication that creates its own reality. The *objets d'art* of the period created their own *ersatz* reality on the other side of the facade.[11] Inside the

---

[9] There is probably no stronger manifestation of this tendency than the multifarious forms of the fête that were perfected during the eighteenth century. Cf. Starobinski's *L'Invention de la liberté* (Paris: Skira, 1964), 100-111.

[10] Lough, *Eighteenth-Century France*, 6.

[11] Cf. Patrick Wald Lasowski's description: "L'aura de l'or a disparu. Et la dorure n'en est pas le triste substitut. Au contraire, assistons à ce fastueux déballement de simulacres où, avec l'effondrement de l'or, s'évanouissent le marbre et la laine, comme si cessait le régime de l'intimidation propre à la vérité qu'ils recelaient, à la faveur d'une prodigieuse économie de l'ersatz, des mélanges, où l'étalage des nouveaux artifices approfondit la satisfaction de leur seule vanité. Gloire du factice: c'est le triomphe

palace walls, we are within a world where artifice rules in the strongest possible way, namely as a matter of course, as an axiom on which the operation of the *monde* is predicated.

It is within the parameters of this region that virtual space is established. The hall of mirrors that contained the hero or courtier's identity at Versailles has now succeeded in duplicating itself across national boundaries. Thus the prevailing conception of geographical alterity at the time sees other spaces as little more than idealised (or satirical) versions of Paris, as witness the *Lettres persanes*. Amidst the explosion of travel literature of the eighteenth century, utopias are thought through in an understated tone that makes them far more powerful than the fantasmagoric spaces that served as a backdrop to the *roman d'aventure*. Similarly, Watteau's painting operates by pushing imitation to the limits of the surreal, whereby ordinary everyday *types* are combined in unlikely combinations to depict a reality that could exist, but only virtually (and therefore, much more persuasively);

> Ont-ils jamais été ainsi mêlés et confondus, ces acteurs, ces grandes dames, ces paysans? Tant de confiance et de tendresse, où les trouvait-on hors du rêve de Watteau? Mais vêtant et coiffant ses personnages à la mode du jour, il donne à sentir la proximité d'un âge d'or, la vraisemblance d'un bonheur désiré. Si ce n'était l'imitation d'un spectacle réel, c'était au moins une image attirante, une promesse qui paraissait pouvoir être tenue: le spectateur s'y croyait aisément transporté. (Starobinski, *Invention*, 64)

Whether the spectator was being transported to Watteau's Cythère or Marivaux's *Ile de la raison*, the process was facilitated by the parallels that existed between the palace and utopia, both of which were variants of the sorts of virtual space that the eighteenth century never tired of inventing and re-discovering for its aesthetic pleasure. The *ersatz* reality depicted therein enabled the spectator's mapping of his or her identity onto that of the inhabitants: Marianne and Jacob read themselves into their (better-dressed) mirror-images, and each of Zéinis's listeners imagines himself to be the lover whose adventures on Crébillon's sofa have just been narrated.

With the expansion of the literary public to accommodate the beneficiaries of the increased social mobility of the age, the concerns that move to the fore are those of an effectively expanded nobility, lacking perhaps the

---

du Stuc!... [L]'épée est devenue une parure, les emblèmes disparaissent, jusqu'à cette consommation finale: le cartouche réservé à la devise perd sa fonction emblématique pour n'être plus traité que comme une forme vide et élégante parmi d'autres." (*Libertines* (Paris: Gallimard, 1980), 23-25). The use of the sword as *parure* is especially important for Marivaux's paysan parvenu, Jacob, who sees it less as a weapon than as part of a costume that aids and abets his social ascent.

mythic *éclat* of the court of the Sun King but no less zealous in its addiction to ritual and exclusion. With the parallel shift in emphasis from bombastic heroes to more quotidian figures,[12] literature becomes a mirror both in reality and on the conceptual plane: insofar as one is a member of a given group, one is always, de facto, on display. The eighteenth century presents us with the vindication of the précieuses ridicules, a society on permanent display to and for itself. Standards, both intellectual and aesthetic, migrated from Versailles back to the salons of Paris after 1715. Coupled with the impact of increased trade and industry, the rise of the bourgeoisie, the acceptability of mercantile careers among the nobility and an increase in the literacy rate this shift gave rise to a new literary community.[13] Henceforth, as Fréderic Deloffre puts it, "on n'écrit plus en France pour la cour, mais pour la ville."[14] The impact of this republic of letters spread far beyond the borders of France, to re-create the *monde* of Paris in the French countryside and in the capitals of continental Europe. Consequently the form of the dramatis personae, so to speak, changes. Thus it is with some distaste that Rousseau describes the limited range of backgrounds from

---

[12] On this point, see Georges May's *Dilemme du roman au dix-huitième siècle* (Paris: PUF, 1963) and Lough, *Eighteenth-Century France*, 276-299. It bears pointing out that that in relative terms, the encanaillement or plebeianisation of protagonists was slight and that, by and large, most of the reading public preferred to save its attention for the inhabitants of le monde. Lower-class protagonists were usually introduced in French fiction with a view to the depiction of the improvement of their social standing (as in *Le Paysan parvenu*).

[13] These claims should be attenuated somewhat: the rift between the old nobility, bent as it was on re-asserting its presence after Louis XIV, and the bourgoisie and annoblis led to inreasing resistance in the upper strata of society to the admission of new members. It is not insignificant that by 1789, all the ministers (with the exception of Necker) were noble. If there was to be intercourse with a different class, it was to be the nobility of another country in Europe. Cf. Lionel Gossman, *French Society and Culture: Background for Eighteenth-Century Literature* (Englewood Cliffs: Prentice, 1972) pp. 50-60. Furthermore, despite the increase in rates of literacy, the composition of the French reading public remained fairly traditional, which may help explain the tenacious insistence in French aesthetics on characters' being born into the appropriate rank. If anything the eighteenth century's greatest impact on the literary community seems to have been in sheer number due to the overall increase in the population of France and the growth of the pirated book trade beyond the French border. This issue has seen an explosion of very informative studies in recent years, and no attempt has been made to take issue with the many schools of thought here. Especially helpful were François Furet's seminal essay, "La "librairie" du royaume de France au dix-huitième siècle" in Bolleme et al., *Livre et société dans la France du dix-huitième siècle* (Paris: Mouton, 1965-1970); Daniel Roche's *Les Républicains des lettres. Gens de culture et Lumières au dix-huitième siècle* (Paris: Fayard, 1988) and Robert Darnton's "Reading, Writing and Publishing in Eighteenth-Century France" in *Daedalus* 100 (1971).

[14] In his *Marivaux et le marivaudage* (Paris: Les Belles lettres, 1955).

which the characters of eighteenth-century comedy arise and with some outrage that he uncovers the reasons behind this tendency:

> Molière osa peindre des bourgeois et des artisans aussi bien que des marquis... Mais les auteurs d'aujourd'hui qui sont des gens d'un autre air, se croiraient deshonorés s'ils savaient ce qui se passe au comptoir d'un marchand ou dans la boutique d'un ouvrier; il ne leur faut que des interlocuteurs illustres, et ils cherchent dans le rang de leurs personnages l'élévation qu'ils ne peuvent tirer de leur génie... Les spectateurs eux-mêmes sont devenus si délicats qu'ils craindraient de se compromettre à la comédie comme en visite, et ne daigneraint pas aller voir en représentation des gens de moindre condition qu'eux. Ils sont comme les seuls habitants de la terre; tout le reste n'est rien à leurs yeux. Avoir un carosse, un suisse, un maître d'hôtel, c'est être comme tout le monde... et l'on dirait qu'un carosse n'est pas tant nécessaire pour se conduire que pour exister. (*OC* 2:252)[15]

The theatrical production of the self, reaches new heights in the eighteenth century. The implications of Rousseau's vitriolic denunciation of the mores of his age are quite clear: attending the theatre is less an exercise in cultural refinement or even entertainment than a crucial mechanism used to maintain and confirm one's social persona and status. Not only is social station mirrored onstage, it is also mirrored, as we have seen, in the audience. The continuity between identity and theatrically-represented self is especially important in Marivaux's theatre, where the "jeu de l'amour" consists in  re-casting oneself as a member of the lower orders and the "autre monde", and allows its participants to reach a state of lucid authenticity where they can say, "Ah! je vois clair dans mon cœur."[16]

The plots change as well: no longer concerned with the hot-headed vindicators of a past generation's wrongs or the plight of young couples with no authority, the new generation of protagonists is endowed with all the trappings of a socially determined subjectivity. In the eighteenth century we move from one conception of literature and fiction to another; the *romanesque* of the eighteenth century is "non plus le romanesque du sacri

---

15 It is interesting to note that this quote throws Rousseau's prescription regarding popular festivals (in the *Lettre à d'Alembert*) into an interesting perspective: if, in fact, the solution to the theatre's corrupting influence is to "donner les spectateurs en spectacle" it is precisely because eighteenth-century French society had, by that point in time, come close enough to this state of affairs to allow the change, if implemented, to come about effortlessly and imperceptibly.

16 In *Le Jeu de l'amour et du hasard*, II.xii.

fice et du dépassement héroïque comme au dix-septième siècle, mais le romanesque de la conquête du bonheur et des obstacles qu'elle affronte."[17] This new brand of identities is defined under the gaze of a panoptic group. Most of the activities of the *libertin* or the *habitué* of a given salon would make very little sense without an equally obsessive group of *libertins* to surround, watch and validate the events that constitute the plot at hand. Thus there is a certain group expansion of the individual.[18] Hence the central importance accorded to conversation in the literature of the period, presenting a scenario where the identity of every participant oscillates between individual and collective space as he or she revives, with every utterance, the social relationship that determines identity and status.[19] The touchstone of appropriate social behaviour moved from the court back to the salon. Thus the theoreticians of fiction turn to conversation as a reference-point in legitimating the upstart genre: if the novel can instruct, it is by initiating the reader into "l'usage du monde."[20]

Accordingly, the undertakings that took Rodrigue and Horace to the battlefield take the protagonists of the later era to the *boudoir*. This shift entails a transposition of the self-fashioning process (as applied to Corneille's heroic warriors) from the battlefield to the myriad virtual spaces of the eighteenth century: the *salon*, the bedroom, the park and so on. Seduction replaces war as the shortest path to glory among the mem-

---

[17] Henri Coulet, *Le Roman jusqu'à la révolution* (Paris: Armand Colin, 1967) 1:311.

[18] On the extent to which the novel has served as a medium of exploration of the relationships between group an individual, see Michel Butor's "Individu et groupe dans le roman" in *Répertoire II* (Paris: Editions de Minuit, 1964), 73-87.

[19] On the importance of conversation in the eighteenth century Philip Stewart's *Le Masque et la parole. Le langage de l'amour au dix-huitième siècle* (Paris: Corti, 1973), 59-89.

[20] Crébillon's preface to *Les Egarements* has already been mentioned in this respect, but Lenglet DuFresnoy's *De l'usage des romans* is more explicit: "Enfin il y a un usage du monde, qu'il n'est pas permis d'ignorer; cet usage n'est ni dans la pratique de la vertu, ni dans les moeurs, ni dans la suite des passions; ce sont des grâces, mais qui ne sont pas tout à fait personnelles. C'est un talent qui consiste plus à faire valoir les autres qu'à se faire valoir soi-même; il consiste dans un tour adroit à faire sentir sans affectation ni fades loüanges combien on doit estimer ce que les autres disent ou font de bien; à leur déferer sans s'y soumettre bassement; à parler à propos, mais toujours juste et en termes convenables; à s'expliquer même ou par un sage, ou par un ingénieux silence. On n'a pas toujours l'esprit assez vif pour prévoir sur le champ tout ce qu'il faut faire là-dessus dans les entretiens particuliers, il est bon de s'y préparer; et c'est par les Romans seuls qu'on peut le faire: c'est sur quoi tous les autres livres sont en défaut; les situations où l'on représente les acteurs donnent lieu de se préparer pour une pareille occasion." (292-293)

bers of a nobility cut off from its violent, feudal origins, as Michel Butor reminds us in his reading of *Les Liaisons dangereuses*:

> Qu'à partir du moment où sa liaison avec les armes disparaît, la noblesse transpose dans un autre domaine cette "guerre" qui la justifiait, voilà qui est facile à comprendre, mais il appartenait au génie de Laclos de nous faire saisir pourquoi cette transposition devait se faire sur le terrain de la "séduction". Cessant d'être alimentée, entretenue par l'ennoblissement pour fait d'armes, la seule "raison" de la noblesse devient l'hérédité, la naissance... La notion de "vertu" se dégrade alors en virilité au sens purement sexuel du terme.[21]

Even more interesting is the fact that the procedures involved in this sort of self-fashioning are still as verbal as they were in the preceding century: seduction, glory and social identity are all precipitated from the matrix of narrative. *Les Liaisons dangereuses* stands as a first-rate parody of the idiom of chivalry and feudal conquest that held an earlier nobility together. Valmont and the Marquise engage in seduction not out of boredom, but, to borrow a phrase, "pour avoir de quoi fournir à leur caquet," to have something to write about and thus maintain the social configuration that supports their status. The corporeal dimension is almost entirely lacking from the seducer's undertaking.[22] When the *libertin* does deal with the body, it is only insofar as the latter catalyses the writing process, as when Valmont writes letters on Emilie's back.[23]

---

[21] Michel Butor, "Sur *Les Liaisons dangereuses*" in *Répertoire II*, 148.

[22] On the deliberate avoidance of the feminine body by the male libertin, Cf. Lasowski's commentary: "Ausi le dialogue, chez Crébillon, est-il par lui-même l'expression de l'irritation libertine. Libertine par excellence, cette oeuvre nous fascine, autant par ses héros que par sa forme structurante: incapable d'accéder jamais—fût-ce par le biais du Conte—aux plages délicieuses du continent romanesque, le lieu donc d'une certaine jouissance. Mais retombée toujours, extrêmement tendue, dans les filets serrés d'une conversation qui ne cesse de dire l'absence du sexe féminin." (*Libertines*, 64)

[23] This habit seems to have extended to real *libertins* as well as ficticious ones, as witness the opening of Voltaire's bawdy mise-en-scène of the writing process:

> Que devient donc mon Cideville?
> Et pourquoi ne m'écrit-il plus?
> Est-ce Thémis, est-ce Vénus?
> Qui l'a rendu si difficile?...
>
> Il faut que loin de m'oublier
> Il m'écrive avec allégresse,
> Ou sur le dos de son greffier
> Ou sur le cul de sa maîtresse.

As a result of the importance of the group, plot construction often suffers in favour of a series of contrived events culminating in the confirmation of a given individual as a legitimate member of a given social group: *Les 120 journées de sodome* is a series of initiation rites, the evolution in extremis of the histrionic rituals that animated *Le Bourgeois gentilhomme* and *Le Malade imaginaire*.[24] Apart from ritual, however, history is often the component lacking in these identities, and it is this lack of personal history that much eighteenth-century fiction sets out to remedy since, in a group where all ranks are equal, history is the only effective strategy of legitimation and source of distinction between the members. The hierarchies that determined social identity in the seventeenth century are mapped onto the genealogies and narratives that a given participant brings to a given gathering. A character's status within that gathering is assured as long as he or she maintains it by telling the appropriate stories.[25]

---

Ah datez du cul de Manon,
C'est de là qu'il me faut écrire
C'est le vrai trépied d'Apollon,
Rempli du feu qui vous inspire.

Ecrivez donc ces vers divins,
Mais en commençant votre épître
La plume échappe de vos mains
Et vous foutez votre pupitre. (*Correspondence*, 1:632)

[24] Cf. Claude Reichler's description in *L'Age libertin* (Paris: Minuit, 1987): "L'époque "classique" a inventé une disposition qui se prête admirablement à cette dialectique de l'individuel et du collectif: du "rond" des précieuses à l'espèce du théâtre en rond des *Cent vingt journées de Sodome*, pendant deux siècles le langage et ses échanges ont été manifestés dans l'espace quasi rituel du cercle." (29)

[25] One of the most interesting cases of group narration in this respect is Challe's *Illustres françaises* (1713). Challe takes the *Héptameron* as his model but is especially innovative insofar as (a) the narrators and actors of his novel focus primarily on the formation of their narrated historical selves and, (b) all the stories feed into one another so that a given narrative (and, ipso facto a given identity) never really ends, subject as it is to the changes in the greater narrative entitled *Les Illustres françaises* in which it is contained. On this point, see Coulet, *Roman*, 1:309-315. The structure of the "endless narrative" becomes especially important with Marivaux, whose Marianne and Jacob owe their social status to their self-narration and risk losing their status if and when their tales come to an end. This is, in fact, what sets them apart from the heroines of Mme de Lafayette, whose status is assured and whose lives necessarily end with the end of the narrative. Cf. Aron Kibédi-Varga's excellent analysis of this phenomenon in the context of the shift from the seventeenth to the eighteenth century in his "La désagrégation de l'idéal classique dans le roman français de la première moitié du dix-huitième siècle" in *Studies in Voltaire and the Eighteenth Century* (henceforth SVEC) 25 (1963).

Subsequently, we see a steady loosening and expansion of the definition of history during the eighteenth century. The significance of personal histories in society, coupled with the strong realist tendencies of the novel and the rational "de-sacralisation" of history, contributes to the increasing permeability of the border between history and fiction.[26] This development has as its consequence the establishment of narrative as an epistemological category made manifest by the novel on one hand and history on the other. Fiction and historiography are, at the start of the eighteenth century, united by their opposition to the *romanesque* excesses of the traditions that inform them,[27] and the rest of the century spends most of its time moving from one to the other; "le dix-huitième siècle, qui romance l'histoire et historise le roman, a discuté avec passion du parallélisme des deux genres."[28] The temporal dimension so sorely lacking from Corneille's theatre is re-introduced with a vengeance in the literature of Marivaux and Crébillon, who fit quite neatly in the space that separates the *Discours sur l'histoire universelle* from the *Siècle de Louis XIV*. (By and large the eighteenth century's interest in history could be read as a reaction to the anti-historical bent of Louis XIV's reign, when the movement of history was systematically negated in order to fuel a royal mythology that made the regime not only the inheritor of Augustan Rome, but, through a perverse reversal of historical reason, its progenitor,[29] The appearance of various suppressed

---

[26] On the relationship between history and the novel in the eighteenth-century novel, see Furet, "La "librairie" du royaume de France"; Lenglet-Dufresnoy's *De l'usage des romans*; Lionel Gossman's "History or Literature: Reproduction or Signification" in *The Writing of History: Literary Form and Historical Understanding*, ed. Robert Canary and Henry Kozicki (Madison, WI: University of Wisconsin Press, 1978); Suzanne Gearhart's *The Open Boundary of History and Fiction: A Critical Approach to the French Enlightenment* (Princeton: Princeton UP, 1984) and Georges May's *Dilemme du roman*. On the relationship between history and fiction in the seventeenth century, the reader is referred to Erica Harth's fine analysis in *Ideology and Culture in Seventeenth-Century France* (Ithaca: Cornell UP, 1983), 129-179.

[27] As witness Voltaire's many remarks in the *Essai sur les moeurs* that evince a greater interest with everyday events as opposed to the verbal and military bombast, e.g.: "Je voudrais découvrir quelle était alors la société des hommes, comment on vivait dans l'intérieur des familles, quels arts étaient cultivés, plutôt que de répéter tant de malheurs et tant de combats, funestes objets de l'histoire, et lieux communs de la méchanceté humaine." (*Essai sur les moeurs*, Pomeau ed. (Paris: Garnier, 1963) 2vols. 1:757).

[28] Furet, "La "librairie" du royaume de France", 25.

[29] I am thinking of Perrault's observation in the "Parallèle des Anciens et des modernes"; "C'est nous qui sommes les anciens." On this point, Cf. Jean-Marie Apostolidès' commentary: "Le savoir sous Louis XIV est plus lourd qu'au temps d'Auguste; le temps présent a atteint les plus hauts sommets; on a fait des découvertes que ni les

memoirs narrating the history of the seventeenth century in scandalous detail, such as those of Saint-Simon after 1715, added to the French reading public's interest in the history of its immediate past.) The vector of history—in both its orthodox and fictitious variants—is now oriented towards the laws of human conduct, both collective and individual, that are to be deduced from the study of the past. Soon enough it is the authority claimed by a text with a narrative structure rather than history in the received sense that is to become the central definition of the word *histoire*. Thus in Du Plaisir's rigorous and methodical "poetics",[30] we find the terms "Histoire" and "Historien" used as synonyms for "roman" and "romancier" respectively. Moreover, the twin expansion of the notions of history and theatre were eventually to give the age its more idiosyncratic moments: if fiction and oratory were the two genres that were not banished from Rousseau's republic it is because they embodied, in their eighteenth-century form, the conferral of the authority of history on the histrionic sincerity of public performance. Eventually fiction would explicitly gain the upper hand, as the *Eloge de Richardson* makes abundantly clear:

> O Richardson! j'oserai dire que l'histoire la plus vraie est pleine de mensonges, et que ton roman est plein de vérités. L'histoire peint quelques individus, tu peins l'espèce humaine; l'histoire attribue à quelques individus ce qu'ils n'ont ni dit ni fait: tout ce que tu attribues à l'homme, il l'a dit et fait; l'histoire n'embrasse qu'une portion de la durée, qu'un point de la surface du globe: tu as embrassé tous les lieux et tous les temps... Si l'on appliquait au meilleur historien une critique sévère, y en a-t-il aucun qui la soutînt comme toi? Sous ce point de vue, j'oserai dire que souvent l'histoire est un mauvais roman, et que le roman, comme tu l'as fait, est une bonne histoire. (*Œuvres*, 1097-98)

The eighteenth century thus inaugurates the reign of fiction. Imitation overtakes the real because fiction is truer than the truth.[31] The central focus

---

Grecs ni les Romains n'auraient pu imaginer. Ces arguments constituent la poutre maîtresse de l'édifice théorique des Modernes qui, à la suite de Descartes, reprennent le même motto: "C'est nous qui sommes les Anciens."" (*Roi-machine*, 119)

[30] Du Plaisir, *Sentiments sur les lettres et sur l'histoire avec des scrupules sur le style* (Paris, 1683; re-edited by Philippe Hourcade, Genève: Droz, 1975).

[31] Cf. the following self-congratulatory passage from Restif de la Bretonne's *Les Françaises*; "Rien de plus utile, pour l'instruction des hommes, que l'histoire vraie, ou simulée, mais que dis-je! simulée? Elle est toujours vraie dans les romans naturels comme ceux de Jean-Jacques, de Richardson, de Marmontel et de La Bretone; n'a-t-on pas reconnu tous les héros de ce dernier lors même qu'il ne les connaissait pas? Ne s'est-il pas lui-même surpris en prophétie lorsqu'il voyait arriver postérieurement les faits qu'il avait décrits? Personne n'a voulu croire que la Julie et la Claire de Jean-

of the new brand of history becomes the operation of virtual spaces in which object and copy or mask and persona are accorded equal status. Similarly, the proliferation of rococo artifice—stucco, chinoiserie, lacquer and so on—marks the mapping of this tendency onto the arena of social exchange. These art forms all operate as markers of a virtual space that supplements and eventually substitutes for the real. Marivaux's plays and novels are made intelligible by the existence of this procedure of fictionalising reality: it is no accident that Jacob, the upstart peasant, first acquires a sense of himself in the imaginary space on the other side of the mirror, or that the Europeans shipwrecked on the Isle of Reason "become" themselves because of their location. Soon enough the scenarii of legitimation thus sketched would translate into the revolution's more memorable moments, if only for all their comic import, as witness the Feast of the Supreme Being.[32]

This new brand of history is paralleled by the development of two new sub-genres within the space of fiction: the false memoirs and the epistolary novel.[33] The former is concerned primarily with the forging of a private history for oneself, taking such seemingly trivial details as geographical location and human emotion into account. It is not insignificant, however, that the claim made to the authenticity of the memoirs was often made pro forma: what would by present-day standards be called real autobiography only barely fits into this category. What matters is the casting of an identity (any identity, the author's included) in the mould of narrative; the emulation of history through the laying of claims to factual truth-telling is as ancillary as it is particular to the convoluted plots of the age. Furthermore, the genre of the fictional memoir is interesting insofar as it traces the production of an author and how he or she reaches the position of the narrator/historian of the self with all the trappings of authority that such a posi-

---

Jacques fussent des êtres imaginaires; tout le monde s'est écrié: Jean-Jacques nous a peint celles qu'il a vues et peut-être il a aimées." (*Œuvres complètes*, Henri Bachelin ed., Genève: Slatkine, 1971, 2:360.)

[32] Cf. Lionel Trilling, *Sincerity and Authenticity* (Cambridge: Harvard UP, 1972), 70-71. It bears pointing out that as a concept, temporality does undergo a few sea changes as it is thought through. Thus we move from the concept of time as a discrete series, a succession of moments in which sentimental pleasure peaks and where "le bonheur était representé... sous l'aspect d'une énergie tout entière occupée à se dépenser dans la grâce instantanée du geste" (Starobinski, *Invention*, 95) in the earlier part of the century, to the concept of time as a continuous duration and, finally, to time as the intrusion of History onto virtual space in 1789. See Lasowski, *Libertines*, 28-37, for an excellent reading of the opposition between *le moment* and temporal *durée*.

[33] On the importance of these two sub-genres, see Vivienne Mylne's *The French Eighteenth-Century Novel: Techniques of Illusion* (Cambridge: Cambridge UP, 1965), 20-49.

tion implies. As such it is emblematic of the new mode of self-fashioning that becomes dominant in the eighteenth century.[34] The process of mirroring is still central, but the mirror in which the mask is set forth is inscribed in a (temporal) narrative rather than an (instantaneous) theatrical process. Becoming is placed on a par with being.

The other prevailing sub-genre is, to a certain extent, an extension of the first. Epistolary forms enact a mise-en-scène of the dialogues and conversations that were the central tenet of the histrionics of the period.[35] Letter-writing emblematises the gesture of self-designation if not the very procedure of self-fashioning itself: one becomes oneself by narrating a history (usually one's own) to someone else. Should either end of this communicative model fail, the consequences can prove rather desperate, as is the case at the end of *Les Liaisons dangereuses*.

In view of the importance of narrative, much time and attention is devoted to the telling of the tale, to the control of the history at hand. The roles that were once defined in a holistically structural manner typical of rigid hierarchies, are now mapped onto a bi-polar model, with the teller at one end and the listener at the other. Each end of the teller-listener relationship is foil to the other: in *Jacques le fataliste et son maître*, Jacques does the telling and his (nameless) master the listening, thereby effecting, in the virtual space of Diderot's narrative, a sort of social upheaval that would have been impossible elsewhere. Similarly, the libertine fictions of the period translate this model into the rapport between seducer and seducee, so that a text like Crébillon's *La Nuit et le moment* focuses more on narrative than sexual intercourse. Everyone plays parts, granted, but plays one of two roles: narrator or narratee, seducer or seduced, master or slave.[36] Needless to say, each of these roles depends on the other for its proper functioning: every seducer needs someone to seduce, and no tale would cohere without a listener.[37]

---

[34] Due to the links between history and narrative outlined up to this point, the two terms will henceforth be used interchangeably.

[35] Cf. Rousset, *Forme et signification*, 65-103.

[36] These oppositions matter more as functional abstractions rather than illustrations of mastery and servitude per se. In fact, the relationship between master and servant as such carries a great deal of weight during the seventeenth century, and the device of master and servant swapping places is more frequent than its occurrence in *Dom Juan* and *Le Géôlier de soi-même*. In the hands of someone like Marivaux, this device gains some originality by becoming a crucial step in a character's *Bildung* as in *Le Jeu de l'amour et du hasard* or *L'Ile des esclaves*.

[37] For an account of the extent to which this structure becomes pivotal in the formation of the self in a more recent context, see François Roustang's account of the

It is also important to note that the exchanges between teller and listener (or any of the synonymous pairings) are exchanges of fictions and of personal histories. The multiplicity of roles is recoded into a multiplicity of narratives and narrative voices that weave the fabric of the mask. The continuity thus established between self and story translates into another major preoccupation of the period, namely the tale told in confidence. Once the grandeur that was the Sun King has passed, the entire country seems to delve into its historical self, and the reading public, composed as it was of newcomers and upstarts, necessarily tried to partake of the forms and authority of historical discourse as its modus operandi with a view to legitimating its social status.[38] It will perhaps stand as one of the supreme ironies of literary history that the age that invented de-mystification (Diderot was Marx's favourite prose writer) should also be the one that saw the most ardent return to the quixotic self invented during the preceding century, the one that took every novel at its word. Not only does role-playing become a way of life, but the roles themselves are defined by a narrative, by a series of events: here if one is at all, it is only insofar as one identifies with a fictional character, insofar as one can see oneself reflected in some fictional situation. The most surprising effect of sympathy, to borrow Marivaux's phrase, is the one that transforms the reader into a writer through the identification with a character, the one that transforms the seducer into an object of seduction through the mediation of the mirror of fiction.

Narrative identity thus operates as an extension of the author's role and as an exchange mechanism within the space of narrative: selves are forged and characters reflected in the mirror of fiction, the virtual space par excellence. There results from this a number of thematic preoccupations, all revolving around the central concern of re-casting the reader in the same mould as the characters in the book. Foremost among these are metempsy-

---

real necessity of the disciple or listener as someone who keeps the master-teller's fictions in check: "Finalement, la question est de savoir pourquoi on devient disciple ou, ce qui est correlatif, pourquoi on fait des disciples. Cette question à double face est... susceptible d'une seule réponse: pour ne pas devenir fou... Le délire, c'est la théorie d'un seul, tandis que la théorie est le délire de plusieurs, susceptible de se transmettre. Mes disciples, ceux qui retiennent mes paroles et les répandent, me libèrent de ma parole solitaire, la transforment en science et en principe de communication; ils sont eux aussi pour moi mes garde-fous." (*Un destin si funeste* (Paris: Minuit, 1976), 51-53)

[38] On the legitimating power of narrative, see Michel Butor's "Individu et groupe dans le roman"; Marthe Robert *Roman des origines et origines du roman* (Paris: Grasset 1972) 41-78, and Louis O. Mink's "Narrative Form as a Cognitive Instrument" in *The Writing of History*.

chosis and sympathy.[39] Both are concerned with the valourisation of
empirical knowledge and *Erlebnis*, which in turn is the most important step
in the formation of the author. The narrator depends on his experience; he
can only narrate by virtue of his having sympathetically identified with, or
his being metempsychotically metamorphosed into, everyone (and, in the
case of Crébillon's *Sopha*, everything) else. Rousseau validates his massive
project of self-documentation by arguing that he has known all states because he has no state of his own.[40] The magician in Marivaux's *La Voiture
embourbée*, an alias for the narrator, expounds his powers in similar terms:

> [I]l est peu de choses que je ne sache, peu de plaisirs que je n'aie
> goûtées, peu d'états que je n'aie éprouvés... J'ai le secret de changer
> de corps, quand le mien est usé, et comme l'âme ne viellit point, je me
> trouve quand je veux tout aussi beau, tout aussi frais qu'un homme de
> vingt ans... [E]n prenant le corps du jeune homme, je sais tout d'un
> coup ce qu'il savait; j'ai les mêmes connaissances, les mêmes
> maîtresses; et quand la fantaisie de vivre de cette manière m'est
> passée, je pars par la voie la plus courte, et je me dérobe tout d'un
> coup à l'amour d'un père et de parents que la ressemblance abuse pour
> jamais: je deviens femme, si je veux; en un mot, j'ai le choix libre sur
> les corps.[41]

This description is not insignificant, coming from the future author of
*La Vie de Marianne*, a narrative where Marivaux metamorphoses into a
woman, and *Le Paysan parvenu*, where he metamorphoses into a young
man of (about) twenty. Similarly, Montesquieu's *Histoire véritable* claims
its truth-value by virtue of its subject-matter, metempsychosis, which it
uses to stage the act of narration incessantly. Similarly sympathy stands as
a figure for the opposite procedure, namely reading oneself in(to) the mirror of fiction. Every narrative is constructed with cut-out slots, as it were,
into which the reader can insinuate his—or herself *après coup*. Thus we see
a number of heroines start their textual existence like Marivaux's Clorinde
or his *fille séduite*, both of whom say, "I am the person who has just been
narrated."[42] If no-one can claim, as Rousseau's preamble to the *Confes-*

---

[39] For an excellent account of the functioning of sympathy as a literary mode in
eighteenth century literature, the reader is referred to David Marshall's *Surprising Effects of Sympathy: Marivaux, Diderot, Rousseau and Mary Shelley* (Chicago: U of
Chicago P, 1988) to which the present study is deeply indebted.

[40] "[S]ans avoir aucun état moi-même, j'ai connu tous les états." *OC* 1:1150.

[41] *Romans* (Paris: Gallimard, 1949), 54-55.

[42] The paradigmatic situation here is that of Marivaux's Clorinde telling Clorante in
a letter that she recognises herself in the fabric of his fiction; "Je suis la personne à qui

*sions* dictates, that they were better than he, it is because sympathetic self-fashioning does not admit of such hierarchies. A sympathetic reading, which is to say, any reading of the text, will depend first and foremost on the reader's being placed in the same place as the narrator. Similarly, the self advanced by the libertine fictions of the eighteenth century is one that can be defined, in prototypical existential terms, as the sum total of a series of *moments* or seductions, each of which mirrors in no uncertain terms the reader's desires.

As a result of this specular aesthetic, reading comes to mean more than decoding; through the mechanisms of sympathy and metempsychosis reading transports selves between real and virtual spaces across the mirror of fiction. Self-designation no longer occurs through the bombastic locutions of Corneille's heroes: rather than say "I am what I am" the characters of Marivaux and Crébillon *fils* say, "I am the entity mirrored by this story." Similarly, the fictitious autobiographies and false memoirs so typical of the age operate by virtue of this new mechanism of self-designation mediated by narrative: the only way for Meilcour, Marianne or Amanzéi to become themselves is to narrate themselves, to construct a mirror of fiction into which they can see themselves reflected adequately. Having done so, they can take their place in the virtual space behind the mirror, the space known as *le monde*, the stage of society. In *Le Paysan parvenu*, Jacob is to La Vallée as real is to virtual space. The two are mutually constitutive: neither without either could or would obtain. Hence the essentially specular status of the artistic production, both plastic and literary, of the early eighteenth century. The spectacle of pleasure was not without its value as something that engenders what it represents:

> Un jeu de miroirs; un art qui veut dispenser le plaisir, en prenant le plaisir même pour sujet; des peintures qui cherchent à séduire en représentant des scènes de séduction. Le tableau plaira, à la condition de figurer la volupté... Tous les arts de séduction voient leur fonction conservée dans la séduction supérieure du tableau qui les rassemble.[43]

Similarly, the autobiographical texts constructed by Amanzéi, Meilcour and Jacob aim at bringing about the formation of a self through the representation of that formation. Seduction, *qua* act of self-appropriation through an other, becomes a variation on the act of reading and writing, all of which are self-conscious meditations on the process of self-construction through the fictional other reflected in the mirror of fiction. Thus Crébillon

---

tantôt vous avez raconté vos aventures; j'en étais le sujet..." in *Les Aventures de* \*\*\*\* *ou les effets suprenants de la sympathie* (in *Romans*, 1077).

[43] Starobinski, *Invention*, 64.

Ziad Elmarsafy

was right to speak of the novel as the "tableau de la vie humaine" in his preface to *Les Egarements*. The tableau seduces (instructs, forms) its reader by drawing him or her into the virtually real space that it depicts. Seduction—aesthetic or literary—is a formative step that necessarily involves a passage through virtual space, the space of the novel, of the painting, of the stage, of the other side of the mirror.

# Chapter Five

# Marivaux: How One Becomes What One Is

As I approach Marivaux's work I would like to juxtapose a quotation and a stylistic remark. The quotation comes from *L'Ile de la raison*, where Frontignac, a Gascon peasant stuck with eight other Europeans in a Swiftian context is told that he must become "reasonable" in order to grow back to his original size and liberate himself from the island's curse. Frontignac's response is, "Qué beut donc dire cé vouffon, avec son *débénez raisonnavles*? Peut-on débénir ce que l'on est?"[1] The question sums up very elegantly the themes with which Marivaux concerns himself. The other question, the question of style, is simpler: despite his prolixity Marivaux was incapable of completing the narratives that he started after 1735, *La Vie de Marianne* and *Le Paysan parvenu*. The serial style established in his one-man journals, though no great novelty in its own right, seems to

---

[1] In *Théâtre Complet* (Paris: Gallimard, 1949), 498. All future references to the plays will be to this volume, and will be given in shortened form as *T* followed by a page number.

My reading of Marivaux is indebted to a number of sources: on the question of sympathy, Marshall's *Suprising Effects of Sympathy* is indispensable; on the issues of Marianne's *mondanité*, Peter Brooks's seminal, *The Novel of Worldliness: Crébillon, Marivaux, Laclos, Stendhal* (Princeton: Princeton UP, 1969); on the question of style, Deloffre's *Marivaux et le marivaudage*; Jean Rousset's "Marivaux et la structure du double registre" in *Forme et signification*, 44-64, and Leo Spitzer, "A propos de *La Vie de Marianne*" in *Romanic Review* 44 (1953); on the marivaudian narrator's "double vision" and its affinities with Sartre's concept of *mauvaise foi*, Josué Harari's *Scenarios of the Imaginary: Theorizing the French Enlightenment* (Ithaca: Cornell UP, 1987) as well as Felicia Sturzer's "*Marivaudage* as Self-Representation" in *French Review* 49 (1975); on the links between speech patterns and character formation, Henri Coulet and Michel Gilot's *Marivaux. Un humanisme expérimental* (Paris: Larousse, 1973); on the operation of theatricality in his works, Robert Tomlinson, *La Fête galante. Watteau et Marivaux* (Genève: Droz, 1983); Bernard Dort, "A la recherche de l'amour et la vérité: Esquisse d'un système marivaudien," in *Théâtres* (Paris: Seuil, 1986) 25-59; Marie-Paule Laden, "The Pitfalls of Success: Jacob's Evolution in Marivaux's *Le Paysan parvenu*" in *Romanic Review* 74:2 (1983); Philip Koch's "On Marivaux's Expression, `se donner la comédie'" in *Romanic Review* 56:1 (1965); John Fleming,"Textual Autogenesis in Marivaux's *Paysan Parvenu*" in *SVEC* 189 (1980); Lubbe Levin, "Masque et identité dans *Le Paysan parvenu*" in *SVEC* 79 (1971); Marie-Hélène Huet's *Le Héros et son double. Essai sur le roman d'ascension sociale au dix-huitième siècle* (Paris: Corti,1975); on the operation of seduction in the text of *Le Paysan parvenu*, Roger Kempf, *Sur le corps romanesque* (Paris: Seuil, 1968) and Pierre Saint-Amand, *Séduire, ou la passion des lumières* (Paris: Klinksieck, 1987).

take precedence over such concerns as consistency of character, plot coherence and the sense or even the possibility of an ending. At the nexus between the axes of style and transformation unfolds the Marivaudian opus, one predicated on an aesthetics of becoming and improvisation.[2]

So deeply entrenched is this tendency towards becoming and away from being in Marivaux's idiom that it is hard not to read his intention or project as a reaction—strong in some areas, weak in others—to the classical features of rigidity and steadfastness of the preceding century. In French classical theatre, much depended on remaining true to oneself, and on this consistency's transcending each and every situation in order to remain itself. Marivaux's worldlier manner presents us with the more realistic development of such stiff characterisations; the meta-theatrical dimension is still very much there, but the premises on which it is predicated are different. In *le monde*, where his works unfold, people are what play their parts in the hope that everyone around them has consented to theirs with the best of intentions, or, as Marivaux himself would put it, "de la meilleure foi du monde". This ethical code thus encourages this world's inhabitants to make certain assumptions about each other and act accordingly, safe in the knowledge that their behaviour adequately displays what is proper to them.

Or is it? This ethical code, born as it is at a time of great social mobility, also gives rise to a great deal of deception, and not a little mutual observation carried out with a view to ensuring that the assumptions people make about each other—and, indeed, about themselves—are in fact reliable. The apparent inconsistencies that mark Marivaux's characters in the eyes of traditional readers[3] result from the relentless rigour of their meditations on how they appear to themselves and how they appear to each other, on the viewpoints of the actor and of the spectator. His best-known "autobiographers," Marianne and Jacob, are motivated by these two foci. To take one example: as she describes her first make-up session, Marianne says, "Il me prenait des palpitations en songeant combien j'allais être jolie."[4] Now, if the narrator's claims to absolute veracity are to be believed, there is really no way that the young (narrated) Marianne could know,

---

[2] In connection with Marivaux's improvised narration, Rousset mentions the following citation from *Le Spectateur français*: "Je ne sais point créer, je sais seulement surprendre en moi les pensées que le hasard me fait, et je serais fâché d'y mettre du mien." (*Forme et Signification*, 45).

[3] I am thinking in particular of Georges Poulet's analysis of Marianne in *La distance intérieure* (Paris: Plon, 1952), 1-34, and Leo Spitzer's response in "A propos de *La Vie de Marianne*."

[4] In *Romans*, 117. All future references to this edition and will be rendered by *R* followed by a page number.

"combien (elle) allait être jolie." What Marianne experiences is the combination of the two aformentioned foci—her own and that of her narrator—in the virtual space provided by the mirror. Marianne becomes herself through the synthesis of the viewpoints of the narrating and narrated Mariannes.[5]

Thus it comes as no surprise that we are presented with a theatre that foregrounds the contractual and therefore contingent nature of the relation between two poles of the theatrical identity, master and servant. It would be quite out of place and character for Sganarelle or Sosie, say, to embark upon a discussion of voluntary servitude with Dom Juan or Amphitryon. This is due, in part, to their status as indispensable constituents of their master's identities. When it does occur to them to swap places or experience displacement of some sort, the experiment itself proves either maddening, leading to a near-total loss of identity or trivial enough to be glossed over. In neither case does the swap prove decisive, in neither case does either side of the bargain deceive the other. Emphasizing the voluntary aspect of this relationship would have been irrelevant: Sganarelle is "useful" as Dom Juan's other and vice versa, but not quite as a servant who would betray his master or himself.

With Marivaux things change slightly, as they are bound to do with the new patterns of social mobility that prevail during the eighteenth century. The fact that the servant can no longer be taken for granted as a second self prompts a closer look at the links that bind him or her to the master. Consequently the formative mirrors of Marivaux's idiom are drawn along class lines: the ties examined not only link self to other as other, they not only investigate the beneficial effects of an evolution from a state of servitude to a state of mastery, they stage the vacillation from one stage to another. Equally important is the use of servants as witnesses to the contained play and to the "internal" (sentimental, emotional, formative) of which the main characters remain unaware.[6] The apparent predictability of Marivaux's theatre is very important in this respect: it matters, of course, that Dorante and Silvia swap places with Arlequin and Lisette in *Le Jeu de l'amour et du hasard*, but what matters more is the stylised subversion of the game of love and chance by the fact that class will out and blood will tell, that the masks eventually fall and that all return to their stations in life. To take a

---

[5] This self-construction through the virtual also explains the resonances that Marivaux's vocabulary has with Sartre's concept of *mauvaise foi*, whereby the self is appropriated through its theatrical representation and a certain "double vision" develops: "As Sartre points out, in 'bad faith' the combination of deceiver ('le trompeur') and deceived ('le trompé') into a single unit results in a hybrid product—a vision which is halfway between a lie and the truth." (Felizia Sturzer, "*Marivaudage* and Self-Representation", 214-215). Cf. Harari, 26-37 and 67-68.

[6] Cf. Rousset, *Forme et signification*, 54-64.

different example, it matters more that the erstwhile slaves redeem themselves in *L'Ile des esclaves* by finding out just how good being virtuous can feel ("qu'il y a de plaisir à bien faire" (*T*, 448)) than that they avenge themselves. It could of course be argued that Marivaux is trying to placate his audience by assuring a return to order once the *égarement* that warrants the play at hand is over and done with, all the more so in view of the revolutionary implications of his plots. In so doing, however, he foregrounds the incessant because necessary fluidity of identity in a world where the old order seems to be breaking down (although the order is preserved in the fact that there are only two roles that operate as paradigms, master and servant). Marivaux's mastery makes itself felt in his translation of these concerns into a certain situational facticity rather typical of his idiom: with the possible exception of *Annibal*, Marivaux's stage does not offer very much in the way of dramatic monologue. None of his characters, moreover, is ever onstage for very long, as though the social mobility that marked the age were figured in the constant comings and goings of the background players.

As he asserts a new sort of selfhood, one produced in an improvised rather than a conformist mode, Marivaux postulates a different problematic for its construction. This is, in fact, what enables the circulation of a certain critical vocabulary between his theatre and his fiction: Marivaux was far ahead of his time in laying out the apparatus necessary for the transformation of a problematics of sincerity into one of authenticity. The distinction between the terms is clarified if we postulate the transformation of a situational into a narrative aesthetics (and ethics). Sincerity is to theatrical role and situation what authenticity is to narrative. If we define authenticity as the quality that allows one's being to shine forth through their person, then it becomes difficult not to read the repeated emphasis on Jacob's candour or Marianne's face as an investigation into the effects of authenticity, or of what is taken to be authenticity, in the world of manners. If Jacob and Marianne operate as they do, as both characters and narrators, it is because their looks (their *paraître*) are suggestive of what they are (their *être*), and what they are is their narrative. If the latter suffers from excessive complications it is because of the implication of the narrator therein.

Further evidence of this paradigm shift is to be found in Marivaux's theatre, where the new framework results in the development of two more stylistic insignia. First, the authenticity of the servants vis-à-vis the masters: a cursory reading of *Le Jeu de l'amour et du hasard*, *La Double inconstance* or *L'Ile des esclaves* makes quite clear that the world of the masters, the *monde*, functions primarily as a stage and is unabashed in its display of its theatrical underpinnings. Irrespective of the attitude of the servants vis-à-vis this world, be it one of superiority (*L'Ile des esclaves*, *Les Fausses confidences, L'Ile de la raison*), complicity (*Le Jeu de l'amour et du hasard, Les Sincères*) or exemplary servitude (*Les Acteurs de bonne foi*), they are usually farther removed from the logic of the mask than their masters. Which is not to say that Marivaux's idiom reserves the histrionic way of life for the happy few. It is, however, to argue for the servants' position as that which privileges narrative history over the mask: they make better storytellers than the masters. Blaise and Colette's history as well as the history of the characters in general interrupts all of the rehearsals of Merlin's impromptu in *Les Acteurs de bonne foi*, and Dubois goes his erstwhile employer one better through his ability to construct narratives that effectively explain the most awkward situations that populate *Les Fausses confidences*. What matters, both on- and offstage is the story, (as against the previous century where the play was the thing), a fitting preoccupation for a one-man journalist. In most of his plots, the character who succeeds in topping the hierarchy and pulling all the strings will usually be the one who masters narrative. Which mastery is, more often than not, the lot of the Arlequins and Blaises rather than the Dorantes and Erastes of Marivaux's works.[7]

Together with this mastery of narrative and authenticity among society's rank and file is the question that haunts the earlier narratives, namely the question of sympathy as a theory of reading and writing. Here fiction acts as a mirror indispensable to the forging of the subject; the ability to put oneself in the place of the hero or heroine counts for much more than what they are like, *a fortiori* if the hero or heroine in question is oneself. The essence of Marivaux's accomplishment inheres precisely in his having spelled out the logic of a necessary doubling and concomitant alienation that inscribe themselves at the heart of each and every project aiming at authenticity and a good faith rendition of the self. To a certain extent this is underscored by the links between subjectivity and narrative, the overlap between books and people: the answer to Frontignac's question ("comment peut-on débénir ce que l'on est?") is the confessional; one becomes oneself by narrating oneself, turning oneself into a story. Furthermore this "entry into consciousness" is occasioned by the narratives that circulate and implicate but do not do justice to the self: Marianne comes into herself once she overhears Madame de Biran and Madame Dorsin talking about her. Jacob is only made aware of his position as himself once he sees himself addressed as "Mons Jacob". The identification between fiction and subjectiv-

---

[7] The superiority of the servant as manipulator and "meneur de jeu" is of course present in Molière's theatre, as witness *Le Malade imaginaire*. Here, however, the weight is attached to the narrative rather than the theatrical dimension of the theatrical "jeu" in question.

ity is also foregrounded in the preface to *Les Effets surprenants de la sympathie*. Here the tone ostensibly echoes the traditional prologue ("Va, livre…" and so on) but the idiom is quite telling: at the first significantly autobiographical moment of his career, Marivaux creates a fictional double of himself and describes how he "overheard" the preface as its author produces it in a different context; "L'avant-propos que l'auteur de ces aventures fait de lui-même en parlant à une dame pourrait leur servir de préface. Il écrivit ces mêmes aventures pour amuser cette dame qu'il aimait."[8] Even more revealing is his evaluation of the novel itself;

> Ainsi j'abandonne ce roman à ses risques et fortunes, persuadé qu'il méritera l'éloge bon ou mauvais qu'on en fera. J'ai cependant dans le fort de la querelle appelé certains beaux esprits pédants, et voilà les ennemis que j'ai suscités à l'auteur… Ils regardent quelquefois un livre sans aveu comme un (*sic*) espèce d'enfant trouvé que quelque misérable auteur a fait perdre, et n'a point osé déclarer pour sien par une honte qui, à l'avis de ces messieurs, le caractérise lui et son ouvrage." (*OJ*, 8)

The novel, in a literary historical context, is a sort of Marianne *avant la lettre*; Marianne is herself a novel. She (like Jacob, like any of Marivaux's narrators and like Marivaux himself in this instance) is the narrative that she signs with her own name.[9]

In order to trace the functioning of this quixotic sense of the self-as-fiction in Marivaux's work, I would now like to turn to one of his earlier stories, one that appeared in the ninth issue of *Le Spectateur français* (1722) and to which Marcel Arland has given the provisional title of *Double histoire de la fille séduite et de la demoiselle avisée*.[10] Ostensibly a short moral tale about the dangers of seduction and all the reasons for which gallant young men are not to trust, it illustrates very well the operation of sympathy and its Marivaudian variant, exemplarity. Like so many narratives of his this one is an allegory of reading, one based on the model of the hall of mirrors to a certain extent and on the image of chinese boxes to an even greater extent.

---

[8] In his *Œuvres de Jeunesse* (Paris: Gallimard, 1972), 3. All future references will be to this edition and will be indicated by *OJ* followed by the relevant page number.

[9] Cf. Marshall, 9-49.

[10] In *Romans*, 829-843; rpt. *Journaux et œuvres diverses* (Paris: Garnier, 1969) pp. 154-172. References will be to the latter and will be given as *J* followed by a page number.

The tale divides into two separate stories, one of which reads like a commentary on the other. The plot is a typically marivaudian tale of seduction, abandonment and suffering. The first half of the narrative presents the story of the *fille séduite*, who arrives at a friend's country estate on the eve of the latter's marriage. The ensuing events can be summed up by the friend's seduction (by her future groom), her running off to a Carmelite nunnery and the *fille séduite*'s suffering the very same fate. The second half of the story narrates the hesitation of a young Polish lady, Eléonore, before a similar prospect, and her deciding against it on the advice of her servant and confidante, Fatima. Fatima's instruments of persuasion are a young slave girl and a stable boy, Viniescho. She advises Eléonore to substitute her slave for herself before Her suitor (Mirski's) ardour and has Viniescho present a candid presentation on pre-marital sex from a male viewpoint, thus convincing Eléonore not to give in to Mirski's impatience.

The doubling mentioned in the title is significant in view of its anticipation of the bifurcation fundamental to Marivaux's later novels, the one between the older Marianne and the Marianne who wrestles with the moral implications of wearing a dress, or the one that divides Jacob the narrator who draws moral portraits *après coup* from Jacob the upstart peasant featured in that narrative. The difference between the first and second halves of the story thus corresponds to the difference between the two voices—that of the narrator and that of the narrated self, the voices of being and of becoming respectively—involved in any autobiographical project. Thus the establishment of the two halves as exemplary opposites is not without its reasons: the story and its telling function as a narrative mirror mediating between and linking the *fille séduite* to the *demoiselle avisée*.

The narrative starts off with a scene of reading, an editor being made privy to what would otherwise have remained privileged information (namely the editor of the *Spectateur français* reading the *fille séduite*'s autobiographical letters). It is clear from the outset that the narrative and its publication are aimed at someone, are deliberate acts performed with the intention of revealing a certain reader to his- or herself; with the intention, that is, of starting the chain reaction of the effect of recognition known as sympathy. Indeed, the editor underlines the fact that this is a narrative seeking a readership: "J'exhorte les personnes que deux de ces lettres regardent, à les lire avec attention quand je les donnerai: je ne leur demande que cela, persuadé qu'elles produiront l'effet que cette infortunée en attend." (*J*, 154) The text then proceeds to another reading, or rather a misreading, of the seducer's character by the *fille séduite*. They first meet through the mediation of her friend who is supposed to marry the seducer in question, Monsieur de ****, a starting condition that enacts another situation into which our unfortunate heroine is to read herself, aided and abetted by her friend's designs and indifference to her suitor; "Tout ce qui me reste à vous dire, c'est que je vous aime; et voudrais que l'epoux qu'on m'avait destiné devînt le vôtre..." (*J*, 157) As the wife-to-be proves the amiability of the young man in question, the *fille séduite* quite literally finds herself in the narrative: "Je m'intéressais à tout ce qu'on m'avait dit, sans pouvoir encore demêler pourquoi, il me semblait que c'était de moi que nous avions parlé, que c'était sur moi que roulait toute l'aventure." (*J*, 158) Interestingly enough, Monsieur de *** still behaves in a manner consistent with his former indifference to his bride-to-be, and yet the *fille séduite* mistakes the signs of indifference for those of passionate involvement. This misinterpretation is due, in part, to her quixotic outlook: from her perspective, now that she has replaced her friend, all is as it should be and Monsieur de *** is enamoured, all appearances to the contrary. The extent to which this identification is carried only becomes clear at the end of the episode, by which point both of Monsieur de ***'s victims become Carmelite nuns, one merely having passed the torch to another.

The second half of the *Double histoire* presents us with another scenario of reading, one threatening to move in the same direction as the first. The scenario of reading is further concretised here by the (presumably) realistic detail, but this realism is undermined by the relatively fabulous status of the characters who inhabit this second half. They are in Poland, which is to say, nowhere, in the land of fiction. Poland is used as a virtual space that informs the real, anticipating Marivaux's use of insular atopias in *L'Ile des esclaves* and *L'Ile de la raison*. Furthermore, the status of this second half as a lengthy intervention on the part of an author concerned with keeping his reader's interests by raising the entire account to the level of exemplary generality suggests that the second half is more of an extension of the principles laid out in the first as opposed to a departure therefrom. The addition of names and places eventually serves to accentuate the specular relationship that links the two halves of the story. Eléonore and the *fille séduite* are related not just as text and reader but as self and (specular, autobiographical) other. This specularity is of course accompanied by some of the reversals that one might expect, although the reversals do little more than accentuate the similarities between the two halves of the narrative. The sort of transposition that turns Eléonore into the counterpart of the *fille séduite* and Viniescho into that of Monsieur de *** is one that will motivate the later changes of state between masters and servants in Marivaux's theatre. Even more important, however, is the introduction of Fatima, the narrator who teaches Eléonore how to read rather than leave her to indulge her misreading. This she does by relating the exemplary narrative of the first half of the story and then bringing it to life in the person of Viniescho. To a certain extent the entire second half of the story is a de-metaphorisation of the first. Fatima is, in a manner of speaking, in the position of the editor of the *Spectateur français*, presenting cases on a tale-by-tale basis. So close is this identification that, two pages after he has praised Eléonore's sagacity as ideal, Marivaux takes the trouble to distance himself from Fatima's ruses; "Qu'on ne se scandalise pas ici de l'expédient que va donner Fatima, il n'est pas chrétien, je ne l'approuve point, et ce n'est qu'une histoire que je rapporte." (*J*, 169) And, not unexpectedly, the ruse that the editor finds so reprehensible is none other than that of acting out the mechanisms of identification and sympathy that have motivated the plot so far. Fatima suggests that Eléonore send her twin (slave) to Mirski in order to placate him. She suggests, in other words, that she deceive Mirski, but that she do so in a manner commensurate with the fairy-tale world of the *Double histoire*: she proposes that Eléonore substitute a fictional version (if not *the* fictional version; the *fille séduite*'s ruined state brings her closer to the slave of the second half) of herself in the narrative that (of) Mirski desires. This is the real reason for calling on Viniescho: in the world of Marivaux's fiction, one fictional example deserves another. Self-designation and self-fashioning would be impossible without the passage though the mirror of fiction and the filter of virtual space. The spectacle of fictional alterity—Viniescho and the slave are fairy-tale characters come true—enables the staging of fiction in a mode that allows Eléonore to come into her own as a social entity (by regaining the upper hand) and as a narrator in her own right. So impressive are her narrative skills that once she informs Mirski of her ruse he dies. Eléonore can take life as easily now as tales, a condition created by her ability to divide herself into a self that lives out her narratives and a self that makes them.[11]

The *Double histoire* illustrates the salient feature of Marivaux's histrionics: a consistent meditation on the tangible reality of the narrating and narrated selves, on the narrator as puppeteer and the space of fiction as a stage. Much time and attention is devoted in his fictions to the life of textual characters, to being in the word. Marivaux de-metaphorises and makes quite literal the parallels between narrative fiction and "reality" in the context of his novels: fiction and reality, or virtual and real space, are related in a manner similar to dreaming and consciousness, insofar as one "works through" the other, like the two halves of the *Double histoire*.

---

[11] This theme of the mirror of fiction as a hinging-point for the subject is quite common in Marivaux's incidental fiction. One of the strongest examples of this division between "real" and "fictional" selves as seen through the mirror of autobiographical fiction is a story that appeared in *Le Cabinet du philosophe* (1734) and which Arland provisionaly entitled *La Veuve et le magicien* ( *R*, 967-973; *J*, 419-425).

The mirror of fiction becomes with Marivaux a portal onto a virtual space where the social antinomies and contradictions of real space are resolved. It is therefore no accident that this mirror is oriented along the lines of class and gender in Marivaux, for whom the act of narration itself suffices for these lines to be crossed and a new identity forged. The accidental and circumstantial grounds that enable narrative production will eventually dominate Marivaux's style, to the point of being thematised in the later novels in the form of the narrator performing what he or she narrates. Before that stage, however, Marivaux expounds his views on the narratorially improvised self in his many plays, most of which deal with the same issues as the *Double histoire* in more direct (because less prosaic, because the stage speaks for itself) terms.

One of the more striking aspect of the *Double histoire* is the relative ease with which the servant, Fatima, produces her narratives. This facility with narratives on the part of the servants is something that occurs frequently in Marivaux's idiom. One of the reasons for the "sham" quality of the masters and servants' apparent authenticity can be ascribed to the parallels and constant oscillation between the two sides of the mirror of fiction. In Marivaux's idiom the cleverest, and consequently the best-rewarded servant will be he who can best engage in narrative production to control the situation at hand and help save the day. To a certain extent such impromptu narration is entailed by the change of status central to most of his plots, but as characters Merlin (*Les Acteurs de bonne foi*; henceforth *Les Acteurs*), Dubois (*Les Fausses confidences*) and Blaise (*L'Ile de la raison*) do stand a notch above the rest. This improvised narration is not without its importance. To this end I would like to examine in some detail *L'Ile de la raison* and *Les Acteurs*.

The other places, the ones featured in Marivaux's three theatrical utopias (*L'Ile des esclaves*, *L'Ile de la raison* and *La Colonie*) function as virtual spaces, as stages within stages, spaces where fiction is realised and history re-written, where certain restrictions are lifted and new axioms emerge.[12] In this respect they are also de-metaphorised versions of the spaces that are de facto transformed from real to virtual but nevertheless retain their quotidian airs: the reversals of *Le Jeu de l'amour et du hasard* do not suddenly transform Monsieur Orgon's house into a stage although that is, for all intents and purposes, what it becomes.

The impact of these contained stages on their inhabitants is demonstrated by Frontignac's question: these are loci ideally suited to the forma-

---

[12] The status of these virtual spaces as a locus that takes on all the trappings of the real but is not necessarily real places can be linked to Marivaux's use of *mauvaise foi* insofar as the latter is aimed at representing a situation between truth and falsity.

tion of identities, where one can "débénir cé qu'on est." Unlike the contained stages of the previous century, these are not without a narrative dimension: the freedman's island where Arlequin and Cléanthis attain their freedom (something they would never have had at home), the Swiftian isle where Blaise and Frontignac attain their humanity, the charmed circle in *La Surprise de l'amour* where Lélio and the Countess find their enamoured selves (despite Lélio's disillusionment) all deal extensively with what has gone before the arrival of the characters within their boundaries.[13]

This historical component of the virtual space provides the answer to Frontignac's question: on the island of reason, subjectivity is attained through the production of narrative and the presentation of what preceded the Europeans' landing. Indeed it is insofar as they can attain authenticity in some form that the stranded travellers can attain their freedom. This task can only be accomplished through confession: once they narrate themselves as they have been the trapped Europeans can become themselves again. It is, moreover, not insignificant that the act of narration, usually an owning up to past sins, is performed in the presence of someone else. Indeed, the logic operative on the isle of reason anticipates to a very large extent the relation between analyst and analysand. Marivaux's use of this transferential aspect of human behaviour is counter-balanced by the island's initial curse: one narrates to become what one is, but this condition becomes necessary due to the starting condition: "ceux-là qui n'étiont pas raisonnables, deveniont bian petits en la présence de ceux-là qui étiont petits." (*T*, 499)[14] The medium of this cure is also spelled out by Blaise: "Les gens de ce pays l'appelont l'île de la Raison, n'est-ce pas? Il faut donc que les habitants s'appelaint des Raisonnables, car en France il n'y a que des Français, en Allemagne des Allemands, et à Passy des gens de Passy." (T, 499) In other words, the process by which subjectivity is forged is verbal, depending first and foremost on a continuity between a word and its bearer. What allows soul and body to operate as metaphors for one another ("La petitesse de vos corps n'est qu'une figure de la petitesse de vos âmes") is the verbalisation of the link between them. Henceforth soul and body will only adequate one another insofar as the narrative associated with one cor-

---

13 Cf. Tomlinson, 143-145.

14 In his preface to a recent edition of *L'Ile de la raison*, Fréderic Deloffre points out that the association of small minds and small bodies is a marivaudian topos, citing as evidence a passage from the *Télémaque travesti* in which a philosopher, "qui croyait avoir plus d'esprit que tous les hommes de la terre", receives the following judgement in hell; "on l'attacha à un pilier, et on lui mit devant les yeux un grand miroir, où, quand il se regardait, il se voyait petit comme un ciron, et il reconnaissait par ce miroir aussi, que c'était là la véritable figure qu'il avait eue sur la terre." (*OJ*, 917; qtd. *Théâtre complet* (Frédéric Deloffre & Françoise Rubellin eds., Paris: Garnier 1989), 1:581-582)

responds to or proves compatible with the narrative associated with the other. The reign of the word also extends to the lives that the Europeans led before reaching the island, since most of their misdemeanours were verbal rather than literal: Frontignac was a flatterer, and the poet was a poet. The fact that the narrated identity is something fluid and susceptible of a certain quantification is foregrounded by Marivaux's ingenious *coup de théâtre* whereby the characters actually grow in direct proportion to their self-narration rather than doing so in the blink of an eye (which would not be unexpected in the fabular space that he constructs).

The exemplary case on the Isle of reason is that of Blaise, who is the first to become himself and to teach the others how to do so. Rather than focus on him and his paradigmatic authenticity, however, I would like to examine the case of Spinette and her mistress the Countess. Their case is interesting primarily because of its apparent subversion of the rules of the island, insofar as they transform the primacy of the verbal into the priority of the visual, as well as the fact that Spinette seems to do all the narrating for the countess.[15] This introduces a new model of "reading" that will find its apotheosis and final development in the later novels, specifically in the scenes involving Marianne before the mirror or Jacob as he meditates on his costumes. The countess's sin was the most Marivaudian of all sins, the sin of *coquetterie*, of wearing a mask of her own making. The terms in which this *coquetterie* is described are quite revealing. They indicate, first, that the coquette's face is her medium of self-fashioning and second, that the procedure executed before the mirror implicates and incriminates any spectator who might be found therein (in this case, Spinette herself):

> Bon! est-ce que le visage d'une coquette est jamais fini? Tous les jours on y travaille: il faut concerter les mines, ajuster les oeillades... N'allai-je pas répéter toutes vos contorsions? Il fallait me voir avec mes yeux chercher des doses de feu, de langueur, d'étourderie et de noblesse dans mes regards. J'en possédais plus d'un mille qui étaient autant de coups de pistolet, moi qui n'avait étudié que sous vous. Vous en aviez un qui était vif et marrant, qui a pensé me faire perdre l'esprit: il faut qu'il m'ait coûté plus de six fois ma vie, sans compter un torticolis que je me donnai pour le suivre... ne vous troublez point, Madame; c'est un cœur tout à vous qui vous parle. (*T*, 523)

Spinette means what she says quite literally, for in exercising one's profession as a coquette's aide one risks losing oneself to the coquette, whose *praxis* has already claimed Spinette's heart (by her own admission) and

---

[15] Of course Spinette is not unique among the cast of characters in this respect, and the same could be said of Frontignac vis-à-vis the courtesan. If anything this further emphasises the peasants' and servants' authenticity in relation to their masters.

eyes (by Blaise's: "Velà une terrible condition que d'être les yeux d'une coquette!" (*T*, 523)). The shift in grammatical subject that occurs halfway through Spinette's tirade implies that, in the course of her reading the mask (persona) under construction, she loses her own identity and becomes what she sees. The countess's attitude as she makes herself (up) is predatory. Anyone who reads her persona, be it a young *étourdi* at the opera or Spinette in the bedroom, is in danger of losing his or her being for the benefit of the mask. In alienating herself the countess alienates everyone else; her *aliénation* is contagious, whence her confession; "J'ai vécu comme une folle." (*T*, 525) Her modus operandi approximates that of Eléonore, which is not surprising since what the countess really stands accused of is the sin of (false) narration. The cruelty of her idiom rivals that of the other narrators (manipulators) that we have seen so far as witness what she does in her own style to the spectacle of society:

> Sans compter cette rancune contre tous les jolis visages que l'on va détruisant d'un ton non-chalant et distrait. Combien en avez-vous trouvés de boursouflés, parce qu'ils étaient gras?... A vingt-cinq ans, on approchait de sa quarantaine. Une petite fille avait-elle des grâces? oh! la bamboche! Etait-elle grande et bien faite? oh! la géante! (*T*, 523-24)

It is, of course, only fitting punishment that, having sacrificed so many identities to her narrative idiom, she be narrated in turn on the Isle of Reason and that she be forced to recognise herself in the narrative mirror drawn by Spinette.[16] In Marivaux's idiom, therefore, *coquetterie* and narration are synonymous. It is also worthy of note that Spinette's (enforced) alienation and inauthenticity necessitated by the countess's excesses pre-figure the development of Jacob, the upstart peasant.

In *L'Ile de la raison*, as well as most of the earlier comedies, the social hierarchies dictate and condition the staging of the narrative and the *Wirkung* of the interior stage. The events of the "real" world translate into a situation that is resolved and brought to an acceptable end in the virtual world. Once this resolution has been accomplished, the players step off the stage in order to return to a new world, one shorn of the antinomies that made an existence there intolerable. Thus at the end of *L'Ile de la raison*, we see all conditions return to normal, with the courtier coming dangerously close to his erstwhile Parisian gallantry in the course of his wooing Floris, and *Le Jeu* end safely in a way that proves that blood will tell and

---

16 Thus adding to the transferential mechanism operative in *L'Ile de la raison*. The countess, in effect, gets her story straight by being narrated, by having her identity appropriated by another narrator. To make matters worse, Blaise takes over the narration after Spinette.

class will out on planes both linguistic and emotional. What links the real and virtual worlds, the near and far side of the mirror is a dialogic exchange rather than a uni-directional metamorphosis.

Towards the end of his life, however, Marivaux changes his thoughts on the subject, and the possibility of closure, of a return to the real or even of an ending *tout court* is called into question. The possibilities implicit in these games of love and chance harden to become part and parcel of the plot of *Les Acteurs*, a compact investigation of the consequences of improvisation, together with the concomitant construction of an identity. This play reverses the conditions of its forebears: whereas earlier being (character, narrative) was a necessary constituent of what happened on-stage, here it is merely a by-product, a theatrical effect. Hence the arbitrariness of social standing imposed by the demands of the genre. *Les Acteurs* sees everyone's rank displaced according to the whims and fancies of the contained playwright(s). As a whole *Les Acteurs* reads, in some respects, like a reductio ad absurdum of the conditions underlying and the topoi inhabiting Marivaux's theatre.

The complex plot turns on a demetaphorisation of the expression, "se donner la comédie." Mme Argante is to marry her daughter Angélique to her daughter's beau, Eraste, whose family stands a few notches above his fiancée's on the social scale. Eraste wants to thank his aunt, Mme Amelin, for helping him financially ("je ne suis que son neveu," he says, "et elle me donne tout son bien pour me marier avec Angélique que j'aime." (*T*, 1455)) and decides to offer her a theatrical *divertissement* (il veut lui donner une comédie). And so he has Merlin, his clever *valet de chambre*, direct a play for her viewing pleasure. Merlin stages what seems to be an autobiographical scenario: he scripts an impromptu of his affair with Colette, the gardener's daughter, who is now engaged to Blaise. Thus we have a play-within-a-play featuring the traditional pastoral *Liebeskette* structure (Blaise likes Colette who likes Merlin who likes Lisette) put on by the servants for the viewing pleasure of the masters.

But then things change: Mme Argante decides that she does not want a theatrical production staged at her home, since gaiety is not her strong suit. Mme Amelin bristles at Mme Argante's refusal and decides to turn the whole thing into a farce: she pretends to change her mind and "arranges" another marriage for Eraste to a mutual friend, Araminte, without due regard for Mme Argante, Angélique or even Eraste himself. In other words, we have an aristocratic impromptu that isomorphically mirrors the plot staged by Merlin: in both cases we have a young engaged couple threatened by the machinations of an *intrigant(e)* who uses them as characters in his or her own play. The resulting confusion lasts until the end of the play, when the entrance of a *notaire ex machina* assures a happy end for all and sundry.

Thus the viewer is presented with not one but two comedies, a situation offering two conclusions. First, there is the familiar thesis that the real world is no less theatrical than the virtual, that the ostensible locus of authenticity (the world of the servants and spectators) entertains a continous rather than merely specular relation with the stage. The other, more troubling conclusion derives from the form of *Les Acteurs*. Each of the plots is divided along a central axis between players and spectators, and the succession of scenes implies that the histrionic mode could conceivably continue ad infinitum, thus calling into question the possibility of making distinctions between real and virtual, player and audience, authentic and inauthentic.

Merlin is, to a certain extent, the apotheosis of the Dubois of *Les Fausses confidences* and the Fatima of the *Double histoire*, acting as a marriage-broker for his social superiors by using his social inferiors as puppets in an exemplary narrative. His plot presents and develops an ostensibly false situation that turns out to have some truth in it: initially we assume that Merlin is faithful to his betrothed Lisette and that Colette is faithful to Blaise. Eventually, however, we learn that Merlin and Colette do have some inclination for one another, and that the concerned responses on the part of Blaise and Lisette are not unwarranted. It is difficult, however, not to read this developing inclination as the result of the rehearsal, thus linking *Les Acteurs* to the tradition of Rotrou's *Saint Genest*. Merlin's ruse is very similar to Hamlet's: in his impromptu (which, he claims, holds the mirror up to nature; "dans le plan de ma pièce vous ne sortez point de votre caractère," (*T*, 1457)) he reveals a hitherto secret infidelity. His rather questionable motives are revealed by his prefatory discussion with Eraste: "J'oublie encore à vous dire une finesse de ma pièce; c'est que Colette doit se faire mon amoureuse, et moi je dois faire son amant. Nous sommes convenus tous deux de voir un peu la mine que feront Lisette et Blaise à toutes les tendresses naïves que nous prétendons nous dire." (*T*, 1456) It is not unreasonable to assume that the meeting between playwright and actress involved more than a discussion of the conventions of the impending impromptu. The assumption, suspicious though it may seem, is warranted in view of Merlin's later admission; "elle est si jolie que je n'ai pu m'en empêcher." Thus the general trend of this reading is re-confirmed: Merlin's impromptu is a play planned with Colette staged for the viewing benefit of the two *cocus* in order to keep them abreast of current developments. Furthermore, since we only see them flirting onstage, Merlin's and Colette's brand of rehearsal provides a very good example of improvised narration at its best, one where the author (Merlin) oscillates between his status of writer and character at every moment of the impromptu.

Thus we see a transformation of the paradigm established on *l'Ile de la raison*. On the Isle of Reason, the characters narrated themselves directly. In *Les acteurs de bonne foi*, on the other hand, Merlin stages his narrative; he writes a play in order to narrate himself. The sort of self-fashioning that occurs in *Les Acteurs* is framed by both theatre and narrative: Merlin is both autobiographer and director of a play in which Blaise, Colette, Lisette and Merlin all play themselves. The scene of Colette's seduction is a confession that only becomes intelligible (and only elicits a concerned response from Blaise, Colette's current beau) once it is staged. Despite the fact that anyone can see that Merlin has really seduced Colette, it is only the theatrical narration of this act that counts, as opposed to its observation as historical fact: as Blaise himself points out, "maugré la comédie, tout ça est vrai... car ils font semblant de faire semblant." (*T*, 1474) The virtual, in a way, determines the real; life imitates art.

The movement from the servants' plot to the masters' plot in the second half of the play marks the passage from a deliberate conscious, "reasonable" theatricality to a theatricality gone awry, a theatricality of an unconscious, most unreasonable sort. Consequently, there is a very real sort of suspense created in *Les Acteurs de bonne foi*, a suspense worthy of a whodunit without a crime, since we, the readers and spectators, really have no idea as to what will happen until the end of the play. One can no longer speak of a reflection or a specular doubling between the real and the virtual, but rather of a proliferation of modalities between one framework and another, of an invasion of the real by the virtual: Mme Amelin takes over the direction of the play and by staging events as she imagines them annuls the marriage of Angélique and Eraste. The domination of the narrative staging process by Madame Amelin underlines what we know about narrators as they operate in Marivaux's idiom: everyone else becomes a puppet, an object of narration, including her homonymic companion, Araminte (the two are rather difficult to distinguish) who functions as her second, "fictional" self, and Eraste, who becomes a character as pliable as the quartet that staffed Merlin's impromptu. Insofar as it is as unpremeditated as Merlin's, Mme Amelin's play continues the tradition of improvised storytelling ever aware of the eye of the beholder (even when this spectator is included in the form of the indignant Madame Argante or the wide-eyed Eraste). It also foregrounds the fact that identity in general, and Eraste's in particular, depends in no small part on who is controlling the narrative and who is pulling the strings. Equally worthy of note is the ease with which Mme Amelin steers her plot, thus intimating the fact that the space surrounding the lovers was already shot through with theatricality and lends itself to constructions of that sort. The author's subjectivity thus becomes an effect of the situation that he or she claims to narrate: like everyone else, she is a product of her narrative.

Marivaux's text puts an end to spectatorial complacency. Past a certain point we no longer know whether the marriage will take place, who has seduced whom, who likes whom (Araminte, after all, really does seem to have fallen in love with Eraste), who is playing what part for whose benefit, and, last but not least, whether there will be a return to order at the end of the play (after the *notaire* leaves, will Eraste and Angélique's life together follow the same farcical lines as the wedding?) Far from suggesting a return to order, as did *L'île de la raison* and *Le Jeu de l'amour et du hasard*, *Les Acteurs de bonne foi* suggests the absolute triumph of comedy, of the order of virtual space. When Eraste asks his aunt whether she wants his life to depend on a play ("voulez-vous qu'une comédie décide de mon sort, et que ma vie dépende de deux ou trois dialogues?"(*T*, 1473)), her response is negative but the response that Marivaux implies is very much in the affirmative. Theatre takes precedence over distinctions of class and seniority. Insofar as he has been reduced to a complete ignorance of the possibility of life being a comedy, not to mention the de facto existence of hypocrisy and bad faith among the inhabitants of *le monde*, Eraste has in effect been reduced to the lowest possible level of social existence, that of being subject to someone else, like a character to an author, like a child to a mother. As his subjectivity oscillates between the twin foci of mastery and servitude, the trajectory that it traces is dictated as much by the facticity of theatricality and the inevitability of the histrionic as by social and economic power.

What Marivaux describes in *Les Acteurs* is the foundation of a society (since the central event is a marriage) where theatre and role-playing constitute social and existential norms. The formulation of an identity now depends not only on narrative discourse but on staged narrative, relentlessly re-inscribed in the framework of the histrionic sensibility. One can no longer speak of an individual except in the sense of a role, which role is bound inextricably with the narrative dimension. And the text that bears witness to this theatrical individuality plays its arbitrary, carnavalesque hand incessantly: as the peripeteias multiply, we lose sight of the status of Angélique and Eraste's marriage; half-way through the play, it is still on; by the end of the seventh scene, it has been cancelled; at the start of the eleventh scene it seems to have been restituted; is apparently cancelled again with the entry of the notary; is re-established at the end of the play, and if the text continued for ten more lines, it would probably have been cancelled yet again. This oscillation could easily have continued indefinitely: there is a *marivaudage* on the level of the plot as well as the level of dialogue. The play has, as it were, neither beginning nor end, it is always there. The gap between stage and spectator is bridged so frequently that it gives way to a seamless continuity. *Les Acteurs* is less what Robert Nelson has called a play within a play within a play within a play than play *tout court*.[17]

Thus *Les Acteurs* takes to a logical extreme all the hidden implications of the earlier plays: where once the auctorial function was anterior to its product, we are presented with a context in which narration is improvised to the point of making the priority of the narrator over the narrative impossible. Where once the real and virtual came into close contact and then separated from each other, we are presented with a spectacle of the sort of damage wrought when the principles of the virtual are let loose upon the world of the real, and with the establishment of the histrionic as a norm in the real and the dependence of "real" subjectivity on performance. The extension of the code of play-acting to the ostensible audience effaces the boundary between stageboards and orchestral pit, making good and bad faith indistinguishable and elevating play-acting from the pastime of the privileged to the necessity of the many. The persuasive depiction of this state of affairs and its attendant anxieties in *Les Acteurs* makes it a very useful introduction to our treatment of Marivaux's novels, ones that explicitly make theatricality laudable and improvised narration essential. It comes as no surprise that both *La Vie de Marianne* and *Le Paysan parvenu* centre on people with no past, no subjectivity, merely the one role that they can prescribe themselves in the eighteenth century, that of the narrator.

In approaching *Le Paysan parvenu* I would like to quote Frontignac once again. As he reminds the courtier of his past, he turns to Blaise and asks, "Qué dités-bous de ces gens qui n'ont qué des mensongés sur lé bisagé?" (*T*, 535) This question introduces the most important issue that is brought into play in the novels of maturity, the adequation of essence and appearance and the verbal structure of the mask. In *Le Paysan parvenu*, every face tells a story, and appearances translate into narratives. Small wonder, then, that Jacob spends much of his time discussing his appearance and contemplating the mirrors where it hardens into a social station. His project entails the effacement of one identity and the construction of another, as is indicated by the gradual lightening of his complexion as the novel progresses: early on in the first part he makes a point of mentioning the fact that, "Mon séjour à Paris m'avait un peu éclairé le teint; et, ma foi! quand

---

[17] In *Play Within a Play: The Dramatist's Conception of his Art from Shakespeare to Anouilh* (New Haven: Yale UP, 1958), 82.

je fus équipé, Jacob avait fort bonne façon!"[18] (P, 14) There is an added layer of significance in the shift from first to third person: in considering the status of his mask, Jacob holds himself at a distance in a rhetorical twist corresponding to the replacement of oneself by a double in one's own narrative. The rest of *Le Paysan parvenu* is an account of Jacob's improvisation and refinement of his own narrative skills, showing and telling a self under construction.

Probably the most obvious indication of Jacob's identity and social status (the two are essentially synonymous) apart from physical appearance is verbal appearance or style. Jacob creates himself in the space of language. This process is carried out on two levels; the diegetic level, the level of the narrative proper, through his exchanges with the other characters in the text, and the meta-diegetic, on the level of his exchange with his readers, the level that mediates Jacob and his autobiographer. The narrative conveys the distance travelled in the process of social climbing; the style of the parvenu constantly hints at the start and end of the voyage he has made up the social ladder. Indeed, without these termini Jacob's "becoming" would be indefinite and would not lend itself to narration.[19] This discrepancy between the old and new Jacob manifests itself in two aspects of *Le Paysan parvenu*: the unrealistic development of characterisation (in Jacob's idiom) and the performative tone in which this narration is carried out.

The very facticity of the act of narration weighs heavily on the *paysan*. In the words of Marie-Hélène Huet, "son langage ne *dit* pas, son discours ne *rapporte* pas, il transforme, il recrée, il provoque le geste." (37) To this end Jacob's use of language aims primarily at the legitimation of his social transformation from his interlocutors' viewpoint: he is quick to mention his peasant origins where they come in handy (with the female characters) and is just as quick to disavow it when it proves embarassing (primarily with

---

18 References will be to the Deloffre edition (Paris: Garnier, 1959) and will be given by *P* followed by a page number. Roger Kempf correctly identifies Jacob's problem as one of appearance primarily: "Ce n'est pas le villageois, mais l'*air*, l'écriture d'une condition." (35)

19 Cf. Huet, 31-50 as well as Laden, 180-182. Huet and Laden approach the opposition between Jacob and de la Vallée differently: Huet emphasises their separation, reading the final scene at the theatre as the final triumph of the peasant over the *parvenu*. Laden, on the other hand, gives Jacob's *marivaudage* its due and reads his development as a *fuite en avant*, leading to a conclusion that recognises the peasant's necessary failure: "The more La Vallée succeeds in hiding Jacob, the more the vitality of the peasant is eroded: as if... the mask had devoured the face wearing it, until with nothing left to support it, the mask drops away to reveal the emptiness staring out behind." (181)

the male characters).[20] It is through his listeners' belief of his narrative that he becomes what he is. Whence the importance of Mlle Habert as Jacob's first "convert" and the catastrophic impact of the recognition scene at Mme de Rémy's. This leads to a partial explanation of the lack of closure at the end of the fifth part of the novel: in order to become a "parvenu" Jacob must necessarily narrate himself, either to other characters or to his reader, as long as possible. *Le Paysan parvenu* deals less with his "being" La Vallée than with his becoming La Vallée through the enactment of his autobiography. Indeed, once this phase of becoming is complete, Marivaux stops adding to the novel, thus bearing out the observation that Marivaux's interest in his characters only lasts as long as they are in this transitional phase.[21]

The movement of *Le Paysan parvenu* is of a piece with the movement of *Les Acteurs*. In both cases, the text becomes a virtual space that turns author, reader and character into entities engaged in the same mode of existence. The virtual space, in all of its forms (the mirror, the stage, the text) thus becomes a locus ideally suited to the construction of authorial identities. *Le Paysan parvenu* combines its operation with the image of the text making place for its narrator. Jacob spends most of his time improvising a character that he only comes across accidentally. But Jacob is also a reader, insofar as he reads himself into the text of the social fabric. He "reads" his own candor and assumes that it implies a real rather than imaginary nobility. His candor also allows him to be read as a text, and to be mistaken for a dead or missing husband by all the female characters in the novel (thus acquiring the costumes that add to his "act"). Finally, he is invited into the circle of a nobleman for these same reasons. Jacob's tale is Quixote's revenge: he insinuates his masked appearance into the space of the virtual and manages to re-fashion himself as a legitimate inhabitant of that world instead of his own. Jacob can only "become" in a space where the distinctions between classes and between the mask and its bearer are nominally erased.

Nevertheless, in order to maintain his narrative agenda, Jacob needs to keep the distinction between the real and the virtual, the provincial and the Parisian, the narrator and the narrated entity, alive (otherwise there would be nothing left to narrate). Indeed, his project stands as an incessant re-iteration of the passage from one space to the other, from a point where the two spaces are declared separate and discontinous to one where they are bound inextricably with one another through Jacob's agency. Thus *Le*

---

[20] Cf. Laden, 174.

[21] Cf. Felicia Sturzer, "Exclusion and Coquetterie: First-Person Narrative in Marivaux's *L'Indigent Philosophe*", *French Review*, 55:4 (1982), 475.

*Paysan parvenu* moves beyond the ostensible goal of narrating social ascent to a higher aim of developing a narrative meditation thereupon.

Consequently Jacob's status, *qua* parvenu, depends to a greater extent on his adequacy as a narrator than his appearance alone. Consider the account he gives of the evaluation of his relationship to the younger Mlle Habert, and the extent to which events are constituted in and through their narration:

> Plus elle riait, plus je poursuivis. Petit à petit, mes discours augmentait de force; d'obligeants, ils étaient déjà devenu flatteurs, et puis, quelque chose de plus vif encore, et puis ils s'approchaient du tendre, et puis, ma foi, c'était de l'amour, au mot près que je n'aventurai point, parce que je le trouvais trop gros à prononcer, mais je lui en donnai bien la valeur et le reste. (*P*, 76)

The final "ma foi!" sounds like a theatrical declaration. Jacob sounds no less surprised than his reader at this sudden outburst of love from the text. This section shows us the operation of a *marivaudage* of sorts, only rather than being used as an expository tool between two stage characters it is applied to Jacob himself. His final conclusion, the word, "love", only takes place at the moment of the utterance of his autobiography, at which point he, in Frontignac's terms, becomes what he is: Jacob-who-once-loved-Mlle Habert. This is, in effect, the novel's answer to Silvia's "Ah! je vois clair dans mon cœur!" (from *Le Jeu*): Jacob's insight and perspicacity vis-à-vis the motives of his conduct with Mlle Habert speak legends about the innately aristocratic merits of Jacob, as it implies a certain inauthenticity and propensity towards alienation from the self that would be incompatible with his standing as a peasant. In uttering the word "love", Jacob passes a contemporary judgement on a past situation. He deals with himself, in other words, in the same way that he deals with his characters, as witness, to take one of a number of examples, the following rejoinder appended to his portrait of Mme de Ferval, "Telle était la dame d'auprès de qui je sortais; je vous la peins d'après ce que j'entendis dire d'elle dans les suites, d'après le peu de commerce que nous eûmes ensemble, et d'après les refléxions que j'ai faites depuis." (*P*, 143) Now, since the "peu de commerce que nous eûmes" is the least reliable source of evidence for Jacob's views on Mme de Ferval, it is obviously only on the "refléxions" that his judgement rests. Characterisation, therefore, takes the form of a collapsed analeptic moment in the narrative, a pocket in the narrating trajectory that looks both forwards and backwards. So Jacob's performative rhetoric is not without its uses insofar as it allows the doubling and separation that render Jacob narrateable and through this narrative a *parvenu*. It is clear that, given this structure of performed eventuality, Jacob does nothing other than become the *paysan parvenu* and the act of coming through socially (*parvenir*) partakes of its own narration. Jacob does not come through until he becomes a character, until he sees himself in the mirror of his own narrative, until he attains Eléonorean duality.

In this respect Jacob's social standing is bound inextricably with his alienation from himself. Obviously it is rather difficult to square this separation with the image of rustic candour and naïveté with which everyone associates him. The two are juxtaposed in the final state of Jacob's face (and of his soul) with its *hétéroclite* character. To a certain extent the adjective reflects the division that Jacob epitomises; he is part human (narrator), part puppet (character). This division can be aligned with the other one that subtends Jacob's development: he is part *parvenu* and part *paysan*. The first part of the novel, the account of his experiences with Geneviève, illustrates the making of the puppet. Jacob's change upon arriving in Paris is as material as it is metaphysical, especially when he is confronted with the more traumatic facts of life (infidelity and the *droit du seigneur*), as witness his consistently corporeal response to everything he hears: "Je restai comme un marbre à ce discours..." (*P*, 26) and "Ce discours me glaça jusqu'au fond du cœur..." (*P*, 34). In both of these cases Jacob hardens into his second, fictional self almost as a way of dealing with (appropriating and assimilating) the formative moment. This is further supported by the lack of narrative continuity with the rest of the novel.

The time that Jacob spends discussing costumes and appearances thus amounts to a critical history of that puppet, a sequence of interpretations of each of his appearances. This is not without importance, for in order to rise socially Jacob must read himself into such social "slots" as may exist at any given time. The costumes thus act as markers of the virtual space in which Jacob is trying to make a name for himself, promising aristocratic fortune with every perfect fit. Like the act of narration, the accoutrements of Jacob's enactment of his transformation into La Vallée hold a certain transformative power, propelling him farther up the social ladder. The first glimpse that we are offered of this process is during Jacob's first (and only) day in the Habert kitchen, where Catherine tells him that, "vous ressemblez comme deux gouttes d'eau à défunt Baptiste, que j'ai pensé épouser, qui était bien le meilleur enfant, et beau garçon comme vous." (*P*, 49) It is not insignificant that the marriage between Catherine and Baptiste never came off. The unresolved nature of the emotions involved lends a certain depth to what would other wise have been a domestically farcical situation. A very similar sequence of events takes place in another, somewhat wealthier household a few days later. Mme d'Alain tells Jacob that because of the resemblance between them, she will give Jacob her husband's *robe de chambre*, an item essential to Jacob's well-being, since he is only comfortable when he is playing the gentleman; "je vais vous en chercher une qui est presque neuve, mon pauvre défunt ne l'a pas mise dix fois; quand vous l'aurez, il me semblera le voir lui-même." (*P*, 166) Soon thereafter Jacob procures a suit through a similar procedure: M. Simon, the tailor with lodgings at Mme d'Alain's, offers him another man's suit; "j'ai chez moi un habit tout battant neuf à qui je mis hier le dernier point, et que l'homme à qui il est me l'a laissé pour les gages, à cause qu'il n'a pas pu me payer l'avance que je lui en ai faite." (*P*, 166) The sword that he dons later "pour être M. de La Vallée à forfait" acts as yet another signpost pointing the way to the virtual space where Jacob's aristocracy is to be legitimated. With every acquisition, Jacob moves forward to incorporate the rank implied by the costume, to play the part that he looks. It is the recently-acquired sword that inspires his saving the comte d'Orsan's life.[22] Indeed, things reach the point where dressing the puppet by inserting himself into other gentlemen's attire becomes Jacob's raison d'être, and the separation between character and narrator becomes crucial as the sole source of self-definition;

> Comment donc, des pantoufles et une robe de chambre à Jacob! Car c'était en me regardant comme Jacob que j'étais si délicieusement étonné de me voir dans cet équipage; c'était de Jacob que M. de la Vallée empruntait toute sa joie. Ce moment-là n'était si doux qu'à cause du petit paysan. (*P*, 248-49)

The apparent collapse of self and other (or costume and character) in the space of the mirror is balanced by Jacob's taking stock of how far the "petit paysan" has come. The distance between object and mirror-image or Jacob and de La Vallée renders the peasant's identity narrateable.

Divided though he is, Jacob still worries about consistency. Insofar as he behaves in a manner consistent with himself, he can be called authentic if the term is taken to mean a conformity with a certain fictional narrative. Jacob reads himself incessantly into pre-existing fictional situations (to a

---

22 Cf. Laden's account of this movement between the two spaces:

Jacob's outfits are not a sign of his present condition, they herald a future one... The sword soon becomes much more than Jacob intends it to be. Like his words, it is a sign without substance, but soon communicates to him a courage of which he was unaware, as he draws his brand-new sword to rescue the comte d'Orsan... When Jacob talks himself into loving Mlle Habert or rescues the count, the usual distinction between appearances and reality makes no sense. In light of such instances, critical disputations as to whether Jacob, M. de la Vallée or te narrator are sincere or hypocritical are inevitably fruitless: they ignore what we must perorce call, in such illustrations, appearing reality or real appearances. (175-176).

The last pair of terms (appearing reality/real appearances) could be treated as a description of the axioms of virtual space.

certain extent all the suits, gowns and slippers that he inherits evince this tendency). The strength of his leaning towards a manner consistent with his fictional self emerges during the phase that follows his mistaking himself for a nobleman, a rank that he obtained by donning M. Simon's suit. He continues, for one thing, his problematic policy of candid resemblances, allowing him to insinuate himself anywhere. Mme de Fécour tells him that, "Le premier homme pour qui j'ai eu de l'inclination vous ressemblait tout à fait." (*P*, 185) Even more important is his growing awareness of himself as he develops in the fifth part of the novel, the part where the puppet moves into the corridors of power only to be found out at Mme de Rémy's and the Comédie française. Both the scenes at Mme de Rémy's and the theatre are especially significant insofar as they seem to indicate the failure of Jacob's project, although it is, I should like to argue, a necessary failure if he is to adequately indicate where it is he came from and if he is to effectively (re)present himself as a narrator engaged in improvised narration.

The intruder at Mme de Rémy's who recognises both Jacob and Mme de Ferval as well as what they are up to, is a major source of irritation to Jacob, in part because he provides the only de-mystified reading of the situation. It is, moreover, significant that he is the only character in the novel who does not mistake Jacob for someone else (including Jacob himself). This is precisely what bothers Jacob: the intruder's reading does not misplace Jacob into some other narrative full of ardent glory, he sees him for what he is, "Mons Jacob." Indeed, Jacob finds the shock of being recognised and found out far more intolerable than any other situation that he encounters, and the only one calling for an immediate escape, "ce nom de Jacob, qu'il m'avait rappelé, me tenait en respect, j'avais toujours peur qu'il n'en recommençât l'apostrophe; et je me songeais à m'évader du mieux qu'il me serait possible; car que faire là avec un rival pour qui on ne s'appelle que Jacob?" (*P*, 227) Precisely, not because of the rival's bid for the affection of Mme de Ferval, but because of his capacity as a witness, because of Jacob's transparency before him. The witness destroys Jacob's act as M. de la Vallée by calling attention to the fact that it was an act, one preceded by a narrative that subverts its claims. The witness thus replaces Jacob vis-à-vis himself (knowing himself as Jacob the *petit paysan* was Jacob's only privilege). This structure of displacement by a witness echoes in strict formal terms the demystification of the countess by Spinette in *L'Ile de la raison*, together with all the concomitant conclusions: that social rank is a role and mask, that the border between history and fiction is very problematic, that the gaze of the witness can easily turn the appropriative gaze of the narrator against itself. In the narrative of social mobility, the only crime is the recognition of the hero's or heroine's origin under all the layers of accumulated wealth.

As against the frustration offered by this setback, consider Jacob's tone as he gleefully throws himself into the arms of danger for the sake of falling back into his chosen role of de la Vallée, a nobleman whose actions speak for themselves (and will, hopefully, erase irritating, accidental details like the fact of his humble birth and so on). Jacob describes the young count's peril as a mere one among many distractions on the streets of Paris to which the public responds as they would to a staged performance; "en pareil cas le peuple crie, fait du tintamarre, mais ne secourt point: il y avait autour des combattants un cercle de canailles qui s'augmentait à tous moments, qui les suivait, tantôt avançant, tantôt reculant, à mesure que ce brave jeune homme était poussé et reculait plus ou moins." (*P*, 250) Jacob's admiring tone implies that the brave young man in question is another version of himself, a product of the other side of the mirror of fiction. The crowd is literally following the young man's performance. Not content to see so much attention focused elsewhere, Jacob throws himself into the narrative as it unfolds before him. He makes quite clear the fact that performing in this way comes quite naturally to him, that he comes into himself (or rather back into himself) as he fights alongside his other self;

> [C]'est ici où je me sentis un peu glorieux, un peu superbe... Tout distrait que je devais être par ce qui se passait encore, je ne laissai pas que d'avoir quelques moments de receuillement où je me considérais avec cette épée à la main, et avec mon chapeau enfoncé en mauvais garçon; car je devinais l'air que j'avais, et cela se sent; on se voit dans son amour-propre, pour ainsi dire; et je vous avoue qu'en l'état où je me supposais, je m'estimais digne de quelques égards, que je me regardais moi-même moins familièrement et avec plus de distinction qu'à l'ordinaire; je n'étais plus ce petit polisson surpris de son bonheur, et qui trouvait tant de disproportion entre son aventure et lui. Ma foi! j'étais un homme de mérite, à qui la fortune commençait à rendre justice. (*P*, 252)

This is a very explicit proclamation of his identity as circumscribed by this moment of theatrical triumph: after the shattering experience of recognition, Jacob returns to find himself in the mirror of his *amour propre*. Moreover, his vision of himself, sword in hand and all aswagger with self-confidence is very much in keeping with his tradition of analeptic character-formation: he does not become this man equal to his situation until the moment of narration.

Thus we see him spend the rest of the novel re-confirming what he has just stated so unequivocally. His embrace of his chosen role continues, despite the visibility of his peasant origins, out of what can only be called Marivaudian authenticity: Jacob, as he sees it, fits in better in the world of the nobility. This is the case not because of his comfort there, as his reception by his future peers makes obvious, but rather because the role (and the accompanying suit) fits him better than any other narrative slot. His narration of this point is typically pro-jective, making itself manifest through his discomfort at the d'Orvilles':

> Et en effet, ces-choses-là se sentent; il en est de ce que je dis là-dessus comme d'un homme d'une certaine condition à qui vous donneriez un habit de paysan; en faites vous un paysan pour cela? Non, vous voyez qu'il n'en porte que l'habit; sa figure en est vêtue, et point habillée, pour ainsi dire; il y a des attitudes, et des mouvements, et des gestes dans cette personne, qui font qu'elle est étrangère au vêtement qui la couvre. (*P*, 254)

Jacob thus retains the gap dividing his origins from his terminal station so that both are visible in his final situation, the one from which he narrates his narrative. When he presents himself to the Comte d'Orsan, he does so as a negative double, with the meeting only showing Jacob what he is not; "Quant au manque d'education, il n'y paraît jamais tant que lorsqu'on veut en montrer... Mon nom est la Vallée, lui dis-je, vous êtes un homme de qualité, et moi je ne suis pas un grand monsieur..." (*P*, 264) And when he does accept Orsan's protection and friendship, every step up the social ladder proves embarrasing: in the lobby of the Comédie, Jacob's face, once the epitome of candour, takes on a different aspect. He literally does not know what to do with his appearance; he tries to compose a new one and fails:

> Que vas-tu faire de toi, me disais-je?
> Aussi, de ma contenance, je n'en parlerai pas, attendu que je n'en avais point, à moins qu'on ne dise que n'en avoir point est en avoir une. Il ne tint pourtant à moi de m'en donner une autre; mais je crois que je n'en pus jamais venir à bout, non plus que d'avoir un visage qui ne parût ni déplacé ni honteux... [J]'étais une figure de contrebande... ils [Orsan and his friends] parcouraient donc mon hétéroclite figure... (*P*, 265-66)

The more he is on display, the more Jacob feels the nakedness that comes with being out of his social place. Jacob's face is *hétéroclite* because its origins and artifice are no longer hidden. As how could they fail to reveal themselves: much of his development has depended on his revealing his "true" personality up to this point, embarrassing though some of the details may have been. But now, in the social comedy that precedes the evening's performance, a different sort of behaviour is called for, namely the sort of theatrical behaviour in which the wealthy indulge, and none of the courage or authenticity that helped Jacob to *parvenir* will help him now. What he has to do is play a role.

Thus Jacob ends his life much as he started it (if his account is to be believed): as a performer, forced to improvise a social status and a history not quite his own but still defining himself as the sum of his actions as presented by the text of *Le paysan parvenu*. It is no accident that Jacob ends the Fifth part in a hall of mirrors; each of the men in the count's entourage effectively compares himself to and with Jacob, down to the level of movement (Jacob looks at himself as a trained puppet). This is, of course, the same mode in which he started, but something has changed: the act of rising above the social hurdles that block his path is nowhere near as innocent as he makes it out to be. His *hétéroclite figure* is marked by his *mensongés sur lé bisagé*.

The closing scene of the fifth part shows us the protagonist in a state of near panic because of his *hétéroclite figure*; "je tremblais qu'on ne connût à ma mine que ce monsieur-là avait été Jacob." (*P*, 266) This situation marks the visible incorporation of the real into the virtual, the provincial into the Parisian. The gap between point of arrival and point of departure that made Jacob narrateable has now become permanently inscribed on his face. Rather than argue that the mask has entirely devoured its wearer, it would make more sense to argue that the two are fused onto one another in a space that proves the opposition between essence and appearance to be quite senseless. It is no surprise that the novel ends there because of the collapse of the opposition between paysan and parvenu—the mask and its bearer—effectively closes, on the level of appearances, the gap that motivated the novel hitherto. Jacob has "become" de la Vallée, figuratively speaking, not only in his own eyes but in those of the spectators of the virtual space mapped out by his autobiography. Once closed on this level, however, the gap remains open on another: Jacob may look like de la Vallée, but he certainly does not feel like la Vallée; his history differs significantly from a nobleman's. "J'avais sauté trop vite," he says, "je venais d'être fait monsieur, encore n'avais-je pas la subalterne éducation des messieurs de ma sorte..." (*P*, 265-6). In attempting to represent this flight into the virtual, the narrator is still struggling with the paradoxical nature of a narrative traced around the two foci of actor and author. There is still a great deal left to be said. This is why the novel ends on one level (Marivaux only wrote five parts) but is nowhere near attaining closure on another.

It would seem therefore, that a reassessment of what the terms becoming and "parvenir" really stand for in Marivaux's idiom is in order. Vis-à-vis society, Jacob's *modus operandi* is the same as that of the countess before the mirror, avowing what is manifestly not the case (his *honnêteté*) and tirelessly disavowing what is the case (the inscription of his history as a peasant on his face, his language and so on). His existence through others is clear from the very beginning, as is its independence of any effective action taken on their part. "Rien ne rend si aimable que de se croire aimé," (*P*, 76) he remarks during the early phase of his romance with Mlle Habert, and with good reason: the reflexive pronoun refers to Jacob the puppet, not the narrator. His mode of "becoming" is no less improvised or narratorial than that of the Europeans on the island, as witness his constant references to himself as "petit homme". The term functions as more than an intertextual link, for it refers to his station as a character in his own fiction. Furthermore, the novel presses forward with the same urgency as *Les Acteurs* towards virtual space, which is what the aristocracy has become for Jacob. Still, the intrusion of Jacob into La Vallée's world is by no means anomalous: the price that Jacob pays for becoming de la Vallée is his eternal reassessment of himself, his condemnation to measuring the distance travelled across the ranks of society with each and every person that he meets. His closing the gap between himself and La Vallée is never complete, which incompletion is indicated by his hétéroclite figure. His accounting for himself must necessarily continue *ad infinitum*. Jacob has opted for the thankless task of identifying narrator with character, and thus finds himself prey to the restrictions of bad faith and inauthentic narration. His is the serio-comic embarrassment of the dedicated dramatist who, in trying to attempt his condition of estrangement from the truth, is doomed to fail the more he succeeds. If the *Paysan* were a play, it is quite reasonable to assume that Marivaux would have made the most out of the convention that Jacob be unmasked and that he return to a state of primeval innocence at the end of the play, that the threat of his disarming charm be removed. This is not the case, however: the logic of *Le Paysan parvenu* is of a piece with *Les Acteurs de bonne foi*, letting loose the virtual on the banality of the real. The unspeakable result of all this is Jacob's reappropriation of his fictional double as he makes him, that despite his candor, his honesty and the seemingly natural style he is as much a product of bad faith as he is its sworn enemy. As the novel and its writing make clear, a full autobiography, an autobiography of both self and other (or real self and virtual self), entails the necessary undoing of the Penelopean web of narrative, in an eternal reassessment of the self, in the incessant return to the mirror, in an endless narration, self-fashioning and self-unravelling. By rigorously investigating authenticity, "de la meilleure foi du monde", Marivaux stumbles upon its other and the inevitability of their parity.

Jacob and his *hétéroclite figure* —a mask that expresses the many *historiettes* cobbled from here and there in his life—demonstrate a contrario the new conception of identity in the France of the 1730s, and the extent to which the processes of narration and role-playing are bound inextricably with one another. We have come a long way from the dynamics that accompanied the construction of the self in the seventeenth century. Tartuffe, it will be remembered, played his part to perfection, to the point where no distinction between his real and false selves was possible without the artificial intervention of the king. The crisis of faith of which *Tartuffe* was symptomatic is resolved in *Le Paysan parvenu*. Marivaux's point seems to be that the *paysan* —the "real", originary self—will always show through the mask of the *parvenu*, that class will out despite the ubiquity of the theatrical because of the importance of historical narrative. Narrative is now an integral part of the social mask that one presents in everyday life. In addition to simply demonstrating a given set of values concomitant with one's social status, one is now called upon to tell one's story as a means of entering society. Moreover, the story that one tells has to be adequate to the social mask that one presents.

This adequacy is to be gauged by society, now conceived as a vast mass of spectators before whom one plays and narrates oneself. It is their criteria of credibility that determine whether a self is properly constructed, or will, at the very least, be deemed socially credible. This is the most important measure of identity, namely its social acceptance in *le monde*. The question that haunts *Le Paysan parvenu* is precisely that of credibility, or authenticity: How believable is Jacob in his reincarnation as M. de la Vallée? Do the theatrical laws of virtual space allow transformations like these? The answer would seem to be a decisive, "No, but…" Jacob may not have had the history of a man of leisure, but he could, presumably, pass for one through the right combination of playacting and storytelling. The problem, however, is that Jacob's stories interfere with his playacting: everyone at the Comédie française can see that Jacob is an upstart, not because he plays his part badly—if anything, his having saved Orsan's life and his many "courbettes de corps courtes et fréquentes" (*P*, 266) attest to the contrary—but because his lack of experience and utter discomfort with the history that he tries to pass off as his own are blatantly obvious. Furthermore, the source of this discomfort is not Jacob but French society: the arbiter of the "fit" between the teller and the tale is not the teller but the listener. It is the latter who decides that the niche that Jacob tries to carve out for himself in the virtual space of the nobility is not of the right size, that the shoes of de la Vallée are too big to be filled by the *petit paysan*. Jacob, in other words, creates a narrative with a slot into which he tries to insinuate himself but cannot because society has deemed that slot inappropriate.

Thus the last word would seem to go to those who, like Mme Amelin of *Les Acteurs*, valourise the virtual space where "[l]a vie dépend[e] de deux ou trois dialogues," and master the production and circulation of narratives therein. The dialogues are, of course, the sources of those narratives, the fictions that regulate society and social behavior: reputations, gossip, intrigue, all depend on the observation and operation of a code that synthesises the participants' narrative and theatrical skills. Jacob's problem inheres in his management of the parts and stories that he tells, as well as the many dialogues and *discours* that circulate about him. He might think his narrative is good enough to pass social muster, but the reception of his *hétéroclite figure* makes abundantly clear that this is not the case. Society is now the mirror of fiction and the anchor of identity. Unless one's history passes the social test, the identity that one attempts to construct through that history collapses. One is completely at the mercy of the "deux ou trois dialogues" that society scripts and performs.

The result is an extremely conformist social ethic, one far less individualistic than the one that went before it: whereas once the king was needed as *the* criterion of all values and touchstone with which one could distinguish true from false, society now reigns supreme. Where once all that mattered for the acquisition of prestige, rank and status was pleasing the king, there is now the vastly more complex task of pleasing *le monde*. Unlike the world of Corneille, where social power meant scripting one's own role, social power in the early eighteenth century means mastering one's own narrative and the narratives of those with whom one comes into contact. The greater the number of narratives that one controls, the more power one wields over the other members of one's social circle, members whose fortune, in turn, depends on their reputations and on the narratives that circulate about them.

The use of society as a mirror of the self is a question treated by a number of writers apart from Marivaux. The importance of the issue comes across with especial clarity in Montesquieu's *Lettres persanes*, where Rica, a Persian in Parisian society (i.e. a total outsider) is confronted with the social conformist imperative when the Parisians ask him, "Ah! monsieur est persan? Comment peut-on être persan?"[23] This is basically a pre-figuration of Blaise's question, "how can one be what one is?" How can one be a Persian in Paris? In fact, how can one be anything other than a Parisian in Paris? How can one be someone without one's social group, one's society? Montesquieu calls attention to the rather problematic nature of the French understanding of identity in the early eighteenth century, and the conception of the self as something entirely dependent on one's aptitude for dealing socially. The fact that the question is posed at all means that society—this society, French society in 1721—cannot cope with outsiders like Rica, or, for that matter, anyone with a *hétéroclite figure*, anyone with a different narrative, anyone who does not conform to its rules and

---

[23] Cf. Harari, 67-101.

expectations. Society, itself a web of interconnected narratives, dictates where and whether room will be made for those who seek a space therein, by they outsiders like Rica, or upstarts like Jacob. More often than not, of course, room is not made at all, and it is up to the individual seeker in question to cope with the process as best he or she can. Such are the ethics of the society of the salon. Marivaux depicts them with admirable precision, but it fell to another writer, a contemporary of Marivaux's, namely Crébillon *fils*, to abstract the principles of their operation into a more systematic idiom. It is to his work that we now turn.

# Chapter Six

# Crébillon fils:
# Carnal Knowledge and Narrative Knowledge

Whereas Marivaux tries to answer the question of how one can be what one is, Crébillon's project is more ambitious: he asks how a group of people, a society, can be what it is. Specifically he addresses the question of how *le monde*—understood as a network of interconnected personal histories and narratives—operates, and tries to formulate the laws of its functioning with respect to the two poles of narrative, the teller and listener of the tale. Marivaux describes the phenomenology of *le monde*, focusing as he does so on its relationship with other social spaces (island utopias, countryside chateaux and so on). Crébillon, on the other hand, takes the de facto primacy of *le monde* for granted, and writes texts that focus exclusively on the individual's relation to the web of narratives that constitutes the social space.[1]

Crébillon completes the displacement from theatre to fiction that began with Marivaux: it is not insignificant that he did not write any plays.[2] Still, one of the more powerful metaphors for the social stage is the closed circle of Parisian society in which the novels of Crébillon fils are rooted. The theatre that he affected to disdain returns like a repressed motif in the setting that he used for nearly all of his works, *le monde*. In this space, repu-

---

[1] My reading of Crébillon owes a great deal to Peter Brooks's *Novel of Worldliness*, a text whose influence is ubiquitous in this chapter and which I shall cite directly only in case of a direct quotation. On the technical and rhetorical aspects of *libertinage* and its fictions, Sturm's *Crébillon fils et le libertinage au dix-huitième siècle*, Reichler's *L'Age libertin* and Lasowski's "Crébillon fils et le libertinage galant" were especially useful. On the formal aspects of Crébillon's fiction, P.V. Conroy's *Crébillon fils: Techniques in the Novel* is indispensable.

[2] Crébillon's relationship to theatre was quite ambiguous: his father was one of the foremost tragedians of his time, but he himself was fairly disdainful of the medium as a whole (despite his anecdotal "formation dans les coulisses"). Cf. Mercier's description of his attitude: "Un jour, il me dit en confidence qu'il n'avait pas encore achevé la lecture des tragédies de son père, mais que cela viendrait. Il regardait la tragédie française comme la farce la plus complète qu'ait pu inventer l'esprit humain. Il riait aux larmes de certaines productions théatrâles et du public qui ne voyait dans tous les rois de la tragédie française que le roi de Versailles." (qtd. in E. Sturm, *Crébillon fils et le libertinage*, 23). Even more significant is his composing dialogues that occupy the interstitial space between the novel and theatre: *La Nuit et le moment* and *Le Hasard du coin du feu* contain both stage directions and editorial interventions on the narrator's part.

tations are everything, and the fictions that circulate within it determine the identities of its inhabitants and their rank in the social pecking-order. This leads to a literary *œuvre* focused primarily on seduction and narration, which, in the event, emerge as two sides of the same coin. In the libertine text, every sexual relationship—which is to say, every relationship—serves primarily as a pretext for telling stories and thinking through a given social situation. The struggles in which Crébillon's characters engage are struggles for the mastery of a narrative, a *conte*, which will circulate in *le monde* and make or break the reputations of its participants, depending on the parts that they play therein. Much depends on whose version of events is authorised and legitimated by *le monde*, and Crébillon's stylistic subtleties aim primarily at showing the efforts involved in wresting control over the production and circulation of worldly narratives, which control accounts for a great deal of power.

The texts with which we shall be concerned with here all deal with the acquisition of narrative power and the construction of the narrator in the space of *le monde*. In all three cases this construction is successful only due to the would-be narrator's managing to narrate an other in order to narrate his—or herself, or rather to narrate himself as an other. The specular relationships and forms of doubling that we have seen elsewhere become an essential component of the narrator's self-fashioning. Crébillon's seducers—and narrators—all need someone onto whose history they can map their own. Crébillon's texts eloquently demonstrate the fundamental import of the autobiographical instance in the production of fiction, arguing that the only way to become a narrator is to narrate oneself, and the only way to narrate oneself is to double oneself, to narrate an other, a double with whom one can identify.[3] The creation of this double is, moreover, underwritten by the separation of the self into an *être* and a *paraître*, the better to allow that self to function in a world where masquerade is all, where seduction (the copula between carnal knowledge and knowledge of other people's histories) is to be sought at all costs and sentiment avoided like the plague. Or smallpox.

In *Les Egarements du coeur et de l'esprit*, Meilcour's entry into *le monde* is described in theatrical terms: the novel itself is a series of scenes punctuated by the movement of the dramatis personae (in the event, *tout le monde*) in the theatre that is Paris. The salon is the privileged locus of the

---

[3] It bears pointing out that this mapping of the narrator's history onto the character's (and therefore the constitution of the narrator's identity) depends in no small part on the prior existence of a narrative structure that might contain them both. This is, as we shall see, Meilcour's problem at the outset of *Les Egarements du cœur et de l'esprit*: he has no reputation, and is therefore incapable of taking part in the narrative circus called *le monde*.

discovery of the self, now effected through the display of idiosyncrasy with the usual consequences of such close scrutiny. In addition to the theatrical atmosphere there is, in the case of Meilcour's initiations by Versac and Mme de Lursay, the fictional equivalent of Argan's lesson in alterity. Meilcour is society's rattle until Versac teaches him how to behave, which is to say how to act, and Mme de Lursay teaches him how to properly read the history of his interaction with her. At this point he understands—retrospectively—what had been happening to him all along, and can effectively narrate it. Meilcour's incarnation as a narrator therefore depends on his seeing himself as an actor (in every sense of the term) in his own narrative. In a similar vein, *La Nuit et le moment* shows us two characters vying with each other physically and narratologically. Clitandre's quest for the evening is to add Cidalise to his catalogue of seducees, the set of narratives that defines his identity in *le monde*. Cidalise, for her part, only allows this to happen once he has narrated all of his past seductions to her, once she has seen him as both author of and actor in his own narrative. Finally, *Le Sopha*, is a series of lessons in alterity, in how selves are swapped through narrative self-fashioning and self-maintenance. Here the narrator both produces and is produced by his narrative: Amanzéi, technically, only becomes himself once a true exchange of identities (or "premices") takes place before his very eyes. As he narrates, Amanzéi foregrounds his identification with the characters and their history and the fact that he is to be identified with the meta-narrative container. He only metamorphoses into his human self once he is implicated in his own narrative by falling in love with Zéinis and in narrating his desire through *Le Sopha*. In all three cases, the oscillation between the narration of the self and the narration of the other, between narrative mastery and the subjugation to an other's narrative idiom, between *erlebendes Ich* and *erzählendes Ich* is very much in the foreground. As how could it not be, for in each of these narratives, we are shown a character getting his story straight and becoming a narrator in his own right by narrating himself before an audience.[4]

---

4 This aspect of the characters' development is not without affinities with the psychoanalytic scenario. Peter Brooks sums it up thus: "*Mens sana in fabula sana*: mental health is a coherent life story... narratives speak repeatedly of the transferential condition of their anxiety concerning their transmissibility, of their need to be heard, of their desire to become the story of the listener as much as of the teller... Something is being transmitted or transferred from the teller and his told to the listener, and to listening: it has entered into the realm of interpretation. And if the story told has been effective, if it has 'taken hold', the act of transmission resembles psychoanalytic transference, where listener, and reader, enter the story as active participants in the creation of design and meaning." ("Psychoanalytic Constructions and Narrative Meanings", 53-57).

## The Birth of the Narrator: Les Egarements du cœur et de l'esprit

In *le monde*, everyone has a reputation, which is to say, a history, except Meilcour. *Les Egarements* narrates how Meilcour acquires a story.
The greater concern of this text is with the construction of Meilcour
through his narrated identity; it is the story of an "I" recoded into a lesson
on reading identities in general and the narrated identity in particular.[5] This
is the crucial step in the transformation of Meilcour from innocent to experienced *mondain*: Meilcour only learns to narrate by seeing through the
false appearances of those who surround him, by "penetrating" everyone
else in his account. The source of this worldly concern with psychological
penetration is, as we have seen, the product of the legacy of foiling and
mirroring invented by Corneille and Molière. Any anxiety on the part of the
characters on this issue merely reflects the narrator's: Meilcour cannot
become the author of his own life without penetrating everyone else, but in
so doing he leaves himself vulnerable to a similar gesture of knowledge
and narration. The only solution, of course, is to know and narrate others
before they know and narrate him. In order to construct his "je", Meilcour
must learn to act and tell stories in order to take his place in the well-regu-
lated market of narrative and social ritual that is *le monde*.

The novel opens with Meilcour at the gates of *le monde*, an outsider
faced with the sect, a would-be player without a part, a would-be seducer
without a reputation. He is bored and utterly lacking in purpose:

> L'idée du plaisir fut, à mon entrée dans le monde, la seule qui
> m'occupa... Au milieu du tumulte et de l'éclat qui m'environnaient
> sans cesse, je sentis que tout manquait à mon cœur: je désirais une
> félicité dont je n'avais pas une idée bien distincte; je fus quelque
> temps sans comprendre la sorte de volupté qui m'était nécessaire. Je
> voulais m'étourdir en vain sur l'ennui intérieur dont je me sentais ac-
> cablé; le commerce des femmes pouvait seul le dissiper. (48)

Meilcour knows who and what he is insofar as those variables are determined by social status, but not what he wants, because what he wants is
bound inextricably with his historicity (or lack thereof). So unlike the
world of Corneille, say, where a rigid social hierarchy informs every char-

---

[5] Cf. Claude Labrosse's "Récit romanesque et enquête anthopologique, à propos
des *Egarements du cœur et de l'esprit*" in Werner Krauss (ed.) *Roman et lumières au
dix-huitième siècle* (Paris: Editions sociales, 1970), 73-88, and Andrzej Siemek's *La
Recherche morale et esthétique dans le roman de Crébillon fils* in *SVEC* 200 (1980). On
the *récit d'initiation* at the heart of *Les Egarements* see Claude Reichler's *L'Age libertin*, 45-78. On the distinction between empirical self and narrated self (*Erlebendes Ich*
and *Erzählendes Ich*) see P.V. Conroy, 75-86.

acter of his or her role, the world of *Les Egarements* is one where the protagonist does not know how to operate himself. Indeed, all Meilcour knows
is that he is a child of impetuous passion and an active imagination, much
of his account trying to organise these affects into something tangible, intelligible, narrateable. Predictably, this self-delineation will only be brought
about through "le commerce des femmes".[6] Rather than pit himself against
other warriors on the battlefield, the hero of this day and age pits himself
against an emotional partner in the boudoir, where his philosophy will
unfold.

Initially, Meilcour's mirrors are all feminine. He is a virgin without an
erotic history, and assumes the same of his widowed mother. Despite her
beauty, youth and wealth, she dedicates herself to the pleasure of raising
her son, and the possibility of any reluctance on her part is dispelled thus:

> Ce projet, je crois, serait entré dans l'esprit de peu de femmes, et
> beaucoup moins encore l'auraient ponctuellement exécuté. Mais
> Madame de Meilcour, qui, à ce que l'on m'a dit, n'avait point été co-
> quette dans sa jeunesse, et que je n'ai pas vue galante sur son retour, y
> trouva moins de difficulté que toute autre personne de son rang
> n'aurait fait. (47)

My mother, myself: Mme de Meilcour does not remarry according to
her son because she, like him, has no "reputation", no worldly history. It
comes as no surprise, therefore, that his attraction to Mme de Lursay, depends as much on his deliberate disavowal of her *galanteries* as it does on
the friendship between her and his mother:

> Coquette jadis, même un peu galante, une aventure d'éclat, et qui avait
> terni sa réputation, l'avait dégoûtée des plaisirs bruyants du grand
> monde... Malgré l'air prude qu'elle avait pris, on s'obstinait toujours
> à la soupçonner; et j'étais peut-être le seul à qui elle en eût imposé.
> Venu dans le monde longtemps après les discours qu'elle avait fait
> tenir au public, il n'était pas suprenant qu'il n'en eût rien passé
> jusqu'à moi. Je doute même, quand on aurait alors voulu me donner
> mauvaise opinion d'elle, qu'il eût été possible de me la faire prendre:

---

6 Meilcour's exemplarity as an eighteenth century character is further underlined by
his relations towards his parents: here, as elsewhere, the name of the father has been effectively erased, and the figure of the patriarch who sends his children to do battle for
his sake gives way to the interfering mother. Indeed, for Meilcour his father is little
more than a source of wealth, whereas his mother is the real source of his identity: the
question he will ask Versac—"Pourquoi avons-nous besoin qu'une femme nous mette
au monde?" (259)—is to be read both literally and figuratively (the word "monde" signifying both the physical world and Parisian society) bespeaks a very real tension between masculine and feminine authority in this respect. Cf. Labrosse, "Récit romanesque et enquête anthropologique."

elle savait combien j'étais éloigné de la croire capable d'une faiblesse,
et s'en croyait obligée à plus de circonspection, et à ne céder, s'il le
fallait, qu'avec toute la décence que je devais attendre d'elle. (53)

The overriding characteristic of this portrait is Meilcour's unwillingness
to believe that Mme de Lursay is even capable of having an erotic experience. The voice of the narrator freely admits that he was the dupe of an
elaborate stratagem, aimed at perpetuating the myth of Mme de Lursay as
the Diana of le monde by covering up those aspects of her history that do
not correlate with that image.[7] For her part, Mme de Lursay also appeals to
the virtues of virginal ahistoricity as part of her seduction routine, asking
Meilcour at one point to reassure her, "contre tout ce que j'ai à craindre de
votre âge et de votre peu d'expérience." (110-111) There is, therefore, a bi-
directional narcissistic projection of Meilcour's ahistoricity onto both his
mother and Mme de Lursay, a reading aided and abetted by the young
man's self-absorption.

This emotional solipsism also speaks to Meilcour's lack of narrative
sense. He is fundamentally incapable of arranging the events that befall
him in an ordered sequence. As a result, every new object of desire replaces
(rather than displacing) the previous one, a situation that causes our young
hero no end of confusion: "Les sentiments que l'une m'inspirait étaient
détruits le moment d'après par ceux qu'une autre faisait naître." (48-49)

Meilcour's problem is that he has little understanding of the ceremonies
that regulate le monde. As he moves through its many stages, he is utterly
incapable of saying the right thing at the right time, itself a by-product of
his mistaking appearances for reality. Left alone in a room with the osten-

---

[7] Mme de Lursay, for her part, is an eminently theatrical creature, like all the other
inhabitants of le monde. Her knowledge of desire and her knowledge of theatre are
mutually constitutive, as witness her first discussion with Meilcour on the latest comedy. It is no accident, either, that she calls attention to the scene featuring a declaration
of love. From her viewpoint, life imitates art and there is therefore no excuse for Meilcour's reticence; "dire qu'on aime est une chose qu'on fait tous les jours, et si cette situation à de quoi plaire, c'est moins par son propre fonds que par la façon neuve dont
elle est traitée." (59) Meilcour, of course, begs to differ: the distance between his position and Mme de Lursay's corresponds to the one between actress and naive spectator.
The exclamatory declamations in which she addresses Meilcour smack more of the idiom of classical tragedy than the quieter world of the salon. Every time she sees that
Meilcour is speaking rather than performing, every time she perceives the shift from a
performative to a constative mode, she feels compelled to utter a "Ciel!" or a "Juste
ciel!", if only to inspire some verbal banter. Rhetorical questions like, "serais-je re-
servée à ce malheur, et ne l'avais-je évité jusqu'ici, que pour y tomber plus cruelle-
ment?" (121) echo Phèdre's "A quel nouveau tourment me suis-je réservée!". Mme de
Lursay is only lovable insofar as she is onstage; she plays her part in the (vain) hope
that Meilcour will reciprocate.

sibly "peu galante" Mme de Lursay, he can think of nothing to say but "Vous faites donc des nœuds?" (120) Faced with the insurmountabe challenge of speaking to Hortense at the Tuileries, he seeks recourse to the only part of his past with any formative impact, namely fiction: "Je me rappelai alors toutes les occasions que j'avais lues dans les romans de parler à sa maîtresse, et je fus surpris qu'il n'y en eût pas une dont je pusse faire usage." (105)[8] Meilcour, in effect, does not know how to read himself into anything, be it a scene from a novel or a situation in *le monde* where his verbal banter might attract the right sort of attention.

All of that changes after Versac's "intervention", like an absent father, in the third part of the novel. He instructs the young Meilcour in the art of solitary conformity, the art of remaining an outsider (and therefore remaining on display) while assuming the behaviour of the sect—*le monde*—within which one would establish oneself. That Versac is a good actor in his own right is evinced by the fact that his façade persuades even at its most pretentious; "il avait l'air Seigneur, même lorsqu'il l'affectait le plus." (131) Like Marivaux's Jacob, he slips into his worldly identity as easily as he puts on his costume. He epitomises histrionic self-fashioning at its rococo best, setting himself apart with his originality, going so far as to forge an inimitable idiom of his very own:

> Il s'était fait un jargon extraordinaire qui, tout apprêté qu'il était, avait cependant l'air naturel. Plaisant de sang-froid et toujours agréable, soit par le fond des choses, soit par la tournure neuve dont il les décorait, il donnait une charme nouveau à ce qu'il rendait d'après les autres, et personne ne redisait comme lui ce dont il était l'inventeur. Il avait composé les grâces de sa personne comme celles de son esprit, et savait se donner de ces agréments singuliers qu'on ne peut ni attraper ni définir. Il y avait cependant peu de gens qui ne voulussent l'imiter, et parmi ceux-là, aucun qui n'en devînt plus désagréable. Il semblait que cette heureuse impertinence fût un don de la nature, et qu'elle n'avait pu faire qu'à lui. Personne ne pouvait lui ressembler, et moi-même, qui ai depuis marché si avantageusement sur ses traces, et qui parvins enfin à mettre la cour et Paris entre nous deux, je me suis vu longtemps au nombre de ces copies gauches et contraintes qui, sans posséder aucune de ses grâces, ne faisaient que défigurer ses défauts et les ajouter aux leurs. (130-131)

---

8 Crébillon's work would eventually undergo very similar treatment at the hands of Laclos, whose Marquise de Merteuil braces herself for an evening of social activity thus; "Après ces préparatifs, pendant que Victoire s'occupe d'autres détails, je lis un chapitre du *Sopha*, une lettre d'*Héloïse* et deux contes de La Fontaine, pour recorder les différents tons que je voulais prendre." (*Les Liaisons dangereuses*, lettre X).

Versac is mirror and mask to everyone he meets. His is the genealogy of Matamore and Rodrigue: people who talk about their exploits and by pretending make them come true. The "grâces de sa personne" that Versac composes so meticulously are clear indications of the time and effort needed to turn such affectations into a mask that stays with its bearer. Nor is this all. Versac's performances are so convincing that he becomes a universal mirror: everyone tries to imitate him, but necessarily fails, much as one might try to be one's mirror image but finds that one can only approximate it because of the reversal of direction involved in the creation of a virtual image (it is no accident that Meilcour uses the term "copies gauches").

Versac's "lesson" to Meilcour expounds the truism that the only way to *be* in *le monde* is to *seem* in *le monde*. The only way to play the social game is to play a part, and to dedicate oneself to being on display in a world where the display's the thing. In *le monde*, he says,

> [T]out y est mode et affectation. Les vertus, les agréments et les talents y sont purement arbitraires, et l'on ne peut y réussir qu'en se défigurant sans cesse... Il faut étudier avec soin le ton du monde où notre rang nous a placés, les ridicules qui conviennent le plus à notre état, ceux, en un mot, qui sont en crédit, et cette étude exige plus de finesse et d'attention qu'on ne peut l'imaginer.
>
> Ce n'est pas tout: vous devez apprendre à déguiser si parfaitement votre caractère, que ce soit en vain qu'on s'étudie à le démêler. Il faut encore que vous joigniez à l'art de tromper les autres, celui de les pénétrer; que vous cherchiez toujours, sous ce qu'ils veulent vous paraître, ce qu'ils sont en effet...
>
> De tous ceux [les "ridicules"] qui regnent aujourd'hui, le fracas est celui qui en impose le plus généralement, et surtout aux femmes. Elles ne regardent jamais comme vraies passions que celles qui commencent par les enlever à elles-mêmes. (242-252)

Versac is the actor, the magician, the seducer, the one who in effect rules the Parisian *monde* with the illusions that sustain his reputation and power. Versac's world (and it is his world: the narrator of *Les Egarements* describes his domination in no uncertain terms) depends on his annihilating the real to vivify his theatrical show. In this world, if anything exists at all it is only insofar as it lends itself to being staged. A "ridicule" is only as effective as it is found interesting. A private passion is only as real as the fracas by which it is accompanied. Such is the authority of illusion in *le monde*.

Versac's authority also depends on the rumours and fictions that circulate in *le monde* representing him as a master seducer privy to everyone's secrets. The narrator tells us that the women of Paris, l'avaient mis à la mode dès l'instant qu'il était entré dans le monde, et il était depuis dix ans en possession de vaincre les plus insensibles, de fixer les plus coquettes et de déplacer les amants les plus accrédités; ou s'il lui était arrivé de ne pas réussir, il avait toujours su tourner les choses si bien à son avantage, que la Dame n'en passait pas moins pour lui avoir appartenu. (131)

Versac's reputation—and therefore his identity—is maintained and propagated by his audience, the spectators who live only to be seduced by the myth that they forge about him. His system consists of inventing a theatrical "travers" and ensuring its widespread use among his imitators and epigones through an extended worldly game of follow-the-leader: "Moi, par exemple," he asks Meilcour,"qui suis l'inventeur de presque tous les travers qui réussissent, ou qui du moins les perfectionne, pensez-vous que je les choisisse, les entretienne et les varie uniquement par caprice, et sans que la conaissance que j'ai du monde règle et conduise mes idées là-dessus?" (243) Versac's authority is also bolstered by his narrative skills. At Mme de Lursay's he immediately sizes up the situation at hand and includes both Meilcour and Mme de Lursay in the rumour he is preparing to launch:

> Par exemple, j'étais il n'y a pas longtemps avec une de ces femmes raisonnables, de ces femmes adroites dont les penchants sont ensevelis sous l'air le plus réservé, qui semblent avoir substitué aux déréglements de leur jeunesse, de la sagesse et de la vertu [like Mme de Lursay herself]… L'amant [Meilcour] arriva, l'on le reçut froidement, à peine voulut-on le traiter comme connaissance; mais pourtant les yeux parlèrent, malgré qu'on en eût. La voix s'adoucit: le petit homme, fort neuf encore, fut embarrassé de la situation; et moi, à qui rien n'échappa, je sortis le plus tôt que je pus, pour l'aller dire à tout le monde. (141)

Everything becomes grist to Versac's mill of rumours.

Versac's putative "honesty" with Meilcour, a potential rival, raises the question of the purpose behind the master seducer's total self-exposition, especially after his long lecture on the necessity of the mask. Versac himself is aware of the risk he is taking;

> Vous avez dû vous apercevoir que je n'ose parler devant personne comme je viens de le faire avec vous, et quand je vous ai prié de me garder, sur tout ce que je vous dirais, un secret inviolable, c'est qu'il m'est d'une extrême conséquence qu'on ne sache pas ce que je suis et à quel point je me déguise. (268)

Nevertheless, the question is bound to remain without a satisfactory answer unless one postulates that the apparent contradiction serves the ends of narration itself. Versac's presentation—this long verbal fireworks that shows him and shows him up—is the ultimate spectacle from the master of spectacles, performed with a view to confirming his status as master with Meilcour as his disciple. This is, after all, the treatise that opens Meilcour's eyes to all that is going on around him; henceforth he will stop seeing and start reading and interpreting (both of which are implied by the term "pénétrer"), stop being and start acting. Versac himself tells him that his success in *le monde* depends on his being a good student; "ce n'est qu'en suivant mes traces qu'on peut parvenir à une aussi grande réputation." (243) Versac's treatise is part and parcel of his routine of seductions: by placing himself between Meilcour and what Meilcour wants, he ensures himself of a great deal of emulation and mimicry on the part of the hapless young man. As he both shows and tells his "system", he ensures the addition of Meilcour to the ranks of his followers, his imitators. In short, he introduces Meilcour to the science of doubling.

Most of this seems to convince Meilcour, who goes on to Mme de Lursay's salon full of confidence and moral verve, ready to denounce her as nothing less than a hypocrite. In the event, the entire denouement of the novel turns into a festival of storytelling, reiterations and revisions of past misunderstandings. Meilcour enters her salon to find a *tiers incommode* in the person of the marquis de ****, the beneficiary of Mme de Lursay's attention for the evening, and the heir apparent to the lineage that includes Meilcour and Pranzi. Meilcour, having learned Versac's lessons well, judges the situation in the light of history: "Je n'ai été, comme Pranzi et mille autres, que l'objet de son caprice. L'homme qui lui plaît aujourd'hui lui sera inconnu demain et j'aurai bientôt le plaisir de lui voir un successeur." (265) Rather than rest contented with this proof in flagrante delicto of Mme de Lursay's infidelity, our hero decides to stay on and stand, in his turn, between Mme de Lursay and the marquis as a spectator in his own right; "Je me fis un plaisir secret de les gêner par ma présence et de me donner d'ailleurs la douce satisfaction de voir Mme de Lursay se dégrader de plus en plus à mes yeux et justifier tout le mépris que je croyais avoir pour elle." (266) Being Mme de Lursay's lover amounts to little more than playing a part in a historical fiction (insofar as history repeats itself): he sees her flirting with the marquis and sees himself under a different guise, which may explain his enjoyment of what should really hurt his feelings. Now, Mme de Lursay protests her innocence as regards her intentions vis-à-vis the marquis, but the reader is only too well aware of her using him as bait with which to tackle Meilcour. Meilcour, of course, falls for the trick, seeing his double in the marquis. Indeed, Meilcour is only touched once he realises that he is not the only man in her life. "Vous dites," she charges,"que j'ai voulu vous faire croire qu'avant que mon cœur fût à vous, il n'avait été à personne... Non, monsieur, j'ai aimé, et avec toute la violence possible...Il faudrait sans doute, pour mériter votre estime, que je n'eusse jamais été determinée à l'amour que par vous." (284) Meilcour's realisation that he is not alone, and his identification with his doubles in Mme de Lursay's past, activates his sympathy; "Ce discours était si tendre!... Il était soutenu par un son de voix si flatteur, que je ne pus l'entendre sans me sentir vivement ému, et sans me repentir de faire le malheur d'une femme qui, par sa beauté du moins, ne méritait pas une si cruelle destinée. Cette idée, sur laquelle j'appuyai, m'arracha un soupir." (284)

Furthermore, Meilcour's insertion into Mme de Lursay's history of seductions is itself not unrelated to his emergence as a narrator in his own right. Meilcour the author sees himself reflected in Meilcour the character whose status depends on Mme de Lursay's narrative. Mme de Lursay regains the upper hand over the rumours spread by Versac by telling stories that better contain and explain the situation at hand, ones that actually re-enforce rather than contradict Meilcour's case. Once again the dominant factor in her rhetoric is time, the disparity between the narratives represented by herself and by Meilcour (which narratives of course approximate and mirror each other once placed over the common denominator of desire); "Chaque jour que nous passions à nous voir me semblait vous donner des années, ou m'ôter des miennes. L'amour seul pouvait m'aveugler à ce point." (179) To the point, one is tempted to add, where she sees herself mirrored in Meilcour's shorter history in le monde. This is, in effect, how she wins her case: the account that she gives of their amorous misadventures is one into which Meilcour can read himself quite effortlessly. Not only does she re-confirm her previous involvement with Pranzi, but she shows Meilcour that she is only happy to fashion herself in a historical idiom; she shows him a sign, as Peter Brooks puts it, of "sensibility not of debauchery." (Worldliness, 30) Meilcour is taken and held captive by the mirror of fiction; he sees and hears all the details of Mme de Lursay's and his common destiny as he listens to her. Once his history has been assumed and re-processed by Mme de Lursay into a fictional mirror in which he recognises himself, Meilcour's sentimental education is over, and Meilcour the débutant becomes Meilcour the writer.

Thus Meilcour is, as the preface claims, "rendu à lui-même" but to his quixotic, fictitious self, the self that exists in the rumours of le monde, as an object is brought back to its mirror-image. He returns as a fragmented subject, formally speaking, trapped in the web of narrative that engenders him and in the social space wherein the machinations of this web are to be recognised and legitimated. Versac is not mocked: as a concept alterity is alive and well and living in Meilcour the narrator.

Very little happens to Meilcour, therefore, apart from Meilcour himself. The distance that separates Meilcour the character from Meilcour the narrator is the same one that separates self from other and author from text. This is what makes Versac's and Mme de Lursay's lessons so important; Meilcour learns to see himself as an other in order to become what he is; the final summing-up is a gauging of the distance covered by a hero who does nothing but scrutinise himself endlessly. If he does achieve anything by the end of the novel, it is not so much a seduction or a conquest as much as an ability to deal in narratives and narrative selves, as well as a decent standing on the auctorial pulpit. All of the attributes associated with mastery, namely authority, power and seduction, are in this context taken as being synonymous and concomitant with narration. Thus there is more to the invention of this subjectivity than role-playing; what is in order is the construction of a narrative into which one can insinuate oneself. One becomes oneself by being sympathetic to oneself, by putting oneself in the position of Marivaux's Clorinde and saying, "I am the one whose adventures have just been narrated." *Les Egarements* can only end once the narrator himself is implicated as an other (as a character) in the textual mirror thus fashioned, and once the thread of the narrative loops around itself in proto-Borgesian fashion to include the moment of narration.

## II. The Battle of the Books: La Nuit et le moment

Thus the seducers, Versac and Mme de Lursay, fight out their fictions on the battleground of Meilcour's nascent persona, each trying to make his version of events the dominant paradigm in *le monde*. This struggle of narratives and wills is brought into much sharper focus in *La Nuit et le moment*, as are the processes of narrative formation and self-formation. Like the final episode of *Les Egarements*, this text presents us with two people telling each other stories from dusk until dawn. The protagonists are completely alone; there is no-one to mediate their relationship with themselves or with each other, although that will change quickly enough. *La Nuit et le moment* represents what people do to each other, although in a sense that goes beyond the strictly erotic. This is emphasised at the outset by the rhetorical question that Cidalise poses and the implied response thereto; "Vous-même, que penseriez-vous si vous appreniez demain qu'un des hommes, qui sont ici, a passé la plus grande partie de la nuit dans ma chambre? Auriez-vous la bonté de croire qu'il ne l'aurait employé qu'à me raconter des histoires?" (18) The answer, of course, is very much in the affirmative; during the apogee of performative language what comes to pass between any two individuals will have to pass through a decidedly linguistic filter. To a very large extent both Clitandre and Cidalise are on display, Cidalise *négligée* on her bed and Clitandre at its foot playing themselves to each other by narrating themselves to each other. What makes this text unique is the attention it pays to the narrative bases underlying their improvised identities, which exists only in such performances, awash in an ocean of verbal banter. Each protagonist presents his- or herself as the sum of a series of past seductions and more significantly, previous narratives. Seductions are transcoded into a two-step procedure: first, reading or interpreting the other (in much the same way that Meilcour learns to "read" *le monde*) and second, incorporating the other into one's own story, one's own series of seductions.[9] As such seduction and its attendant narratives stand for the formation of the self as narrator through the other as character. The central narrative event is one that marks the completion of the process of self-construction through the other, the moment at which the other becomes a character in one's own narrative and the moment at which one can stake a claim to being a narrator. In the histrionically-determined universe of *libertinage*, seduction exists primarily to make narration, and through narration identities, possible. Clitandre and Cidalise find themselves engaged in a contest to see who can author whom, which one will draw the other into his or her story. The two narrative mirrors thus brought face to face with one another soon synthesise an infinite number of infinite reflections, each at one further remove from its own image in the text of the other.

Once the dialogue is under way, Clitandre and Cidalise foreground the importance of narrative. Clitandre's aim—sex with Cidalise—is blatantly obvious, but the latter resists as best she can until she has heard everything she wants to hear about their mutual acquaintances, all of whom are, of course, Clitandre's former lovers. Naturally what she wants is the ability to control Clitandre, the most notorious *petit-maître* of his day, by using what she knows about him. To this end, she employs and endures all she can in

---

9 Roman Wald-Lasowski's reading of *Le Sylphe* merits quoting at length in relation to this synthesis of narration and seduction: "En parfaite stoïcienne du boudoir, La Duchesse succombe dans sa solitude oisive peuplée de témoins insidieux, à l'appel du Sylphe, un ouvrage de morale dans les mains: "Je cherchais quelque dédommagement dans un *livre de morale* lorsque j'entendis prononcer distinctement, quoiqu'à demi-bas, et avec un soupir, ô dieux que d'appâts."... Souffle doué d'un pouvoir irrésistible d'évocation, le sylphe s'insinue dans le corps de la Duchesse pour la soumettre aux dérobades, aux feintes et aux interjections de sa propre "voix proférante"... Corps subtil que l'âme féminine tisse elle-même *ex elementorum vaporibus*, le sylphe recueille, à force de persuasion et de patience, l'Esprit de La Duchesse dans sa matérialité offerte et ravissante." ("Crébillon fils et le libertinage galant" 90-91). Thus the *sylphe* not only *seduces* but actually *becomes* the duchess.

order to put herself in a position where she can claim to have "penetrated" him psychologically as he pentetrates her physically.

Clitandre, for his part, puts up a good front. Consider his much-quoted dissertation on love in the eighteenth century:

> On se plaît, on se prend. S'ennuie-t-on l'un avec l'autre? On se quitte avec tout aussi peu de cérémonie que l'on s'est pris. Revient-on à se plaire? On se reprend avec autant de vivacité que si c'était la première fois qu'on s'engageât ensemble. On se quitte encore, et jamais on ne se brouille." (20)

As a first-rate exposition and defence of *amour-goût* it hinges on the advantages of keeping distances even during the moments of the greatest possible intimacy. But the patina of casual involvement belies the more rigid rules of social interaction underneath. Cidalise is not duped. Her response to all of this is typically astute: "Assurément, si vous croyez tout ce que vous venez de me dire, vous avez jusqu'ici agi bien peu d'après vos maximes, vous qui n'êtes pas encore consolé de l'inconstance de Célimène, et qui l'avez si tendrement aimée." (21) Clitandre's "performance" of his theory is not adequate because his indifference is nowhere in evidence to his audience of one. Cidalise, accuses Clitandre of *mauvaise foi*, of affecting cavalier indifference in order to hide his lingering predilection for Célimène.

The *petit-maître* who would be the seducer par excellence adopts the tone of synchronic philosophical generality (as witness the present tense that dominates his exposition), while his future *séduite* responds with the discourse of historical or narrative truth. Cidalise does not say that Clitandre is wrong, merely that he is inconsistent, that he will have to construct a series of events to prove what he says (another mirror of fiction). In raising this charge Cidalise uncovers Clitandre's deeper motives and undermines his privileges, most of which exist only by virtue of the powers of narrative. It is only once one narrative has successfully superceded another that Clitandre will be what he claims to be. The crucial point here is that the two of them inhabit a structure that allows this sort of thing to happen; that one person can produce a fiction, convince another of its reality and use it to cover up the truth. The control of the fictions that circulate in *le monde* and in the boudoir is the essential component of the mastery to which both of them aspire.

Thus narrative—the instrument of mastery—is a two-edged sword. Clitandre's mastery is assured if and only if Cidalise believes him. He is mistaken only in having emphasised the ethical rather than the historical component of this theory. Cidalise, too, is a willing listener and disciple; she simply uses the historical side of the issue to examine (and call into question) the master's theory of seduction, ultimately proving that the libertine's indifference is only legitimated once it is narrated before a listener who recognises it as such.

Clitandre gives in to Cidalise's objections some one or two pages later. What is interesting, here as elsewhere, is that the logic of the mirror of fiction permits anyone, in principle, to see his or herself reflected therein; it amounts to a backdrop scenario of seduction with cut-out spaces for anyone to fit themselves in. Thus Clitandre renders his desire for Cidalise in the following manner:

> Je commençais à perdre beaucoup de la douleur que l'inconstance de Célimène m'avait causé, et de jour en jour ma liberté me devenait plus à charge. Je brûlais de me rengager, et si vous me le permettez de vous le dire, mon cœur, qu'à votre entrée dans le monde vous aviez vivement blessé, reprenait pour vous ses premiers penchants; mais vous aimiez encore Eraste. (24)

This marks the fact that Clitandre has translated his project into Cidalise's terms; henceforth the question underlying their dialogue is the one of who is to banish whom from whose heart, and the fiction that is to precede and explain this displacement. Célimène and Eraste are indispensable as doubles for Cidalise and Clitandre. If Clitandre had not been previously enamored of Célimène, he would never have been in a position to desire Cidalise. Similarly, if the latter were not madly in love with Eraste, Clitandre would not have taken it upon himself to revive his interest in affairs of the heart. Furthermore, Clitandre's entire orientation has already been biased by the fact that his heart had already been broken by Cidalise on a previous occasion. Thus the status that one attains and the role that one plays depends in no small part on having an established narrative structure before one's eyes and identifying with the relevant part therein.

The importance of the mirror of fiction forces Clitandre into a metanarrative space in a desperate attemot to keep Cidalise's curiosity at bay. Faced with Cidalise's scepticism regarding his account of Araminte's seduction, Clitandre responds with, "Ils [les faits] sont si simples, que je m'étonne que vous y trouviez de quoi vous faire une histoire." (29) Cidalise, for her part, sees very well that "se faire une histoire" is the only reason behind this exercise. Furthermore, when Cidalise asks Clitandre for the story of his involvement with Julie, Clitandre's response lapses into metanarrative space again:

> Ce serait actuellement l'histoire la plus déplacée qu'il y eût au monde… et si déplacée, que si l'on écrivait notre aventure de cette nuit, et que dans la position où nous sommes ensemble on vit arriver

cette histoire-là, il n'y aurait personne qui ne la passât sans hésiter,
quelque plaisir qu'on pût s'en promettre. (59)

Clitandre can only conceive of himself as the author of himself, and as
such the history of Julie is of no particular interest as it represents a part of
himself that he would rather leave out. Although such strategies of exclusion may work wonders in the world of the theory that he is trying to prop-
agate and impose on his listener's mind, Cidalise helps keep the impulse in
check by reminding her *petit-maître* of all the seemingly trivial details that
he has left out and which problematise his views on seduction.

The final (and longest) vignette in *La Nuit et le moment*, the one that
narrates the seduction of Luscinde, brings all of these strnds to a head.
Once again a narrative backdrop is created to give Clitandre a sense of his
incumbent duties: Luscinde has just had an argument with Oronte, whom it
now behooves our hero to replace. Indeed, the entire episode aims at constructing a narrative mirror for Clitandre through his identification with
Oronte. He builds a framework that inscribes Luscinde, Oronte and himself
in an adulterous triangle with Oronte as a fictional double. The episode
amounts to little more than a practice session aimed at re-evoking the
memories of Oronte, followed by feigned indifference, followed in turn by
boredom that hides itself under a thin veneer of erotic zeal; in other words,
at the alternate creation and annihilation of desire. All of which has the desired effect on Luscinde: her affection leans towards Clitandre with every
mention of Oronte and vice versa, thus turning her into a puppet ready, presumably, for inclusion in Clitandre's array of characters and enabling him
to identify with Oronte as a fictional double. Her predictability provides
sufficient proof, to Clitandre's eyes at least, that manipulation is stronger
than sentiment, the very same truism that his failure with Célimène had
called into question:

> Il me prit envie de voir s'il est vrai que la machine l'emporte sur le
> sentiment, autant que bien des gens le prétendent; et pour m'eclaircir
> sur cela, dans l'instant que Luscinde semblait avoir oublié toute la na-
> ture, ou ne plus exister que pour moi: "Ah! Madame," m'écriai-je,
> "pourquoi faut-il que dans des moments si doux je ne puisse perdre le
> souvenir de mon rival? ou pourquoi du moins ne puis-je vous le faire
> oublier? Car enfin je ne le vois que trop, l'heureux Oronte peut seul
> vous occuper"... "Non, Clitandre," me répondit-elle courageusement,
> "vous ne vous abusez pas, je l'adore." Et ce qu'il y a de remarquable,
> c'est qu'en faisant à Oronte une si tendre déclaration, elle m'accablait
> des plus ardentes caresses, et me donna même les plus fortes preuves
> de sensibilité qu'en ce moment-là je pusse m'attendre d'elle." (120-
> 121)

Such, then, is Clitandre's "triumph": Luscinde becomes narrateable because he himself becomes narrateable, contained as he is in Oronte's narrative. In placing such great emphasis on Luscinde's cutting the figure of an adultress he is really casting her in a mould that would fit in with a narrative bearing his imprint and his alone. Clitandre cannot be Clitandre, the seducer, the narrator, without the incessant remembrance of his double and rival, Oronte. Having thus arranged these characters (Oronte, Luscinde, himself) into a triangle that makes his identity as an author thinkable, he can proceed, re-arrange them at will to bring about a suitable end to the fiction that he steered according to his whims and fancies, all for the sake of emerging as an author in Cidalise's eyes:

> Au reste, pour cesser de vous parler de Luscinde, je lui tins parole dans tous les points. Vous êtes la seule à qui j'aie raconté cette histoire. Je forçai Oronte à s'avouer coupable et l'envoyai aux pieds de Luscinde lui demander pardon de ses injustices. J'intercédai même pour lui, et j'eus la gloire de voir mettre dans le traité qu'ils conclurent entre eux, que c'était à ma seule considération qu'on lui accordait la paix. (122-23)

Clitandre's self-congratulatory pose is hardly surprising: Cidalise is both spectator and therapist to Clitandre, allowing him to (quite literally) get his story straight by seeing himself as another and having the feat recognised. What matters at the end of Luscinde's tale is not the fact that she and Oronte are back together again, but that they do so once Clitandre has displaced Oronte and thanks to his manipulation, which manipulation is really the result of his efforts at creating a narrative structure that frames him and Luscinde. As witness to Clitandre's authority, the agreement that terminates the tale acknowledges his intercession and skill. The same could be said of *La Nuit et le moment* in its entirety: nothing happens other than Clitandre and Cidalise, or rather Clitandre himself, tracing as he does the trajectory from his traumatic experience with Célimène to his triumphant one with Luscinde, from his idiotic ignorance of alterity and his false self-conception to his successful reappropriation of himself by "staging" himself as an other (and staging himself by narrating all of this to Cidalise). Thus, in what is a remarkable pre-figuration of post-Freudian psychoanalysis, Cidalise stands as a sujet supposé savoir of sorts, echoing back to Clitandre his various self-designations as a seducer, narrator and finally autobiographer (i.e. as himself) and allowing him to become what he is. If she did identify with this or that character it was only to help him along; the spectacle of alterity, catalysed by the mechanisms of sympathy and identification, produces further alterity. The confrontation of two narrative mirrors produces a multiplicity of narratives.

### III. Metamorphoses: Le Sopha

It is therefore quite clear that in Crébillon's fiction textual authority goes hand in hand with the fictional translation of histrionics. The better part of valour, in Crébillon's idiom, will be the creation of a place for the narrator, a locus that can only be circumscribed and designated once the mirror of fiction has been set up. Whence the import of *Le Sopha*, a work that stages the twin processes of fictional production and auctorial self-fashioning by taking the concomitant figure of metempsychosis to a literal extreme.

*Le Sopha* also demonstrates the extent to which all fiction is to a very large extent autobiographical, not least insofar as it rests on generic self-reflection and includes the images of the author and the reader. If fiction were defined as that process that turns authors into characters and vice versa, or, in more complicated terms, a procedure for the creation of subjectivity through alterity, then there is perhaps no more adequate representation of this procedure than the sopha's situation and the injunction under which he becomes himself qua narrator: "Il [Brahma] ajoutait que mon âme ne commencerait une nouvelle carrière, que quand deux personnes se donneraient mutuellement, et sur moi, leurs premices." (36) Rather than connote sexual intercourse, "se donner leur premices" actually denotes sentimental involvement: Amanzéi only changes into human form once he falls in love with one of his "characters". Unlike the figures of the narrators that we have seen before, Amanzéi's identity precedes his narrative (he was human -albeit with a different name and gender-before being turned into a sofa). Nevertheless, his identity as the king's *conteur* (a parody of the post of historiographer royal) only comes about as a result of his being implicated in the narrative that he produces. Like Meilcour and Clitandre, he needs a double with whom he can identify. It is only once he loses sight of his libertine self that he is ready for a second metamorphosis.

As a representative of the final culmination of the figure of the narrator, Amanzéi's predicament as the court storyteller is also interesting in its giving rise to a situation where the notion of the mirror of fiction is de-metaphorised: as he narrates (performs) the couples with whom he comes into contact, Amanzéi makes clear his identification with each character and his or her history (and most of them exist only long enough to be narrated, they do not transcend the bounds of the conte assigned to them) and that he, in turn, is to be identified with the meta-narrative that sums them all up. Indeed, the intertext of the *One Thousand and One Nights*, Sultan Schah-Baham's claims of clemency notwithstanding, make clear that Amanzéi's life depends on the moment of narration, that he, for all intents and purposes, has no subjectivity outside of that which we see performed before us in the novel, namely that of the court narrator.[10]

The stories that Amanzéi narrates are mirrors that track his development. His first two adventures are ordinary tales of seduction, the sort of thing that would have involved him had he not suffered Brahma's wrath. Indeed, there is not much difference between Fatmé's or Amine's *mauvaise foi* and playacting and that of Amanzéi's former self; "née sans caractère, j'étais tour à tour ce qu'on voulait que je fusse, ou ce que mes interêts et mes plaisirs me forçaient d'être" (36) is a description that could apply to any of them. Amanzéi, like Meilcour, starts his autobiography by narcissistically identifying with everyone around him.

As the text of *Le Sopha* proceeds, we are presented with lessons in reading and writing. The use of *mise en abyme* is extensive: Fatmé thus paves the way for her lover's (Dahis) visit by indulging in some licentious reading (something that would fall into the same category as *Le Sopha*) that proves absorbing because it reflects her persona (we are told that the book animates her, that she abandons her self to her reading as one would to a lover and so on) as well as her lover's.

The scenarii of seduction of *Le Sopha* proliferate incessantly; the mirror of fiction engenders simulacra ad infinitum. The tale of Moclès and Almaïde further expounds the relationship between narration and seduction through the presentation of a (moral, religious) thesis on the passions, something very much in the style of Clitandre and Cidalise, Almaïde's austerity notwithstanding. Both Almaïde and Moclès are middle-aged, both are famous throughout Agra for "le goût qu'ils avaient pour la vertu," and both spend most of their meetings together proclaiming virtue and decrying vice. They are, of course, aided and abetted in their progress by their self-definition through an ostensibly mortal opposition to pleasure rather than a more honest dedication to virtue. One day, the exchange of self-congratulatory stances turns into a swapping of secrets and "des peintures du vice un peu trop détaillées", a favoured medium for the motivation of seduction in Crébillon's idiom. Moclès uses a ruse to prompt Almaïde's confidence about her erstwhile *galanteries*, and, Almaïde falls for the trick. By playing the confessor to Almaïde's penitent self, Moclès reads himself into Almaïde's tale so that the narrative she spins might contain them both. Almaïde's vivid narration evokes "doubts" in Moclès's soul that can only be put to rest by pitting his virtuous soul against the acid test of temptation, or, in formal terms, reading himself into Almaïde's narrative and playing the

---

[10] The autobiographical component of *Le sopha* is rather strong, and the Sultan does to a certain extent represent Louis XV. Cf. Roman Wald Lasowski's *Crébillon fils, ou le libertinage galant*, 43-53.

same part as her former lovers. The exchange of confidences and secret narratives thus turns into an exchange of selves, an exercise in identification and alterity.

The next step in Amanzéi's sentimental education is provided by the Mazulhim/Zulica saga, a relationship that stretches over the course of four tales (Zéphis-Mazulhim, Zulica-Mazulhim, Zulica-Zâdis and Zulica-Nassès) but centres on the mediation of the Mazulhim-Zulica pair via the intervention of Nassès. The better part of Mazulhim's appeal lies in the rumours that circulate in Agra regarding his sexual prowess. The *Liebeskette* (Zéphis loves Mazulhim who loves Zulica who loves Nassès) underlies the importance of the double in the operations of Agra's *monde*, a fact dramatised in the form of the Mazulhim-Nassès-Zulica triangle. Here, as elsewhere, Amanzéi bears witness to the very mechanisms that will eventually enable his own metamorphosis; each scenario is, as it were engraved upon his soul, couched as it is in the sofa.

In addition to dealing with the relationship between Mazulhim and Zulica, this episode is concerned primarily with the relationship between empirical and narrative selves. Mazulhim's (narrated) reputation as Agra's Don Juan contradicts the (empirical) impotent self that he presents to both Zéphis and Zulica. Similarly, the trick that Mazulhim plays upon Zulica—sending her Nassès in his stead and not intruding until Zulica's "infidelity" has been adequately documented—aims at Mazulhim's creating a fictional double for himself. Nassès himself is well aware of the specular nature of this relationship since what he does is project himself onto the Zulica-Mazulhim scenario as Mazulhim's double: "puisque vous (Zulica) avez aimé Mazulhim, il ne serait pas impossible que vous m'aimassiez aussi." (204-205) Indeed, one is tempted to say that the relationship between Nassès and Zulica is possible only because of the narrative precedent set by her relationship with Mazulhim, whereby Nassès and Mazulhim identify with each other as character and author. It is not insignificant that conversation and gossip far outweigh descriptive scenes of seduction in the composition of this part of *Le Sopha*. Just like Jacob and La Vallée in *Le Paysan parvenu*, Mazulhim is bound to Nassès as a self forged in the mirror of fiction, one in which he can see himself reflected and through which his impotence is "cured." (One would not be far wrong in paraphrasing Marivaux and saying that "C'est de Nassès que Mazulhim tirait toute sa gloire.") The fusion of narrative and empirical selves is crucial to Amanzéi's development: once he "sees" and narrates its operation between Nassès and Mazulhim, he feels capable of entering into a similar rapport with Phéléas (Zéinis's lover) in the final episode of *Le Sopha* and thus manages to effect his final transformation through his identification with a fictional double.

The novel's final episode brings us the expansion of the fiction at hand to the point where it includes Amanzéi himself as a character rather than a narrator *tout court*. Like Célimène in the face of Clitandre's duality, like Meilcour in the face of Versac's and Mme de Lursay's, like Mazulhim in the face of Zulica's, Amanzéi becomes what he sees. Here, however, what would have been a denouement typical of Crébillon is folded back on itself: Amanzéi does not become himself until he is implicated in the tangled web he weaves, but this entanglement does not happen as an event until he insinuates himself in this web qua narrative. In other words, Le Sopha presents us with the account of a therapeutic process whereby Amanzéi makes himself by getting his story straight, which straightness is only achieved through the act of narration before an audience, which comes close to attaining the status of an analyst.

The path to this ending, where Amanzéi goes from being a sofa to the king's storyteller, has of course been paved by all the intermediate steps: the narcissistic reading practices of Fatmé, the translation of this method onto a more human level by Moclès and Almaïde, the quixotic legacy established by Mazulhim and the corollary masking of the auctorial self brought about by the use of the envoy as a living book. Amanzéi, in other words, becomes a writer by creating a literary history for himself. He bears witness to and narrates the tales that constitute Agra's *monde*, but his stepping outside that world as a master narrator depends on his being caught in it by Zéïnis's charms. Indeed, Amanzéi owes most of his seductive ploys to the scene that immediately precedes his own: having seen Nassès seduce Zulica in a contiguous mode,[11] our hero proceeds to do the same with Zéïnis. Here for the first time we have Amanzéi's modus operandi switching from a specular, metaphoric paradigm to a metonymic one based on contact; here, for the first time he seems to feel his body, and the imprint made upon his body by another is of paramount importance: "Je pouvais, malgré la rigeur de Brama, accorder quelque chose à la violence de mes désirs; mon âme alla se placer sur le coussin, et si près de la bouche de Zéïnis, qu'elle parvint enfin à s'y coller toute entière." (285)[12] The word "inspiration" is the only one that comes to mind after the description of the metonymic seduction of Zéïnis, coupled as it is with the images of doubling

---

11 Cf. "Nassès, pour la remercier de cet éloge, voulut d'abord lui baiser la main, mais trouvant la bouche de Zulica plus près de lui, ce fut à elle qu'il jugea à propos de témoigner sa reconnaissance." (213)

12 There are, of course, other instances in *Le Sopha* where the figure of the engraving is used to connote obsessed passion, as witness the following description of Phéléas: "C'est son image, et non mon ardeur, qui l'a enflammée." This final episode remains unique, however, in the use it makes of this figure by including it in the image-complex associated with specular self-fashioning in the mirror of fiction.

and identification usually associated with seduction in Crébillon's idiom:

> Tel est notre sort, que notre âme toujours inquiète au milieu des plus
> grands plaisirs, est réduite à en desirer plus encore qu'elle n'en trouve.
> La mienne, collée sur la bouche de Zéïnis, abîmée dans sa félicité,
> chercha à en procurer une encore plus grande. Elle essaya, mais
> vainement, à se glisser toute entière dans Zéïnis; retenue dans sa
> prison par les ordres cruels de Brama, tous ses efforts ne purent l'en
> délivrer. Ses élans redoublés, son ardeur, la fureur de ses désirs,
> echauffèrent apparemment celle de Zéïnis. Mon âme ne s'aperçut pas
> plutôt de l'impression qu'elle faisait sur la sienne, qu'elle redoubla ses
> efforts... Le désordre qui commencait à s'emparer de celle de Zéïnis,
> augmenta le trouble et les plaisirs de la mienne. Zéïnis soupira, je
> soupirai; sa bouche forma quelques paroles mal articulées, une
> aimable rougeur vint colorer son visage. Le songe le plus flatteur vint
> égarer ses sens... Oui! tu m'aimes! s'écria-t-elle tendrement." (286)

The scenario is interesting as a collage of most, if not all the lessons in
love that Amanzéi has narrated up to this point. The entire passage stands
as an effective summing up of all the lessons in alterity (and in seduction)
that Amanzéi has learned so far. As he maps her body, he doubles it with
the contours of his own. Soon enough what is projected onto a body is projected onto a soul, the fragmentation that qualifies his state at this point
translates into the *égarement* of her senses, until, finally, Zéïnis speaks for
both herself and Amanzéi simultaneously. Zéïnis becomes a medium, as it
were, a channel that undoes the bad effects of metempsychosis through another turn of metempsychosis.

The final and most important lesson comes with the entry of Phéléas.
This is where, having established a narrative precedent, Amanzéi can proceed with the next step, that is, identifying himself through someone else's
identification with him, rather like the introduction of Nassès into the tale
of Mazulhim. (One would not be wrong in arguing that Zéïnis herself reads
Phéléas as Amanzéi's double.) The rhetoric of narration changes at this
point to accommodate this identification: we are told that, "Phéléas, sans
lui répondre, lui saisit une main et la baisa avec toute l'ardeur dont *j*'aurais
été capable." (290, emphasis mine) The most interesting twist added to this
final tale is the phenomenon of Amanzéi's disembodiment that accom-
panies his displacement; "Zéïnis pleurait, et était demeurée sur le sopha."
(296) Now, Amanzéi was still referring to himself in the first person a mere
two pages earlier. This transformation from the first to third person paves
the way for the final replacement; "Phéléas et Zéïnis, tous deux immobiles,
respiraient mutuellement leur âme, semblaient accablés de leurs plaisirs."
(297) Amanzéi's final stance, as he sees himself mirrored and displaced in
(by) his own account, is really the founding moment of a narrated subjec-

tivity: once he sees himself both as himself and as an other, he is ready for the final transformation into an author of himself, which is to say a subject. Thus the sultan was quite right to accuse Amanzéi of a somewhat ego-centric garrulity; "je vous soutiens que cet Amanzéi-là n'est qu'un bavard, qui *se mire* dans tout ce qu'il dit, et qui, ou je ne m'y connais pas, a le vice d'aimer les longues conversations et de faire le bel esprit." (119, emphasis mine) Indeed, Amanzéi's love of long conversation is more than just a vice or a weakness, it is a necessity; indeed one could claim (*a fortiori* in view of the Scheherezadean intertext) that he is only insofar as he narrates. The end of Amanzéi's sofa-dom leads without interruption to his rank as court storyteller. One does, however, get the impression that the text could have gone on forever, a result of the somewhat problematic status of the event in Crébillon's plots.

*Le Sopha* both avoids and clarifies the issue by postulating the spectacle of the re-appropriation of the self as a condition for the construction of identity. Nevertheless, Amanzéi is still at pains, even at the end of the text, to show his displeasure at the prospect of closure, and it is not only because of the loss of Zéïnis to Phéléas. It is, rather, because he would ideally like to go on telling stories. *Les Egarements*, *La Nuit et le moment* and *Le Sopha* are not unrelated: in all three, what takes place goes beyond the formation of a particular character. Crébillon's use of the metanarrative dimension in these texts reduces the central event to character *per se*, the invention of a certain textual subjectivity out of the moulds of narration and desire: the art of conversation, so essential to life in the salon, turns people into themselves. Rather than simply being about Meilcour as autobiographer, Clitandre as *libertin*, and Amanzei as omniscient narrator these texts are about *being about* narrators and narratives during the final phase of the paradigm shift from drama to prose fiction. As such the production of narrative (and character through narrative) is necessarily staged, necessitating the inclusion of the reader or narratee in the text and leading to plots of an unbelievable complexity. The production of the narrator is bound inextricably with his or her inclusion in what he or she narrates. Whence the prevalence of narrative fiction as theme, as concern and as conversational interjection ("Quel conte") in Crébillon's fictions.

Even more important, however, is the relationship of the narrator, pegged as he is before his spectator/narratee to the text that acts as a matrix for his subjectivity; for if the creation and utterance of a fiction that would suitably mirror and contain him is the only appropriate path to self-fashion-ing, then we are fast approaching a complete re-codification of the histri-onic self cast in the seventeenth-century mould. This self is conditioned by its being played as a role, its improvisation, and its delimitation in space and time by the locus and moment of its flourish: the bedroom, the sofa, the drawing-room and so on. A further correlate of the invention of the narrator and the first-person narrative is the immediate transformation of that "I" into a "he", a mirror-image, in a space where the only possible act of self-designation is the designation of the other. Unlike Corneille's Horace, say, who designates himself as one who plays a given role the self under construction in the eighteenth century is designated as the self undergoing narration, or rather the self formed through its narration. None of the characters that populate the three texts studied here say "I am I", but they all do utter variations on, "I have just been narrated."

This rendition of the self performed through the telling of a tale designed as a mirror of ink also provides a tentative theory of reading far removed from the aims of instruction and pleasure dictated by the aesthetics of the age, except, perhaps, insofar as the author/seducer's instructions in pleasure, jouissance or whatever really require the reader's total complicity. Insofar as this is a quality that can only be gauged by the reader's becoming another character, another narrated entity (Cidalise as potential seducee, Schah-Baham as object of ridicule), or in simpler terms, by the narrator's becoming his reader, we are led to a conflation of the auctorial and interpretative functions. If indeed they do result in the production of an identity (through its fictional re-production) it is because the text that leads to this production comes under a rubric reminiscent of the Barthesian *scriptible*. Every story has as many ends as it does readers, and every reader is therefore a writer; every subject is what the seemingly indifferent mirror of fiction tells him or her that he is. It is this aspect of Crébillon's work, perhaps more than any other, that makes it so compelling, both in its own right and from the standpoint of literary history.

Nor are the consequences strictly narratological. The power wielded by effective storytellers in *le monde* was very real: Versac is the most powerful man in Paris (for a time, anyway) because he has stories on everyone, and Amanzéi controls the king—the centerpiece of a society that still defined itself as absolutist—by telling him stories. Crébillon thus works out the rules of social domination and proves that the position of power par excellence is the position of the narrator: this is how society (*le monde*) is controlled, and how kings are led by the nose. Power is the direct result of the production, circulation and management of narratives; he who controls this process controls the world.

The implications were not lost on a younger contemporary of Crébillon's, one who used these conclusions to construct his own discursive system, one comprising all of the genres we have dealt with so far and a few others in addition. This writer is none other than Jean-Jacques Rousseau, and his plays, novels, memoirs and theoretical essays all turn on the mechanisms that we have seen here. Despite his many protests to the contrary,

Rousseau is never far in spirit from the glamorous, seductive world of the salon and its modus operandi. He takes the master-seducer's mode of operation—that is, transforming a sector of the real into an artificial theatre where fiction and illusion reign supreme—and transfers it outside the mirrored bedroom. He de-metaphorises the expression, *le monde*, and emulates the habits of its inhabitants not only within the closed circle of Parisian society but with the whole world (*le monde* in its modern sense). He turns the act of writing into an act of seduction. Like Versac, he circulates fictions about himself and uses them to fool everyone into identifying with him, a task aided and abetted by his identifying with the entire world: "sans avoir aucun état moi-même," he says in his *Confessions*, "j'ai connu tous les états." Like Versac, he is a mirror to all of his readers, which is what allows his superior stance. The exchange between narrator and narratee takes place on an equal footing. No-one can say, "je fus meilleur que cet homme-là" about Rousseau because every reader of the *Confessions* becomes Jean-Jacques and vice versa. Because he has experienced any and every state together with its attendant narratives, because he can thus "become" anyone he writes about, Rousseau is especially qualified to write his *Confessions*, whose encyclopaedic scope is striking. The viewpoints that he invites his sympathetic readers to experience aim at the deification of his individual self, the one that manages this summing-up of all viewpoints. This unfathomable self bears out the relativist *Weltanschauung* of the age as described by Georges Poulet:

> [Le dix-huitième siècle] reste un siècle rélativiste. La vérité consiste en une série de points de vue, et le point de vue suprême, le seul qui puisse embrasser le cosmos, est le point de vue de Dieu. Ce qui n'empêche pas que tous les points de vue soient vrais, et que tous les lieux et les moments soient le centre d'un cercle qui enveloppe quelque part de la vérité.[13]

Thus the timeless hierarchies of Corneille and Molière give way to the historically-determined sense of absolute equality brought about by the possibility of writer and reader becoming one another through their common feeling. And out of this levelling (and undoing) of identities there emerges a new sort of self: the auto-deified individual, the *promeneur solitaire, alias* the Supreme Being under whose auspices French society would break into open revolt and whose genesis and development we shall trace in the following chapter.

---

[13] *Les Métamorphoses du cercle* (Paris: Flammarion, 1979) 29.

# Chapter Seven

## Rousseau: Being Supreme

In his monumental biography of Jean-Jacques Rousseau, Lester Crocker mentions the following apocryphal anecdote from Casanova's *Mémoires*:

> Voici l'exacte description de la visite que lui [Rousseau] fit le prince de Conti père du prince qu'on appelait alors comte de la Marche.
> Cet aimable prince va à Montmorenci tout seul, exprès pour passer une agréable journée causant avec le philosophe qui était déjà célèbre. Il le trouve dans le parc, il l'aborde, et lui dit qu'il était allé dîner avec lui et passer la journée, causant en pleine liberté.
> - Votre Altesse fera mauvaise chère; je vais dire qu'on mette encore un couvert.
> Il va, il retourne, et après avoir passé deux ou trois heures se promenant avec le prince, il le mène au salon où ils devaient dîner. Le prince, voyant sur la table trois couverts:
> - Qui est donc, lui dit-il, le troisième avec lequel vous voulez me faire dîner? J'ai cru que nous dînerions tête à tête.
> - Ce troisième, Monseigneur, est un autre moi-même. C'est un être qui n'est ni ma femme, ni ma maîtresse, ni ma servante, ni ma mère, ni ma fille; et elle est tout cela.
> - Je le crois, mon cher ami, mais n'étant venu ici que pour dîner avec vous, je compte vous laisser dîner avec votre tout. Adieu.
> Voilà des bêtises des philosophes, quand voulant se distinguer ils se singularisent. Cette feme était Mlle Le-Vasseur [sic.], qu'il avait honorée de son nom, masquée en anagramme à une lettre près.[1]

Apocryphal or not, the terms that Casanova's Rousseau uses are interesting. First, he calls the invisible third guest his double, "un autre moi-même." Second, this double is defined in exclusively feminine terms: she is neither his wife, nor his mistress, nor his servant, nor his mother, nor his daughter; she is all of them at once. In Casanova's view, Rousseau's doubles are all feminine; indeed, his wife's name is an anagram of his own. Last but by no means least, this is a scene meant to display the behaviour of a man who, as Casanova himself remarks, sought distinction through singularity, a man who believed that the mere fact that he was different set him

---

[1] Casanova, 2:183-184, qtd. in Crocker, 2:24. Casanova's derivation of Thérèse Levasseur's name is original, to say the least, since the editors of Rousseau's Oeuvres complètes point out that her father's name was François le Vasseur (*OC*, 1:1406). If anything, it proves Casanova's perspicacious insight into the nature of Rousseau's relationship with his wife and himself.

above the rest of the human race.[2] This theatrical display of his singular (in every sense of the word) identity, predicated as it is on the simultaneous presence and absence of a feminine double, is emblematic of the processes by which Jean-Jacques Rousseau constructs and acts out his identity, one so absolute in its hold and yet so fragile in its foundations that he would return to it again and again, growing greater in stature with each and every paranoid (or narcissistic) return. Integrated over the course of his constant self-reinvention, the final product "Rousseau" attains the quasi-divine status of the deity to whose name he had to appeal so often.

Towards the end of Book 1 of the *Confessions*, Rousseau describes what would eventually become his quixotic modus operandi:

> Ce fut de se nourrir des situations qui m'avoient intéressé dans mes lectures, de les rappeler, de les varier, de les combiner, de me les ap-proprier tellement que je devinsse un des personnages que j'imaginois, que je me visse toujours dans les positions les plus agréables selon mon gout, enfin que l'état fictif où je venois à bout de me mettre me fit oublier mon état réel dont j'étois si mécontent. Cet amour des objets imaginaires et cette facilité de m'en occuper acheverent de me dé-gouter de tout ce qui m'entouroit, et déterminerent ce gout pour la solitude, qui m'est toujours resté depuis ce tems-là. On verra plus d'une fois dans la suite les bizarres effets de cette disposition si mis-antrope et si sombre en apparence, mais qui vient en effet d'un cœur trop affectueux, trop aimant, trop tendre, qui, faute d'en trouver d'éxistans qui lui ressemblent est forcé de s'alimenter de fictions. (1:41)

Rousseau's choice of verbs is interesting: "se nourrir", "s'alimenter". Both imply that he vivifies an imaginary persona at the expense of the real. Moreover, his constant rearrangements of the fictional worlds of his readings into spaces arranged to his taste announces what will, in effect, become the adult Rousseau's constant pastime: constructing imaginary spaces and carving out a position for himself as their ostensible lord and master. The motto that he would eventually adopt, "vitam impendere vero", is less about staking his life on *the* truth as staking his life on an imaginary truth that eventually shapes it.

Rousseau's assumption of the make-believe identities suggested by his readings is also of a piece with his activities as an adult. There is ample evidence in the *Confessions* that Rousseau acts his way through his life (at least insofar as it is shaped and represented by that text). The examples are

---

[2] Cf. "Si je ne vaux pas mieux, au moins je suis autre." in his *Confessions* (*OC* 1:5; unless otherwise indicated, all references to works by Rousseau will be to the Pléiade edition of the *Oeuvres complètes* by volume and page number).

not lacking—with every new setting he dons a new mask and a new name: Dudding, Vaussore de Villeneuve, Zanetto, Renou (his mother-in-law's maiden name) and so on. Rousseau pretends in order to be: his identity depends on the mask of the moment. This movement can be traced to his subjugating his identity to the Other: he will be whatever he is asked to be in order to be desirable.[3] As a result his identity is constantly buffeted by the judgement that others pass on him: the terrible things they say about him are threatening precisely because he cannot help but appropriate them and act accordingly. His *Dialogues* are haunted by the fear that their negative judgements will indeed "come true" by his helpless implementation of them, that the diffamation that surrounds him will result in a dreadful—but inevitable—metamorphosis of his person.[4] The only solution is to design his own masks and judgements.

Consequently, Rousseau's *œuvre* is littered with paeans to self-reinvention through the adoption of the appropriate role. He plays a game of *jouer pour mieux ressentir* every time someone proposes a new assignment to him. Every new situation becomes a new role that he rehearses in order to better play the part. The interview that Mme de Warens arranges for him to be assigned a secretary to King Victor Amadeus's bureaucracy prompts one of these fits of other-identification: "J'ouvrois grand les yeux sans rien dire, sans savoir trop qu'imaginer: il s'en fallût peu que l'ambition naissante me tournât la tête, et que je ne fisse déjà le petit Intendant." (1:173-174) At Soleure, when the French ambassador's wife tells him that he has the same name as Jean-Baptiste Rousseau who had also stayed in the same room, he writes a few verses in the poet's style in her honor. When he is sent as an attaché to Colonel Godard's nephew, he immediately loses himself in the part: he pictures himself in an officer's uniform, "avec un beau plumet blanc," and goes so far as to think of his myopia not as a handicap but as an asset by association; "J'avois lû que le Maréchal Schomberg avoit la vue très courte; pourquoi le Maréchal Rousseau ne l'auroit-il pas?" (1:158-159)

With every new location, new situation, new page in the *Confessions* Rousseau's situation changes because of his conceiving of himself in a new setting. He is baptised "avec la même ceremonie à laquelle Henri quatre fut soumis par son Ambassadeur." (1:70) Walking around the royal palace in Turin, he says, "je conceus une grande opinion de moi-même en me trouvant dans ce Palais: déjà je me regardois presque comme un habitant." (1:71) Later he adds, "La seule chose qui m'interessât dans tout l'éclat de

---

3 Cf. Alain Grosrichard's seminal reading of Rousseau's relationship with his father; "Où suis-je?", 357-360.

4 Cf. Starobinski, *Transparence*, 86.

la Cour étoit de voir s'il n'y auroit point là quelque jeune Princesse qui méritât mon hommage, et avec laquelle je pusse faire un roman." (1:72) During the war between France and Emperor Charles VI, Rousseau sides with the French and proceeds to fashion himself anew as a Frenchman by reading the newspapers, "mais avec une telle partialité pour la France que le cœur me battoit de joye à ses moindres avantages, et que ses revers m'affligeoient comme s'ils fussent tombés sur moi." (1:182) He reads Brantôme's *Les Grands capitains* in order to bolster this French sense of himself; adding, "J'étois donc François ardent, et cela me rendoit nouvelliste." (1:184) This Francophile tendency stays with him and lands him in a good deal of trouble during his stay in Venice as narrated in Book VII of the *Confessions*.

The Protean habit by which Rousseau metamorphoses himself into whatever his situation dictates also hangs over his relationship with his authorial persona. We have already seen how his identification with Jean-Baptiste Rousseau leads to his writing pastiche poetry, grafting his name, style and personnality onto those of his predecessor. His tendency to double himself and see his mirror image in other people makes itself manifest in his efforts with his first real love, namely music. Rousseau's model here is one of the many "fripons" that come to Mme de Warens' residence, Venture de Villeneuve. Before Venture's arrival, Rousseau tells us that his passion for Mme de Warens had in effect ruled out his paying attention to anyone or anything else, including intellectual development; "Il est vrai qu'un seul sentiment, absorbant pour ainsi dire toutes mes facultés, me mettait hors d'état de rien apprendre, pas même la musique, bien que j'y fisse tous mes efforts." (1:123) Venture's appearance on the scene troubles this beatific union. Everything about him bespeaks his (putative) falsity: he is polished, pretentious and visibly counterfeit. Indeed, when invited to sing at church the man neither rehearses his part nor does he adhere to any musical topics of conversation at the dinner table. That Sunday, though, the stranger sings "ses deux récits avec toute la justesse et tout le goût imaginables, et, qui plus est, avec une très jolie voix." (1:124) Rousseau is impressed with the stranger's talent and engages in an idealized homosexual attachment to him, echoing (with improvements) his earlier relationship with Bâcle:

> On conviendra, je m'assure, qu'après m'être engoüé de M. Bâcle, qui tout compté n'étoit qu'un manan, je pouvois m'engouer de M. de Venture qui avoit de l'éducation, des talens, de l'esprit, de l'usage du monde, et qui pouvoit passer pour un aimable débauché... J'aimois à

le voir, à l'entendre; tout ce qu'il faisoit me paroissoit charmant, tout ce qu'il disoit me sembloient des oracles... (1:125)

What is worthy of note is Rousseau's attachment to and fantasmatic identification with a fake who turns out to be real, a stranger who may or may not be an impostor but who proves his talent nonetheless, to the point where Venture's every word carries the unquestionable truth-value of an oracular pronouncement.[5]

Rousseau goes on to re-enact this primal scene of composition on a number of occasions. After a mere six months of musical instruction with Le Maître, he tries to pass himself off as a music teacher in Lausanne; "Je me mis en tête de faire à Lausanne le petit Venture." (1:147) It is not insignificant that, in fashioning himself as a music teacher, Rousseau chooses to identify with the possibly fake Venture de Villeneuve rather than the genuine LeMaître. His entire career at Lausanne unfolds as an imitation of Venture de Villeneuve. Rousseau goes so far as to pun on the man's name and adopting a modified version thereof:

> Pour comprendre à quel point la tête me tournoit alors, à quel point je m'étois pour ainsi dire venturisé, il ne faut que voir combien tout à la fois j'accumulai d'extravagances. Me voilà maitre à chanter sans savoir déchiffrer un air... Je m'approchois toujours de mon grand modelle autant qu'il m'étoit possible. Il s'étoit appellé Venture de Villeneuve; moi je fis l'anagramme du nom de Rousseau dans celui de Vaussore, et je m'appelai Vaussore de Villeneuve. Venture savoit la composition, quoiqu'il n'en eut rien dit; moi, sans la savoir je m'en vantai à tout le monde et sans pouvoir noter le moindre vaudeville je me donnai pour compositeur. (1:148)

The name "Vaussore de Villeneuve" says a great deal: Rousseau might as well say that he has become a creation, a child, a copy of Villeneuve, "de Villeneuve". Passing for a composer is neither here nor there, it seems; passing for the talented, sophisticated composer Venture de Villeneuve is what really matters. Venture de Villeneuve dominates Rousseau's imaginary space to the point where his name becomes a verb, "se venturiser."

It comes as no surprise, therefore, that we find Rousseau enacting this identity by taking it outside the realm of mere pretense and rumour and submitting one of his compositions for M. de Treytorens' concert series. The concert proves to be an unmitigated disaster, but what is especially worthy of note is the way in which Rousseau composes his musical oddity:

---

[5] See my treatment of the figure of the legislator below.

> J'eus la constance de travailler pendant quinze jours à ce bel ouvrage,
> de le mettre au net, d'en tirer les parties et de les distribuer avec autant
> d'assurance que si c'eut été un chef-d'œuvre d'harmonie. Enfin, ce
> qu'on aura peine à croire, et qui est très vrai, pour couronner digne-
> ment cette sublime production, je mis à la fin un joli menuet qui
> couroit les rues, et que tout le monde se rapelle peutêtre encore sur ces
> paroles jadis si connues.
>
> Quelle injustice!
> Quoi, ta Clarice
> Trahiroit tes feux? etc.
>
> Venture m'avoit appris cet air avec la basse sur d'autres paroles in-
> fames, à l'aide desquelles je l'avois retenu. Je mis donc à la fin de ma
> composition ce Menuet et sa basse en supprimant les paroles, et je le
> donnai pour être de moi, tout aussi résolument que si j'avois parlé à
> des habitans de la lune. (1:148-149)

As far as Rousseau is concerned, the play's the thing: by pretending that
his piece is "un chef-d'œuvre de l'harmonie", Rousseau assumes that it will
turn into one. Rousseau also plagiarises his model's work and passes it off
as his own. Moreover, Rousseau describes this menuet as a "well-known
song": not only is it Venture's, it is everybody's. Rousseau plagiarises
everyone as he attempts to pass for the author of a popular song "que tout
le monde se rappelle peutêtre encore."

Rousseau pretends to be a maréchal and "becomes" a maréchal in his
mind's eye. He pretends to be a minor composer and he "becomes" a minor
composer, both in his own eyes and in the eyes of at least some of the
inhabitants of Lausanne. This habit of constructing an authorial persona by
pretending, emulating, plagiarising and grafting his name onto someone
else's does not end there. His account of his expriences with opera and
fame are telling in this respect. It is no accident, for instance, that Rameau
accuses him of plagiarism after the premiere of *Les Muses galantes* at Mme
de la Poplinière's (*Confessions*, Book 7). Whether or not the charge is true
(and I would like to believe that it is), Rameau's accusation is certainly
consistent with what Rousseau himself tells us about his compositional
"method".[6] The role of the plagiarist that he carves out in Lausanne hardens into a professional identity in Paris. His collaboration with Rameau and
Voltaire on *La Princesse de Navarre/Les Fêtes de Ramire* allows him to
graft his name onto theirs by adding a mere 57 verses to the text. The reception of the work (as narrated by Rousseau) results in a perfect identity
of pillard and *pillé*: "j'appris que les amateurs n'avoient pas été très con-

---

[6] To a certain extent, Rousseau's behaviour announces Genet's: he becomes a plagiarist by assuming the charge of the plagiarist.

tens de mon ouvrage, et que le public ne l'avoient pas distingué de celui de Rameau." (1:338) Rousseau metamorphoses into Rameau; or rather, Rameau becomes a mask for Rousseau. Rousseau pretends to be Rameau, and he "becomes" Rameau, in his mind's eye and in the space spanned by the "amateurs" of opera in Paris. With every new part, he plays to bigger and bigger audiences.

$$*$$
$$*\quad*$$

Eventually, Rousseau starts pretending to be his sincere, commendable self and playing that self—his most significant composition—to his reading public. His playing the part of Rousseau the sincere has a history documented thoroughly in the *Confessions*. The quixotic mode in which he read and enacted novels in his youth, and by virtue of which he turned fiction into reality, was extended at a certain point to include the fiction of moral superiority as narrated by Plutarch. The young Jean-Jacques' identification with Plutarch's heroes has a palpable physical effect on the impressionable youth: "je me croyois Grec ou Romain; je devenois le personnage dont je lisois la vie: le recit des traits de constance et d'intrépidité qui m'avoient frappé me rendoient les yeux etincellans et la voix forte." (1:9)[7] So much so that he dons the mask of the orator—the legislator of public morality—to seek vengeance on adult tormentors, with cries of "Carnifex, Carnifex, Carnifex" (1:20) (Actually, one might argue that, for the rest of his life, Rousseau did very little other than shout "Carnifex, carnifex" to all of his tormentors, who, by that point, included the entire human race.) The conspicuous display of Rousseau's very sincere, very virtuous self, "dans toute la vérité de la nature," depends in no small part on his adopting any number of roles and acting them out; indeed, that the self's formation inheres in its display. This oratorical drive is of a piece with the sorts of playacting in which Rousseau indulges elsewhere. The role of the orator stays with him, and is singled out for praise even as Rousseau attacks conventional thespians for their falsity. The orator, in effect, scripts and invents his own role and is therefore immune to Rousseau's vitriolic attack on actors and actresses:

---

7 Rousseau's emotional transport is not insignificant: like an actor "getting into" the part à la Stanislavski, Rousseau only has a voice when he is moved emotionally, when he has a part to play; "Quand je me passionne, je sais trouver quelquefois ce que j'ai à dire; mais dans les entretiens ordinaires je ne trouve rien, rien du tout; ils me sont insupportables par cela seul que je suis obligé de parler." (1:36)

L'Orateur, le Prédicateur, pourrat-on me dire encore, payent de leur personne ainsi que le Comedien. La difference est très grande. Quand l'Orateur se montre, c'est pour parler, et non pour se donner en Spectacle; il ne réprésente que lui-même, il ne fait que son propre rolle, ne parle qu'en son propre nom, ne dit ou ne doit dire que ce qu'il pense; l'homme et le personnage étant le même être, il est à sa place; il est dans le cas de tout autre citoyen qui remplit les fonctions de son état. (5:74)

As an orator, therefore, Rousseau partakes of the same modalities as actors and actresses, with the difference that he speaks for himself rather than for the part that he is playing. Or better yet, the self in whose name the orator speaks can only be expressed oratorically once it is "cast" as that orator's role. His eloquence and sincerity derive from the parallel he establishes between his being and his appearance, between "l'homme" and "le personnage". And lest the reader of the *Lettre* should pass over this point too quickly, Rousseau makes clear that this very specific sort of play-acting is part and parcel of a citizen's duties; duties to the regulation of which the Citizen of Geneva devoted a great deal of ink and paper.

The role of the orator, the ethically superior wise man, and the fiction of its "discovery" (or its re-discovery) irrupts at several key moments in the *Confessions*. One such moment is the publication of the text that established Rousseau in the republic of letters, the first discourse. In much the same way that he composed through the "masks" of Venture de Villeneuve and Rameau, he borrows the mask of Plutarch to denounce the faddish mores of the world he inhabits in the *Discours sur les sciences et les arts*. It is not insignificant that the prosopopeia of Fabricius was the first part of the *Discours* that Rousseau wrote.[8] Now, in this part of the *Discours*, Rousseau has Fabricius address the late Romans in the same tones that he would have adopted to address his own contemporaries: "Dieux!... Quelle splendeur funeste a succedé à la simplicité Romaine? Quel est ce langage étranger? Quels sont ces mœurs effeminées? Que signifient ces statues, ces Tableaux, ces édifices?" (3:14) Rousseau then adds, "qu'ai-je fait dire à ce grand homme que je n'eusse pu mettre dans la bouche de Louis XII ou Henri IV?" (3:15) The comparisons are not fortuitous; we have already seen Rousseau compare himself to royalty in Turin. Rousseau is, therefore, setting up a series of homologous relationships: Fabricius would have been to the late Romans what Henry IV or I, Rousseau, would be to contempo-

---

[8] Cf. The second *Lettre à Malesherbes*, "Il n'y eut d'écrit sur le lieu meme que la prosopopée de Fabricius;" (1:1136), and Book 8 of the *Confessions*; "Diderot l'apperçût [Rousseau's agitation]; je lui en dis la cause, et je lui lus la prosopopée de Fabricius écrite en crayon sous un Chêne." (1:351)

rary France. The prosopopeia therefore figures the process by which Rousseau writes: by taking on a mask and speaking through it, adopting another identity as he does so. In other words, the transformation that he undergoes under the oak tree ("je vis un autre univers et je devins un autre homme"(1:351)) where he writes the *Discours* is expressed in the process of Rousseau's donning Fabricius' identity as a mask. The prosopopée is a *mise en abyme* of the composition of the first *Discours*. The central section of that *mise en abyme* is the taking on of the mask and the resulting metamorphosis. Rousseau did indeed become "un autre homme"; he became the Plutarch of his day, the one who re-animated Fabricius. Rousseau's first published work is essentially a pastiche Plutarch, as his first concerto was a pastiche Villeneuve and his first opera was a pastiche Rameau. Instead of Rousseau's being just another reader of Plutarch, Plutarch becomes, via the "prosopopée de Fabricius", one of the many masks of Rousseau.[9]

There is no gainsaying the potential for self-promotion inherent in poses like Rousseau's, nor can one deny the megalomaniacal intention fuelled by his paranoid undertaking in the *Confessions*. Rousseau's writing thus emerges as a series of exercises, essays, attempts at self-promotion and self-invention.[10] The use of the mask and the graft that dominated Rousseau's musical undertakings also dominates his literary and moralistic ones. Indeed, the manifestly oratorical tone and composition of the first discourse can only lead us to the conclusion that Rousseau's writing is a theatrical exercise. As we read Rousseau's text, as we peer into this spectacle of textuality, we can barely make out his identity as a collage of names and faces grafted onto each other to give us the construct, "Rousseau."

\*

\* \*

---

[9] The same model applies to Rousseau's adoption of the mask of virtue as a role: "Jusques là j'avois été bon; dès lors je devins vertueux, ou du moins enivré de la vertu. Cette ivresse avoit comencé dans ma tête, mais elle avoit passé dans mon cœur. ... Je ne jouai rien; je devins en effet tel que je parus..." (1:416) Rousseau finds his voice by enacting virtue. Cf. Starobinski's analysis of this moulding of Rousseau's identity, *Transparence*, 77-82. Starobinksi also cites a most appropriate dictum from Rousseau's correspondence; "Quiconque a le courage de paraître ce qu'il est deviendra tôt ou tard ce qu'il doit être." (82)

[10] I use the term "essays" deliberately, since there is no mistaking the many echoes of Montaigne in the first discourse and in Rousseau's autobiographical project as a whole.

The identity that unfolds at the nexus of fiction and play-acting is reminiscent of themes we have seen elsewhere in this study, as is the figure cut by the seductive models (Bâcle, Venture, Rameau) who mediate Rousseau's desires. For storytelling, play-acting and seduction are the modes of behaviour that dominate *le monde*.

Rousseau's texts feature a number of seducers who captivate the multitude with their skill, and who seem to copy the *monde*'s master seducers. Like the *mondains* they operate by carving out a social space and manipulating it with the fictions that they circulate therein. Rather than taking the form of libertines and *petit-maîtres*, however, they are incarnated as wise authority figures: teachers, soothsayers and the like, variations on the theme of the sage.[11] In the *Emile*, the relationship between pedagogue and student hinges on the latter's seduction by the teacher, who shapes Emile intellectually by dominating his imagination.[12] Similarly, the hero of Rousseau's most successful play, *Le Devin du village*, is the wise old man of the village, the soothsayer whose "art" renders him omnipotent by allowing him to divine the other characters' secrets.[13] The village itself is little more than a sentimental translation of *le monde* where people do nothing other than jump from one love affair to the next. In both of these cases, the figure of authority depends on the manufacture of an illusion and the manipulation of the interlocutor's desires, much as Denon's Mme de T... seduces her young man with the enchanted palace. The soothsayer himself admits in a frank soliloquy that the "art" through which he discovers Colin and Colette's secrets is a theatrical re-presentation of what he knows already:

> J'ai tout sçu de Colin et ces pauvres enfans
> Admirent tous les deux la science profonde
> Qui me fait *deviner tout ce qu'ils m'ont appris.* (2:1102; emphasis mine)

His only other aside -"Sur ce qu'elle [Colette] doit dire allons la prévenir" (2:1104)- shows that Colin and Colette's entire reconciliation is simply a ply engineered by the soothsayer. *Le Devin du village* lays clear

---

[11] It is no accident that, in the comparison between the "sage" and the (military) hero in his *Discours sur cette question: "Quelle est la vertu la plus nécessaire au Héros et quels sont les héros à qui cette vertu a manqué?"*, Rousseau sides squarely with the sage: "Toutes les vertus appartiennent au Sage." (2:1262)

[12] Cf. Harari's seminal reading, *Scenarios* 120-124.

[13] Rousseau's play also invites comparison with Corneille's *Illusion comique*, although the concern with constructing an identity through the theatre is not foregrounded explicitly in *Le Devin du village*.

emphasis on the fact that a familiarity with the idiom of the theatre is essential to the life of any authority figure.

One of Rousseau's more seductive characters is the legislator. The legislator leads the leaders. He is to the collective what the teacher is to the individual. In much the same way that Rousseau "produces" Emile by totally controlling his imagination, the legislator will shape a polity by similarly controlling theirs. This he accomplishes by seeking recourse to the tricks of the actor, from whom he is never far and effectivelyindistinguishable.[14] Like Rousseau's pedagogue in the *Emile*, he replaces the violence of despotic political authority with the verbal violence of the ruse, with the impact of a seductive brainwashing of the "sovereign" (which, in Rousseau's idiom, is just another name for the people). This rather difficult task is accomplished by the legislator's taking over the role of the Gods as lawgivers.

Ideally, the law should come from its true divine source according to Rousseau; "il faudroit des Dieux pour donner les loix aux hommes." (3:381) These Gods are defined by their superior intelligence and impartiality; "il faudroit une intelligence supérieure, qui vit toutes les passions des hommes mais qui n'en éprouvât aucune, qui n'eut aucun rapport avec notre nature et qui la connût à fond, font le bonheur fût indépendant de nous et qui pourtant voulut bien s'occuper du notre." Let us note, in passing, the use of the idiom of desire to articulate his conception of authority, as well as the remarkable similarities between these gods and the man who describes them: their knowledge of the human heart and passions is his own, as he takes pains to make clear in the opening preamble to the *Confessions*; "Je sens mon cœur et je connois les hommes." (1:5) In other words, the mere fact of being in touch with his feelings allows Rousseau to lay claim to being in touch with everyone else's and to an exemplary moral authority. If, as Rousseau argues, no-one can claim to be better than he after reading the *Confessions* it is, in no small part, because he establishes his own divine authority by describing his interior. Once he engages his readers in a game of follow-the-leader, the reader becomes a simulacrum of that leader and finds that he is no better than Rousseau because he has, in effect, become Rousseau: "Que chaque lecteur m'imite, qu'il rentre en lui-même comme j'ai fait, et qu'au fond de sa conscience il se dise, s'il l'ose: *je suis meilleur que ne fut cet homme-là*." (1:1155) Rousseau's self-knowledge, in other words, makes him a god, and entitles him to legislate.

---

14 Cf. Bennington, *Dudding*, 69-90, especially 78-79, as well as Descombes, "La vérité du vrai", 59-61; Bernard Gagnebin's "Le rôle du législateur" and Judith Shklar's *Men and Citizens*, 157-158.

The ideal state where the gods give the law to men directly would only obtain in a perfect world. Life's inevitable complexities raise the need for an intermediary between the gods and men:

> Les particuliers voyent le bien qu'ils rejettent; Le public veut le bien qu'il ne voit pas. Tous ont également besoin de guides; il faut obliger les uns à conformer leurs volontés à leur raison; il faut apprendre à l'autre à connoitre ce qu'il veut... Voilà d'où nait la necessité d'un Legislateur. (3:311)

Rousseau's description of the legislator is not without its affinities with the scenarii of mediated desire that dominated *le monde*. There is a desiring subject—"le peuple"—and an object of desire—"le bien". Like Crébillon's Versac initiating Meilcour, the legislator stands between the people and what they want, turning a bipolar relationship into a triangular one, translating their desire for "le bien" into a desire for "le bien" *as he sees it*, and turning them away from "la séduction des volontés particulières" to the greatest seduction of all, the supremely desirable—because universally desired—"volonté générale." The legislator represents, doubles the general will: as such he himself becomes a universal object of desire. Like the master-seducer, he teaches the social body what to want; he is, in effect, a professor of desire.

As such his power extends to areas well beyond normal jursidiction, to internal, private matters like desire and consciences.[15] A certain facility with the idiom of desire on his part would therefore be desirable, as well as a certain knowledge of human nature: "Celui qui se croit capable de former un Peuple, doit se sentir en état, pour ainsi dire, de changer la nature humaine". (3:313) The legislator's task is indeed difficult; "Ce n'est point magistrature, ce n'est point souveraineté. Cet emploi, qui constitüe la République, n'entre point dans sa constitution. C'est en quelque maniére une fonction particuliére et presque divine qui n'a rien de commun avec l'empire humain" (3:313-4) The legislator literally creates desire, and, in so doing, creates the republic, without seeking recourse to force or reason. Hence the need for illusion, for how else is the legislator to reach deep into men's souls without it? The legislator must present things not only as they are but as they ought to be, reorganise time and space, exaggerate visible

---

[15] Rousseau himself was haunted by the possibility of legislating and enforcing desire, as witness his preoccupation with the "maîtresse impérieuse" and the rather clinical account and the consequences of his initiation by Mme de Warens, "plus fait pour m'instruire que pour me séduire". As one might expect, he projects the nightmare of enforced desire onto the image of oriental despotism: "On dit que chez les mahometans un homme passe au point du jour dans les rues pour ordonner aux maris de rendre le devoir à leurs femmes. Je serois un mauvais turc à ces heures-là." (1:190)

advantages and hidden disadvantages, make illusion a tool in order to make his particular interpretation of the public good seductive to the masses. Hence, too, the need for the simulacrum of a higher authority, "qui puisse entrainer sans violence et persuader sans convaincre;" (3:317) for the legislator cannot reveal himself as the object of the people's desire but only as a means to an end, the ever-elusive "bien". And so, the legislator gives his utterances an authoritative air by making it look as though he were doing nothing but speaking for the gods: "cette raison sublime qui s'élève au dessus de la portée des hommes vulgaires, est celle dont le Legislateur met les décisionsdans la bouche des immortels pour subjuguer par l'autorité divine ceux que ne pourroit ébranler la prudence humaine." (3:317) The voice of the oracle ornaments and legitimates the legislator/priest's "prudence", the curb he places on the social body's desires and his own. Rousseau's legislative space is therefore not far from the seductive châteaux and salons of le monde.

Rousseau, of course recognises the danger inherent in this situation and the potential for deception on a massive scale: "Tout homme peut graver des tables de pierre, ou acheter un oracle, ou feindre un secret commerce avec quelque divinité, ou dresser un oiseau pour lui parler à l'oreille, ou trouver quelque autre moyen grossier d'en imposer au Peuple." (3:317) Both the legislator and the charlatan ("tout homme") set up a theatrical illusion and use it to substantiate their claim to speak for a higher authority. Both pretend to speak for the gods and, by dint of their props ("un oiseau pour lui parler à l'oreille") make that pretense real. Both guard against the seduction of particular desires (volontés particulières) by creating a general, overriding desire (a volonté générale). Both sketch a role for themselves and substantiate that role by acting it out. Both engage in the mode of operation by which Rousseau creates his personae as composer and author: they become what they are by pretending to be what they are.The myth of the legislator's authority and expertise depend in no small part on the effective production of these fictions and simulacra. Vincent Descombes sums it up rather nicely:

> Le savoir n'est pas vision correcte, mais production efficace de simulacres. Ou encore, le savoir est ce qui permet de produire du scénario, des situations simulées, le savoir étant d'autant plus vrai—"fiable"—qu'il permet, par ce déploiement des fictions théoriques, un plus grand contrôle des processus auxquels on s'intéresse...
> ("La Vérité du vrai", 158)

The legislator improvises his role like an impostor, and his efficacy as legislator depends on his ability to perform and the skill with which he manages the spectacle of legislation. How, then, are we to distinguish be-

tween the legislator and the impostor? It is a difficult question that the legislator himself might not be able to answer. During his discussion of the
charcteristics of divine messengers in the *Lettres écrites de la montagne*,
Rousseau addresses the possibility of the prophet's self-deception; "ce n'est
pas un prodige qu'un imposteur abuse des gens de bien, ni qu'un homme
de bien s'abuse lui-même, entraîné par l'ardeur d'un saint zele qu'il
prendra pour de l'inspiration." (3:728) The legislator, then, like the
impostor, could be taken in by his own "lies". In fact, one would not be far
wrong in arguing that the legislator is precisely an impostor who is taken in
by his own spectacle, or, better yet, someone who rules by spectacular
means and whose first subject (and spectator) is himself. The legislator is
an actor who cannot help acting.

The distinction between legislator and impostor is therefore to be drawn
according to internal rather than external factors: "La grande âme du législateur et le vrai miracle qui doit prouver sa mission." (3:317)[16] So the legislator, this quasi-divine personnage, needs to be someone with soul, as it
were, in order to fulfill his mission properly; a soul in touch with the divinity that gives the laws to men. Needless to say, such people are not easy to
find ("s'il est vrai qu'un grand Prince est un homme rare, que sera-ce d'un
grand Legislateur?" (3:313)) One such individual, however, might be
Rousseau himself, who, in one of his few recorded prayers, thanks God for
having taught him the Law: "vous avés gravé dans le fond de mon cœur des
loix à l'éxécution desquelles vous avés attaché le prix d'un bonheur éternel,
loix pleines de justice et de douceur..." (4:1037)[17] Nor is this all. The
similarity between Rousseau and the legislator can be extended to their
modes of operation. The legislator, as we have seen, is a histrion: he sets up
his props, marks out his role and acts it out. Similary, Rousseau chooses his
mask ("virtue") and acts it out. Like the legislator, Rousseau sets himself
apart from the many charlatans and hypocrites around him by alleging his

---

[16] This recourse to the "soul" of the legislator recalls another figure distinguished
by his soul in Rousseau's pantheon, namely the hero: "S'il falloit distribuer les vertus à
ceux à qui elles conviennent le mieux; ...pour la force de l'ame, je la donnerois au
Héros, et il n'auroit pas à se plaindre de son partage." (2:1272)

[17] My identifying Rousseau with the legislator departs from most readings of this
figure, notably de Man's and Bennington's, both of whom argue against it. It is rather
difficult, however, to ignore the megalomaniacal tone running through most of
Rousseau's works, as witness the following fragment wherein he identifies himself with
his legislative "heroes": "J'ai vécu seul sur la terre, au sein d'un peuple nombreux
j'étois seul. Lycurgue, Solon, Numa sont mes fréres. Je viens rejoindre ma famille. Je
viends gouter enfin la douceur de converser avec mes semblables, de parler et d'être en-
tendu. C'est parmi vous, ames illustres, que je viens enfin *jouir de moi*." (3:500; emphasis mine)

sincerity to his "soul"; *intus et in cute*. Both look inwards and act accordingly. The legislator, as producer of simulacra and founding myths for the society that he legislates, is clearly a man of some importance, holding, as he does, the key to what the people want and think with his theatrical displays. As such his de facto status is not very different from the divinity of the gods he claims to represent; indeed, from his point of view they are mere props. So this is the most important person within the imaginary universe that Rousseau inhabits. And not only does Rousseau play the part of the legislator (by taking on the role of latter-day Plutarch, or by undertaking such legislative projects as the Polish and Corsican constitutions) but he defines him, creates him, as it were, by writing the text entitled *Du contrat social*. Rousseau, in other words, seems to be saying that the legislator is (like) a God. And that he, Rousseau, legislates for him.

\*

\*  \*

Thus the legislator's ability to legislate depends in no small part on his theatrical skills. The seductive legislator is not the only character that Rousseau translates from *le monde*. Another significant importation is the figure of the woman who rules over her *salon* or *château*, holding all the strings of power and illusion as did Marivaux's Mme Amelin. Indeed, women make for some of the most exacting legislators in Rousseau's texts, uniting as they do authority and desire, embodying as they do the art of mass seduction (read: acting) so essential to the business of legislation. In Rousseau's idiom, the parallels between stage management and political management are linked to the relationship between women and legislative power, which relationship will, in its own turn, determine Rousseau's relationship to both power and femininity.[18]

Rousseau's obsession with powerful women is documented well enough. His memories of Mlle Lambercier engender a fantasm that will stay with him for the rest of his life, the image of the imperious mistress:

> Etre aux genoux d'une maîtresse impérieuse, obéir à ses ordres, avoir des pardons à lui demander, étoient pour moi de très douces jouissances, et plus ma vive imagination m'enflammoit le sang, plus j'avois l'air d'un amant transi. (1:17)[19]

---

[18] On this topic, see Fried 169-171; Marshall 135-177; Zerilli 30-39 and Coleman 99-119.

[19] For a suggestive reading of the "maîtresse impérieuse" in Rousseau's work, see Zerilli, 16-59.

This figure returns in the description of the *salonnière* in the *Lettre à d'Alembert*:

> ...chaque femme de Paris rassemble dans son appartement un serail d'hommes plus femmes qu'elle, qui savent rendre à la beauté toutes sortes d'hommages, hors celui du cœur dont elle est digne. Mais voyez ces mêmes hommes toujours contraints dans ces prisons volontaires, se lever, se rasseoir, aller et venir sans cesse à la cheminée, à la fenêtre, prendre et poser cent fois un écran, feuilleter des livres, parcourir des tableaux, tourner, pirouetter par la chambre, tandis que l'idole étendüe sans mouvement dans sa chaise longue, n'a d'actif que la langue et les yeux. (5:93)

The men's behaviour in this scene is that of creatures incessantly staging themselves before the evaluative eye of the goddess.[20] Rousseau's macho disapproval of these alleged fops notwithstanding, the feature to which I would like to call attention here is the association between the powerful woman and the deity. The description of the *salonnière* carries resonances of the "maîtresse impérieuse". In both cases, Rousseau situates the image of the powerful woman in the place of the divinity, acting as "maîtresses impérieuses" and queens of the (false) men she surveys.[21]

The feminine and the spectacular are never far from each other in the *Lettre à d'Alembert*, and Rousseau takes a great deal of trouble to detail their role in propagating the theatricality of everyday life. Like the gods of the *contrat social*, their modes of operation are grounded in the histrionic sensibility. In Rousseau's imaginary space, women are "données à voir" almost by definition. The idleness of the idol described above lends her a theatrical quality and an ability to generate fictions and fantasms that, in turn, make her more powerful.

The *salonnière* wields a great deal of social and political power, since the entire apparatus of social life revolves around her. Her influence, like that of the legislator, is of a spectacularly verbal order. She talks, forms public opinion (a close cousin of the general will), sets the tone, makes important decisions, and sets up social hierarchies that put everyone and ev-

---

[20] It bears pointing out that Rousseau finds the behaviour of these *mondains* —these false idolators—threatening, since their superior acting skills allow them to displace better, more "sincere" worshippers like himself, who possess the "cœur dont elle est digne": "Il ne seroit pas difficile de montrer qu'au lieu de gagner à ces usages, les femmes y perdent. On les flatte sans les aimer; on les sert sans les honorer; elles sont entourées d'agréables, mais elles n'ont plus d'amans; et le pis est que les premiers, sans avoir les sentimens des autres, n'en usurpent pas moins tous les droits." (5:95)

[21] Nor are they the only ones: Rousseau's ecounters with these beautiful women are often framed in such a way as to situate him at their knees, as witness the scenes with Mme Basile (1:74-76) and Mme d'Houtetot (1:444-445).

erything in their proper places (5:45). The most powerful woman in Rousseau's scheme is she who capitalises on this theatricality of Parisian life, namely the actress. He describes in no uncertain terms the influence of these female legislators in the realm where they hold the most power, the stage:

> Sur la Scéne, c'est pis encore. Au fond, dans le monde, elles ne savent rien, quoiqu'elles jugent de tout: Mais au théatre, savantes du savoir des hommes, philosophes, graces aux auteurs, elles écrasent notre Séxe de ses propres talens et les imbecilles Spectateurs vont bonnement apprendre des femmes ce qu'ils ont pris soin de leur dicter... Parcourez la pluspart des piéces modernes, c'est toujours une femme qui sait tout, qui apprend tout aux hommes... La Bonne est sur le théatre, et les enfans sont dans le parterre. (5:45)

Like the legislator, the actress Rousseau describes wields her power by invokingand speaking for a higher authority, the knowledgeable discourse of the "philosophe". And the law that she pronounces and ratifies onstage is the law of desire, the same one that feeds and informs the "volonté générale";

> L'amour est le régne des femmes. Ce sont elles qui necessairement y donnent la loi; parce que, selon l'ordre de la nature, la resistance leur appartient, et que les hommes ne peuvent vaincre cette resistance qu'aux dépends de leur liberté. Un effet naturel de ces sortes de piéces est donc d'étendre l'empire du *Séxe*, de rendre des femmes et des jeunes filles les precepteurs du public, et de leur donner sur les spectateurs le même pouvoir qu'elles ont sur leurs amans. (5:43)

The same seductive, theatrical powers that allow women to control their lovers allow them to control the polity. Actresses become de facto political figures by virtue of the fact that all the spectators love and adore them. As they treat these spectators like "imbecilles" and reflect their own "general will" ("ce qu'ils ont pris soin de leur dicter") back to them, women onstage do everything the legislator does: making laws, shaping the polity and reducing the citizens to the status of children.[22]

---

22 It goes without saying that Rousseau himself came under the influence of these actresses, as is clear from the embittered tone in which he contrasts the idealised (and idolised) woman of the theatre from her real counterpart:

> Mais cet objet celeste, où se cache-t-il, et n'est-il pas bien cruel de le contempler au théatre, pour en trouver de si différens dans la société? Cependant, le tableau séducteur fait son effet... Qu'un jeune homme n'ait vu le monde que sur la Scéne, le prémier moyen qui s'offre à lui pour aller à la vertu est de chercher une maitresse qui l'y conduise; espérant bien trouver une Constance ou une Cenie tout au moins. C'est ainsi que, sur la foi d'un

*

\*     \*

Thus the power of women that emerges from Rousseau's idiom is un-
limited: they perform the function of the legislator and of the divinity in
whose name he claims to speak, and under whose auspices he regulates the
public sphere—"les elections se feront dans les loges des Actrices, et les
chefs d'un Peuple libre seront les créatures d'une bande d'Histrions."
(5:112) It comes as no surprise, then, that the sheer exemplarity of these
women leads to their emulation by the men of the republic, and eventually
by Rousseau himself, who adopts the power of these theatrical figures even
as he writes against them.[23]

---

     modéle imaginaire; sur un air modeste et touchant, sur une douceur con-
     trefaite, *nescius aurae fallacis*, le jeune insensé court se perdre, en pensant
     devenir un sage. (5:44)

The effect of the star actress, the elusive "objet celeste", is an obsessive hold on the
spectator's imagination, not unlike the effect of the pedagogue on his pupil in the *Emile*
or the legislator on the public in *Du contrat social.*

[23] Cf. Marshall, 164-165. In Rousseau's utopia, there can only be one source of the
simulacra and fictions on which the discourse of the truth (and consequently political
authority) is predicated. It can be either the theatre, or the state apparatus surrounding
the legislator, but not both. Thus the female idol who presides over her salon and/or
*parterre,* and thereby creates a social order of her own, constitutes a very real threat to
the stage management that goes into the business of managing and legislating a republic.

    The extent to which women play the part of both supreme actresses and supreme
spectators in Rousseau's socio-political imagination is noteworthy. We have already
seen the women of Paris cast in the role of spectator-empresses who watch and evaluate
the men that surround them. Interestingly enough, the women of Geneva, their putative
opposites, perform a similar function. In his discussion of the famous Swiss "cercles"
that he opposes to the Parisian salon, he points out that the sort of gossip fostered by
women's circles fulfills a very important political function (5:97). *Qua* public censors
and spectators, the women of Geneva ensure that public opinion keeps its citizens in
check. As such they manage something that even the laws are powerless to effect.
Rousseau, it will be remembered, lists three sources of political influence in the *Lettre*:
laws, public opinion, and the people's pleasure (5:20-21). The trouble with public opinion and pleasure, however, is that neither can be legislated in orthodox fashion (and
Rousseau mentions Nero to warn against anyone attempting to impose pleasure by fiat).
As censors, therefore, Geneva's women are legislators of a special sort, ones who ad-
minister the "law" of public opinion (in *Du contrat social* we read that, "l'opinion
publique est l'espece de loi dont le Censeur est le Ministre." (3:458)) Furthermore, as
legislators, they have a similar hold on the social imaginary, only they use it with a view
to keeping public morals in check by representing things as they are rather than lying
about them. The only difference between the gossip and social influence of the salon
and those of the circle inheres in the duplicity of the former and the probity of the latter.

According to Rousseau, theatre works by promoting imitation and simulacra. Contact between men and women, those eminently seductive, theatrical creatures, leads, in Rousseau's opinion, to the feminisation and detriment of the former. In the same way that the spectator is caught up in the spectacle before him, the male admirer of the female star/goddess becomes the woman with whom he sympathises and identifies; indeed, he would be feminised by any sort of "commerce" with any woman whatsoever; "nous [les hommes] y perdons à la fois nos mœurs et notre constitution: car ce sexe plus foible, hors d'état de prendre notre maniére de vivre trop penible pour lui, nous force de prendre la sienne trop molle pour nous; et ne voulant plus souffrir de séparation, faute de pouvoir se rendre hommes, les femmes nous rendent femmes." (5:92) Even at its best, Rousseau claims, French theatre is bound to create a similar sort of feminisation, as witness the case of Racine's *Bérénice*; "L'Empereur la renvoye *invitus invitam*, on peut ajouter *invito spectatore*. Titus a beau rester Romain; il est seul de son parti; tous les spectateurs ont épousé Bérénice." (5:49) One might add that by espousing Bérénice they become Bérénice.

This warning against gender-bending is not entirely innocent. Rousseau himself partakes of many of the modalities of the actor and the woman, both in the *Lettre* and elsewhere.[24] The moment of contact with the feminine is highly charged for Rousseau. The masks of the actor/legislator/orator are, as we have seen, part and parcel of Rousseau's self-fashioning. But their realisation is modelled on yet another persona, namely the woman, the figure who subsumes them all and consequently wields a great deal of social power. As a result, Rousseau's construction of

---

Whereas Paris's women represent things differently, the gossip that circulates in Geneva's circles tells it like it is:

> Quoique les Genevoises disent assés librement ce qu'elles savent, et quelquefois ce qu'elles conjecturent, elles ont une veritable horreur de la calomnie, et l'on ne leur entendra jamais interner contre autrui des accusations qu'elles croyent fausses; tandis qu'en d'autres pays [i.e. France] les femmes également coupables par leur silence et par leurs discours, cachent de peur de représailles le mal qu'elles savent, et publient par vengeance celui qu'elles ont inventé. (5:97)

In other words, the Parisian *salonnière* is to the Genevan gossip what the actor is to the orator: the former represents someone else, while the latter represents herself. This seeming opposition between representing the other and representing the self is, however, contained (and undone) by the fact that both involve role-playing and theatrical representation. In Rousseau's scheme of things, even the spectators become actors, an association essential to the proper operation of the *fêtes* that he describes for Geneva, where everyone is both actor and spectator at the same time.

24 Cf. Marshall, 155-165.

his identity becomes a narcissistic exercise aimed at feminising himself; his enactment of himself becomes a pursuit of his femininity.

*

*   *

The specular relationship between Rousseau and the divinity/star/imperatrix is not unique to the *Lettre à d'Alembert*. In both his theatrical and autobiographical works, Rousseau takes pains to stage what Robert Ellrich calls his "androgynous dream": the quest for femininity, understood as a display of the self.[25] Which display, properly staged, will lead to the deification of the displayed entity (in this case Rousseau himself).

The theme of an affective attachment to a feminised double runs through most of Rousseau's plays. In *Narcisse, ou l'amant de lui-même* Valére falls in love with a portrait of himself that his sister, Lucinde, has touched up "en des ajustemens de femme" (2:979) to call his attention to his vanity. Once again, the association between vanity, narcissism and femininity are explicitly foregrounded:

> **Marton**: Le voilà, Mademoiselle, changé dans ses ajustemens de maniére à le rendre méconnoissable. Quoiqu'il soit le plus joli homme du monde, il brille ici en femme encore avec de nouvelles graces.
> **Lucinde**: Valére est, par sa délicatesse et par l'affectation de sa parure, une espéce de femme cachée sous des habits d'homme, et ce portrait ainsi travesti, semble moins le déguiser que le rendre à son état naturel. (2:977)

Furthermore, the events of the play only capitalise on such potential as existed before the first act. Valére, in other words, only "falls in love with himself" once that self is displayed in ornate, feminine form. The theatrical articulation of that fact and the framed display of the self are what constitute his identity as latter-day Narcissus. The modified portrait has the effect of a monstrance that precipitates the adoration and conversion of the beholder. Rotrou is not mocked; just as his Saint Genest had to play a Christian to become a Christian, Rousseau's Valére has to witness the representation of his feminised self in order to become "l'amant de lui-même."

Valére and his portrait are the part of a number of variations on the theme of androgynous doubling in Rousseau's theatrical corpus. In *Le*

---

[25] Ellrich's very suggestive essay is my source for the term "androgynous dream" and the markers of Rousseau's quest for his feminine—or feminised—self. The link between femininity and spectacular display is my own.

*Devin du village*, the protagonists Colin and Colette, are a nominal embodiment of the Platonic ideal of androgynous love. The plot of *Le Lévite d'Ephraïm* turns on the substitution of a woman for a man in a Biblical episode of gang rape. In *Les Prisonniers de guerre*, gentle treatment at the hands of the French, followed by an exchange of prisoners causes Frederic, a Hungarian officer, to declare that "Tous les hommes sont les fréres des François" (2:870). Shortly thereafter, Dorante, his French counterpart, who has fallen in love with Frederic's sister, Sophie, while he was held prisoner by her father, declares, "Belle Sophie! vous êtes pour moi le prix de ce qu'il y a de plus estimable parmi les hommes." (2:874) Now, this rather convoluted turn of phrase rhetorically frames the very real affect that binds Dorante, a Frenchman, to his fellow men, which affect can only be expressed in the form of his love for a Hungarian woman, Sophie, who is the sister (the female double) of his double, Frederic. Dorante's falling in love with Sophie is nothing more than his falling in love with his feminised double. In *Pygmalion* this feminised double, Galathée, actually speaks to its creator and says, "Ah! encore moi." (2:1231)[26]

The paradigm established in *Narcisse* - that of a man chasing his feminine double - can also be traced through the *Confessions*. The emotional cogito that Paul de Man correctly discerns behind Valére's behaviour, "Je m'aime comme si j'étais X", also applies to Rousseau; "Je m'aime comme si j'étais une femme".[27] That Rousseau enjoys himself, and enjoys the verbal display of that self, is evident from the many autobiographical texts he left behind. The pleasure he derives is intense and long-lasting: "En me disant, j'ai joüi, je joüis encore." (1:1174) The depth of this narcissistic pleasure derives in no small part from the model staged in *Narcisse*: Rousseau creates himself parthenogenetically by pursuing and uniting with his feminised self.

Rousseau announces the importance of this feminine double *in nuce* in "Le persifleur": "Rien n'est si dissemblable à moi que moi-même." (1:1108) Later, this fundamental difference from himself is elaborated at greater length and with some insistence:

---

26 For other examples of this theme, see Ellrich, 324-337. This tendency also informs Rousseau's fantasm of incest, which is almost always fraternal rather than maternal. (Cf. Derrida, 372-374 and Kavanagh, 3-11). In *Julie*, an enamoured Saint-Preux cries, "O ma charmante maîtresse, ô mon épouse, ma sœur, ma douce amie!" (2:149) Similarly, in the course of the peculiar anthropology sketched out in the *Essai sur l'origine des langues*, Rousseau surmises that, "Il falut bien que les prémiers hommes épousassent leurs sœurs," and "on devenoit maris et femmes sans voir cessé d'être frére et sœur." (5:406)

27 Cf. de Man, *Allegories*, 165-168.

Je me répéte, on le sait; il le faut. Le prémier de mes besoins, le plus grand, le plus fort, le plus inextinguible, étoit tout entier dans mon cœur: c'étoit le besoin d'une société intime et aussi intime qu'elle pouvoit l'être; c'étoit surtout pour cela qu'il me falloit une femme plustot qu'un homme, une amie plustot qu'un ami. Ce besoin singulier étoit tel, que la plus étroite union des corps ne pouvoit encore y suffire: il m'auroit fallu deux ames dans le même corps; sans cela je sentois toujours du vide.[28]

Thus Rousseau finds himself (in the idiomatic sense) through a narcissistic attachment to the women in his life in much the same way that he reverses the polarities of self and other elsewhere. As a result of this tendency, verbal portraiture of any kind is always necessarily self-portrayal in Rousseau's idiom:

Hommes savants dans l'art de feindre
Qui me prêtez des traits si doux,
Vous aurez beau vouloir me peindre,
Vous ne peindrez jamais que vous.
                    ("Quatrain pour un de ses portraits"; 2:1157)

As a consequence of Rousseau's narcissism and self-dissemblance, no two portraits are ever exactly alike. Not only does each have an elusive subject but each is further modified by the imprint of its maker: "faites tirer le meme visage par divers peintres, à peine tous ces portraits auront-ils entre eux le moindre raport; sont-ils tous bons, ou quel est le vrai? Jugés des portraits de l'ame." ("Mon Portrait"; 1:1121-1122) Like the *Confessions*, one might add.[29]

Rousseau sets up the *Confessions* in such a way as to posit this tendency at its origin.[30] The terms in which he narrates his mother's death and its consequences are revealing:

---

[28] For an incisive reading of the link between Rousseau's self-dissemblance and his feminine doubles, the reader is referred to Pontalis, 21-23. This passage, which Rousseau uses to describe his relationship with Thérèse Levasseur, casts an interesting perspective on Rousseau's fantasm of fraternal incest, since after describing her as his feminine double, he adds; "Que n'auroris-je point donné pour me faire l'enfant de sa mère!" (1:415) This habit of seeing his female lovers as sisters goes back to Rousseau's earliest attachments, as witness his description of his "affair" with Mlle Goton; "Je l'aimois en frére, mais j'en étois jaloux en amant." (1:28)

[29] It goes without saying that this reversal of self and other is the same tactic that Rousseau uses to oppose his detractors. Cf. Pontalis, 10-11; Kavanagh, 102-123.

[30] Thus proving de Man's point about the life of the subject imitating the art of its autobiography. Cf. *Rhetoric of Romanticism*, 68-69.

...[J]e coûtai la vie à ma mere, et ma naissance fut le premier de mes malheurs.
Je n'ai pas su comment mon pere supporta cette perte; mais je sais qu'il ne s'en consola jamais. Il croyoit la revoir en moi, sans pouvoir oublier que je la lui avois ôtée; jamais il ne m'embrassa que je ne sentisse à ses soupirs, à ses convulsives étreintes, qu'un regret amer se mêloit à ses caresses; elles n'en étoient que plus tendres... Ah! disoit-il en gemissant; rend-la-moi, console-moi d'elle; rempli le vide qu'elle a laissé dans mon ame. T'aimerois-je ainsi si tu n'étois que mon fils?
(1:7)

Now, as later parts of the *Confessions* make clear, Rousseau's father eventually did recover from the loss of his wife. The figure of the inconsolable widower reflects Rousseau's desire to detain his father's attentive gaze as long as possible.[31] "Il croyoit la revoir en moi": Rousseau has become a portrait of his mother, which is to say, "himself". The bitterness that makes his father's caresses more tender than they would otherwise have been imply the pleasure that Rousseau takes in being identified as his mother's substitute. Similarly, the rhetorical question that he attributes to his father implies that he is much more a mere son; he "is" his mother. To paraphrase Paul de Man's rhetorical paraphrase of *Narcisse*, one might say that Rousseau is saying; "Il m'aimait comme si j'étais sa femme." Or better yet, "j'étais comme si j'étais sa femme; comme si j'étais ma mère." Moreoever, by susbstituting himself for his mother, Rousseau fills in his father's soul the very same gap that will be filled in his own by Thérèse LeVasseur, his own feminine double. At his own "origin", therefore, Rousseau situates a scenario of identification with a feminine double designed to satisfy the narcissistic pleasure he takes in his father's allegedly morbid attention. To borrow a phrase from Derrida, one might say that "il y a du supplément à la source": Rousseau's identity is grafted onto his mother's in a process of supplementary identification not unlike those that have been commented elsewhere in his work. Thus Rousseau "embarks" on a long journey of identification with nearly all of the women that come his way.

Nor is this his mother's only legacy. Rousseau tells us that she left him some novels, and that their effect on him was not negligible since they constitute his sense of who he is; "je ne me souviens que de mes prémiéres lectures et de leur effet sur moi: c'est le tems d'où je date sans interruption la conscience de moi-même." (1:8) Rousseau's self-consciousness is therefore bound inextricably with the process of reading his mother's books and acting out what is in them. His identification with the characters he

---

31 Cf. Grosrichard, 340-345.

reads marks him for life by consigning to him "de la vie humaine des notions bizarres et romanesques, dont l'experience et la réflexion n'ont jamais bien pu me guerir." (1:8) Thus his readings Plutarch and his casting himself as an oratorical firebrand are based on a histrionism aided and abetted by his identifications with the many others he encounters (starting with his mother) in an idealised synthesis of fact and fiction.[32]

If, as Jean Hagstrum argues, the first part of the *Confessions* reads like an eighteenth century novel of sensibility[33] it is in no small part because of the series of identifications and mappings that Rousseau traces so carefully between himself and his feminine selves. His entire relationship with Mme de Warens is predicated on the perceived resemblances between them. Their first encounter is typical insofar as it metamorphoses Rousseau into his reflection; "Que devins-je à cette vue!" The place where he met her, the location of the interface between Rousseau and his feminine double, attains the status of a portrait decorated and framed like the one in the *Narcisse*; "Que ne puis-je entourer d'un balustre d'or cette heureuse place!" They mirror each other, physically and metaphysically: "elle avoit... une bouche à la mesure de la mienne"; she had converted "par une étourderie assez semblable à la mienne";[34] like him she was born to legislate; "Elle étoit née pour les grandes affaires... à la place de Mme de Longueville elle eût gouvernée l'Etat"; their rapport is the epitome of sympathy: they mirror each other's souls to the point where Rousseau's love for her and his love for himself are synonymous; "C'est une question qu'il ne m'est pas plus venu dans l'esprit de lui faire une fois en ma vie, que de me demander à moi-même si je m'aimois." (1:49-52)

And so it comes as no surprise that Rousseau's feelings on his way to Turin are marked by the sort of affective plenitude that comes with a union with one's "better half":

> ...[J]'étois dans ce court mais précieux moment de la vie où sa pléni-tude expansive étend pour ainsi dire notre être par toutes nos sensa-tions, et embellit à nos yeux la nature entiére du charme de notre exis-

---

[32] In Rousseau's idiom, novels inspire little other than the desire to be other than what one is, as witness his warnings in the *Emile* that all will be lost if Emile "aime mieux être un autre que lui."

[33] Cf. Hagstrum, 224.

[34] Rousseau's use of the term "étourderie" is a not insignificant description of his passive conversion after his "debate" with M. de Pontverre; "Ma faute en cela ressem-bloit à la coquetterie des honnêtes femmes, qui quelquefois pour parvenir à leurs fins, savent, sans rien permettre ni rien promettre, faire esperer plus qu'elles ne veulent tenir." (1:47) In other words, Rousseau arrives at the Catholic stronghold of Annecy al-ready feminised to a certain extent.

tence... Je me regardois comme l'ouvrage, l'elève, l'ami, presque l'amant de Mme de Warens. (1:57-58)

Work, student, friend, lover; these are all overdetermined terms in Rousseau's idiom. They characterise the structure of object and mirror-image that unites Pygmalion to Galathée, Valére to his portrait and Rousseau to Emile. Rousseau might as well have added, "je me regardois comme Mme de Warens elle-même." On his way to Turin, Rousseau resembles nothing so much as Galathée coming to life, looking at her creator and saying "c'est moi."

Henceforth it will be impossible for Rousseau to live outside the imaginary space spanned by Mme de Warens; "Je ne voyais plus dans l'univers qu'elle seule: vivre dans sa disgrâce étoit ne chose qui ne se pouvoit pas." (1:102)[35] The creation exists only insofar as its creator accords it grace; if it *is* at all, it is only in the eye of the beholder. Rousseau is to Mme de Warens as the reflection is to Narcissus, as the portrait is to Valére, as the multitude is to the eye of the sun at the festival that ends the *Lettre à d'Alembert*. Everything is shared: he lives where she lives ("je logeai chez moi, c'est-à-dire chez Maman" (1:176)), he eats what she eats, or rather what she has eaten ("Un jour, à table, au moment qu'elle avoit mis un morceau dans sa bouche, je m'écrie que j'y vois un cheveu: elle rejette le morceau sur son assiette, je m'en saisis avidement et je l'avale;" (1:108)), her appearance is his appearance, her being is his being. It is no accident that Rousseau says, time and again, that his feeling for Mme de Warens is co-terminous with his own life, that he will only stop loving her the day he dies. His sense of himself is determined by this specular rapport with Mme de Warens which culminates in the paroxysm of plenitude and posession he describes during his convalescence:

> Je devenois tout à fait son œuvre, tout à fait son enfant et plus que si elle eut été ma vraye mére... nous nous accoutumames à ne plus penser à rien d'étranger à nous, à borner absolument notre bonheur et tous nos desirs à cette possession mutuelle et peutêtre unique parmi les humains, qui n'étoit point, comme je l'ai dit, celle de l'amour; mais une posession plus essencielle qui, sans tenir aux sens, au sexe, à

---

35 This despite a number of affairs and attachements that intervene under the auspices of resemblance and portrayal. Mme Basile sews and breathes in sympathy with his sighs ("tout ce que je pouvois faire étoit de filer sans bruit des soupirs... cependant, je voyois quelquefois par une sorte de sympathie son fichu se renfler assez fréquemment. Ce dangereux spectacle achevoit de me perdre... C'est peut-être pour cela même que l'image de cette femme est restée empreintée au fond de mon cœur." (1:74-76)); Later, the exchange of portraits (or lack thereof) with Mme d'Epinay shows that resemblance remains the most important factor in Rousseau's emotional involvements (1:436-437).

l'age, à la figure tenoit à tout ce par quoi l'on est soi, et qu'on ne peut perdre qu'en cessant d'être. (1:222)[36]

She has become, as Rousseau makes her, the "depositaire de [s]on être" (1:221). She is his goddess and mistress, the custodian of his being, the index to his elusive self.

Rousseau tells us that he liked talking *en tête-à-tête* with Mme de Warens because he felt none of the usual inhibitions. Talking to her is like talking to himself, talking to his specular double and finally being able to say what he wants to say; "tête-à-tête avec elle j'étois aussi parfaitement à mon aise que si j'eusse été seul." (1:181)

Nor is this the only time that Rousseau feels perfectly at ease. More often than not, he links these moments of uninhibited eloquence to his solitary promenades as narrated in the *Rêveries* and the *Lettres à Malesherbes*. In these texts the fantasms of total control and power are coupled with the fantasmatic invisible presence of that most sympathetic—and most powerful—of interlocutors, Mother Nature.

Scenes of Rousseau bathing, walking, talking, or crying are not uncommon in the autobiographical texts. They do, however, grow in prominence as Rousseau approaches the state of "divine" self-sufficiency and solitude so prevalent in the *Rêveries*, where "on se suffit à soi-même comme dieu" (1:1047). There is not much variation in Rousseau's stage settings: he is alone, all alone ("Me voici donc seul sur la terre," (1:995)) in the forest, "talking" to and communing with Mother Nature.[37] There is self-pity there, certainly, but also a certain satisfaction. In view of the importance of women in Rousseau's imaginary, and knowing the lengths to which he goes to identify with the figure of the woman as deity, it comes as no surprise to hear his thoughts as he wanders on the Ile St-Pierre: "Je m'écriois parfois avec attendrissement: ô nature, ô ma mére, me voici sous ta seule garde; il n'y a point ici d'homme adroit et fourbe qui s'interpose entre toi et moi." (1:642-643) The phrase "point d'homme adroit et fourbe" recalls the many "fourbes" that surrounded his beloved Maman and eventually took his place as her favourite, as well as the "adroit" intellectuals like Diderot and Grimm who precipitated his crisis with Mme

---

[36] On this particular passage, Cf. Kavanagh, 8-9. Rousseau's declaration about loving Mme de Warens "to death" is realised through his purile reaction to his replacement by Wintzenried in Book 6 of the *Confessions*; "Ah! Maman, lui dis-je le cœur serré de douleur, qu'osez vous m'apprendre?... Ne m'avez-vous tant de fois conservé la vie que pour m'oter tout ce qui me la rendoit chére? J'en mourrai, mais vous me regretterez." (1:263)

[37] On the significance of Rousseau's solitude during his promenades, Cf. Starobinski, *Transparence* 315-316.

d'Epinay and nearly (as he saw it) ended his marriage. The fanstasmatic reverie to which Rousseau abandons himself here is therefore one of a life lived under the adoring—and adorable—gaze of the maman who spans his universe. His communion and identification with her are not far off.

The prayers that Rousseau utters in these occasions are marked by a lack of content as such, as witness the following anecdote placed amidst his description of the Ile St-Pierre;

> J'ai lu qu'un sage Evêque dans la visite de son diocése trouva une vieille femme qui pour toute priére ne savoit dire que Ô: il lui dit: bonne mére, continuez de prier toujours ainsi; votre priére vaut mieux que les nôtres. Cette meilleure priére est aussi la mienne. (1:642)

This is, of course, a very odd sort of prayer. Like the prayer advocated by the Savoyard vicar,[38] it is not supplicative; it asks nothing of the deity; its emptiness, both formal and substantive, signifies adoration only.

This adoration, however, is neither innocent nor humble. In the third *Lettre à Malesherbes*, Rousseau narrates another scene of prayer and communion in the woods. He speakes of, "cette etourdissante exstase à laquelle mon esprit se livroit sans retenue, et qui dans l'agitation de mes transports me faisoit écrier quelquefois: Ô grand être! ô grand être, sans pouvoir dire ni penser rien de plus." (1:1141) Here again, the prayer is an act of adoration, but here the prayer has some content; it names its allocutor and deity: ""Ô grand être." Taken in the context of Rousseau's ambulatory addiction, it is clear that the deity being named is Mother Nature, the female double/Other/goddess who is part of the series of identifications that includes Rousseau's human doubles: his mother, Mme de Warens, Thérèse Le Vasseur and so on.

Taken in the context of the third *Lettre à Malesherbes*, however, a more disturbing pattern emerges. This letter, like the *Rêveries*, depicts what Rousseau is like when he's at home. And what he is like is divine. It will be remembered that Rousseau congratulates himself on being judged the most unfortunate of men by Malesherbes; "Je ne saurois vous dire Monsieur combien j'ai été touché de voir que vous m'estimiez le plus malheureux des hommes." (1:1138) Malesherbes, in other words, pities Rousseau. And "pity" is the most fundamental and theatrical form of love in Rousseau's idiom; it, too operates in the mode of specular identification.[39] So in

---

38 Cf. *Emile*, 4:582-600.

39 The reader is referred to landmark treatments of this question in Derrida, *Grammatologie*, 259-272; de Man, *Allegories*, 139 n., and Marshall, 147-149. In the *Emile*, pity is described in terms of an exchange of self and other: "Ainsi naît la pitié, premier sentiment relatif qui touche le cœur humain selon l'ordre de la nature... En effet, com-

claiming that Malesherbes pities him, and finds him the most pitiable of
men, Rousseau is claiming to be the most lovable, the most adorable of
men, a situation aided and abetted by the recognition lent to it by the most
powerful man in Paris, the Président de Malesherbes.[40]

No sooner has Rousseau judged himself to be the most adorable of
creatures than he embarks on a lengthy decription of himself as an entity
worthy of that description, as a god. First, Rousseau equates the imaginary
space that he constructs on his own, in the forest, with all of creation. This
is a fantasmatic world produced and peopled by his desire:

> Ô que le sort dont j'ai joüi n'est-il connu de tout l'univers!... Mais de
> quoy jouissois-je enfin quand j'étois seul? De moi, de l'univers entier,
> de tout ce qui est, de tout ce qui peut etre, de tout ce qu'a de beau le
> monde sensible, et d'imaginable le monde intellectuel: je rassemblois
> autour de moi tout ce qui flattoit mon cœur, mes desirs etoient la
> mesure de mes plaisirs. Non, jamais les plus voluptueux n'ont connu
> de pareilles delices, et j'ai cent fois plus joui de mes chimeres qu'ils
> ne font des realités. (1:1138-1139)

Rousseau goes on to describe the happiest moments of his life as those
he spends "avec moi seul... avec la nature entière et son inconcevable auteur." This epithet, "inconcevable", is not uninteresting, and we should not
lose it from our purview. Then Rousseau reviews individually all the creations of this creator in the virgin territories of the forest, "où nul tiers im-
portun ne vint s'interposer entre la nature et moi." (1:1140) Here again,
Rousseau articulates the fantasm of unmediated contact with Mother Nature. The image complex that predominates this passage, however, brings
into play metaphors of royal pomp and circumstance:

> L'or de genets, et la pourpre des bruyeres frapoient mes yeux d'un
> luxe qui touchoit mon cœur, la majesté des arbres qui me couvroient
> de leur ombre, la delicatesse des arbustes qui m'environnoient,
> l'etonante varieté des herbes et des fleurs que je foulois sous mes
> pieds tenoient mon esprit dans une alternative continuelle
> d'observation et d'admiration: le concours de tant d'objets interessans
> qui se disputoient mon attention, m'attirant sans cesse de l'un à

---

ment nous laissons-nous emouvoir à la pitié, si ce n'est en nous transportant hors de
nous et nous identifiant avec l'animal souffrant? en quittant pour ainsi dire notre être
pour prendre le sien?" (4:505) We are not far here from the sorts of emotions based on
similitude through which Rousseau relates to those he "loves".

[40] On the very trying conditions surrounding the composition of the four letters to
Malesherbes, especially in light of the controvery surrounding the *Emile* and *Du contrat
social* Cf. Book 11 of the *Confessions*, 1:549-588.

> l'autre, favorisoit mon humeur reveuse et paresseuse, et me faisoit
> souvent redire en moi meme: Non, Salomon dans toute sa gloire ne fut
> jamais vétu comme l'un deux. (1:1140)

In other words, Rousseau's sylvan space is a hall of mirrors: he identifies with everything he sees, and by identifying with this totality imagines himself to be king of the world. In his mind's eye he turns the enclosure into a picture of a castle where the flowers become royal robes of gold and purple, the trees turn into columns and the "arbustes" into delicate statues. In effect Rousseau frames the forest, surrounding it with an imaginary "balustre d'or", and turns it into a narcissistic portrait. The biblical citation with which he ends this description might be paraphrased by the emotional cogito; "je m'aime comme si j'étais Salomon dans toute sa gloire."

Still, standing in the place of Solomon is not enough for Rousseau. He proceeds to substitute creation for passive specular identification: "Mon imagination ne laissoit pas longtems deserte la terre ainsi parée. Je la peuplois bientôt d'etres selon mon cœur. Je m'en formois une société charmante dont je ne me sentois pas indigne." (1:1140) In other words, Rousseau creates mirror images of himself, reflections worthy of his status as one on a par with king Solomon "dans toute sa gloire." His narcissistic desire produces as many simulacra as are necessary to populate this imaginary utopia. He is in complete control of the imaginary space that he has carved out.

Suddenly, reality intrudes in the form of a memory:

> Ô si dans ces momens quelque idée de Paris, de mon siecle et de ma
> petite gloriole d'auteur venoit troubler mes reveries, avec quel dedain
> je la chassois à l'instant pour me livrer sans distraction aux sentimens
> exquis dont mon ame etoit pleine. (1:1140)

As Rousseau contemptuously banishes these unpleasant thoughts from his mind, one might well wonder what allowed them to intrude on his beatific imagination in the first place. Why would Rousseau think about Paris during this moment of bliss? The answer, I think, is to be found in the metonymy he uses; "ma petite gloriole d'auteur." The act of imaginary creation by which Rousseau peoples this imaginary space serves as a point of comparison with the "inconcevable auteur" of "la nature entiére." Furthermore, if the image of the "petite gloriole d'auteur" (itself an echo of the crown of Solomon "dans toute sa gloire") is quickly and disdainfully "chassé à l'instant", it is in no small part in order to allow the comparison of Rousseau to God to turn into a full-fledged, unmediated identity.

Soon enough, we find Rousseau using the language of sexuality to narrate the genesis of that identity:

> Bientôt de la surface de la terre j'elevois mes idées à tous les êtres de
> la nature, au systeme universel des choses, à l'etre incomprehensible
> qui embrasse tout. Alors l'esprit perdu dans cette immensité je ne pen-
> sois pas, je ne raisonnois pas, je ne philosophois pas; je me sentois
> avec une sorte de volupté accablé du poids de cet univers... (1:1141)

As he reviews all the reflections of himself in his imaginary space
("tous les êtres de la nature"), Rousseau unites with each and every one of
them in an act of coupling with the universe that weighs down on him like
a lover. The scene in the forest is in effect a one-man version of the village
*fête* described in the *Lettre à d'Alembert*.

We are now better placed to understand the "prayer" with which
Rousseau closes this section. His cry, "Ô grand etre, ô grand etre" marks
the orgasmic culmination of his mystical union and his own birth as the
deity that determines everything within it. As he yells, "Ô grand etre"
Rousseau can only be heard by himself; he is his own interlocutor. Far
from addressing a god or deity situated beyond the real, he is addressing a
deity within himself, he is addressing the deity that he has become; he is
celebrating his own status as the "grand être." Far from being a prayer de-
void of content, this is, in fact, a performative that founds a world.
Rousseau declares himself to be the god of his imaginary world, de-
metaphorising the act of creation to populate it with inhabitants that coincide with his narcissistic desire in a paroxysm of parthenogenesis. His hold
on this world is godly indeed: he alone decides who, or what, will enter his
world and who will not. If, as he says, he shouts his prayer "sans pouvoir
dire ni penser rien de plus" it is because there is nothing left to say. In
naming himself god, he has said it all.

Hence the amazing fantasms of divine power and omnipotence that one
sees in the *Rêveries*. Hence, too, the very real jealousy with which
Rousseau, this *deus zelotes*, watches over this world cast in his image. Now
we can see why he was opposed to the constuction of theatre in Geneva: as
a god, as a maker of fictions in which he is himself engulfed, Rousseau
needs his own theatrical apparatus, his own "ornamentation"; any other
fiction threatens to take his divine status away from him. Anything other
than what Rousseau "creates", any embarassing memory or unpleasant
reminiscence, is threat to this universe that depends on, nay, consists of, *is*
its creator's delirium.

This delirium creates a world guarded by an idol, Rousseau, who, like
the *salonnière* "n'a d'actif que la langue et les yeux." As is the case with
every deity, this idol is marked by self-identity (thus echoing the discourse
of the burning bush), which in Rousseau's idiom translates into absolute
innocence, lack of mystery, coincidence with his real self. Thus even his
persecution complex feeds into his deification;

> Toute la puissance humaine est sans force desormais contre moi... Car
> il est clair que redoutant plus que la mort toute explication avec moi
> ils l'éviteront à quelque prix que ce puisse être. D'ailleurs que me fer-
> ont-ils, m'arrêtereont-ils, c'est tout ce que je demande et je ne peux
> l'obtenir... [M]e feront-ils mourir, Oh qu'ils s'en garderont bien. Ce
> seroit finir mes peines. Maitre et Roi sur la terre tous ceux qui
> m'entourent sont à ma merci, je peux tout sur eux et ils ne peuvent
> rien sur moi. (1:1171)[41]

So much so that the fantasm of persecution has to be expanded indefinitely in order to guarantee the continued existence of Rousseau and the
isolated world he has created for himself. Indeed, Rousseau the persecuted
saint and Rousseau the solar monarch are hitherto inseparable;

> Et quand mon innocence enfin reconnue auroit convaincu mes perse-
> cuteurs, quand la vérité luiroit à tous les yeux plus brillante que le
> soleil, le public loin d'apaiser sa furie n'en deviendroit que plus
> acharné; il me haïroit plus alors pour sa propre injustice qu'il ne me
> hait aujourd'hui pour les vices qu'il aime à m'attribuer. (1:1167)

Both the adoration and the iconoclasm of the beholders are essential to
the idol's survival.

Rousseau, this deity, this idol, writes to display himself and, in so doing, to create and deify himself. Across all of the forms that this protean
divinity assumes—the orator, the actor, the impostor, the legislator—there
is a steady displacement towards a fusion with the feminine double (with
the self as double) in and through the act of writing oneself. By fusing with
this double, Rousseau annihilates his real self in favour of an imaginary
self, effecting what Starobinski called "une dialectique qui aboutit à une
synthèse."[42] In this respect Casanova's anecdote rings true: he shows us
Rousseau staging his identity as master of his space (one who can speak to
kings as though they are underlings, "Votre altesse fera mauvaise chére")
and as one who is incomplete without his essential—but invisible, because
imaginary—feminine "tout." This act of auto-creation in a primary imaginary space affords Rousseau a position of absolute authority over the text
and the identity he creates therein.

Hence the frenzied claim with which Rousseau ends his *Confessions*:

> J'ai dit la vérité. Si quelqu'un sait des choses contraires à ce que je
> viens d'exposer, fussent-elles mille fois prouvées, il sait des men-
> songes et des impostures, et s'il refuse de les approfondir et de les

---

[41] Cf. Grosrichard, 363-365.

[42] *Transparence* 109.

> eclaircir avec moi tandis que je suis en vie il n'aime ni la justice ni la vérité. (1:656)

Precisely. In the imaginary space that Rousseau rules, the truth is whatever he declares it to be. This is, of course, typical of someone who routinely pushes facts aside in favour of the imaginary spaces where he reasons ("Commençons donc par écarter tous les faits" he says at the start of the second discourse. (3:132)) Rousseau's identity thus plays itself to produce a totalitarian master of games and illusions, a god in his own machine,[43] carefully regulating its operation and jealous of anyone or anything (*mondains*, actors, women) who would take his histrionic prerogative away from him.

\*

\*   \*

With Rousseau, most of the overriding themes of this study come to a head. The equation between self and mask that started with Corneille and Molière and was subsequently projected onto the space of prose fiction is extended here to include all of creation. The histrionic sensibility traces a widening gyre from the theatre to *la cour*, from *la cour* to *la ville*, from *la ville* to *le monde*, and, finally, from the figurative *monde* of eighteenth-century Paris to the world as a whole. The play-acting and doubling that determined the functioning of the Horaces and the Curiaces and informed Versac's control over his circle now feeds into the formation of a supreme being who controls everything by identifying with and mirroring everything. Rousseau's auto-deification is the start of much lively speculation. In his wake, modernity's project will be to worship at the temple of the self, straining to interpret the oracular soundings made every time it adores its strange new god, the individual. "Moi seul."

### The Revolution and I:

Two issues remain: the socio-historical and the literary consequences of Rousseau's delirium. My diction is, to a certain extent, misleading, since the two are bound inextricably with one another; neither without either could or would obtain.

---

[43] Cf. his description of the legislator as "le méchanicien qui invente la machine." (3:381)

Rousseau's histrionics created many an idolator, the most significant of whom was Robespierre. Like Rousseau, the latter played parts and played them well. Not unexpectedly, they coincided with the parts left behind by the *promeneur solitaire*: the sincere Alceste, the legislator, the dandified political performer, the "seagreen incorruptible".[44] Furthermore, Rousseau's view of the theatre, whereby the festive atmosphere of *le monde* was transferred back to a pastoral setting, engendered lots of spectacles in its own right. One would be hard pressed to find a better example of the feasts that Rousseau advocated—where people became actors and spectators for each other in an imaginary space dominated by the legislator—than the feasts of the Supreme Being held during the revolution, as described ironically by Mona Ozouf:

> A qui est familier des utopies du siècle, la fête de l'Être Suprême fait la savoureuse surprise d'une Arcadie incarnée. Ce défilé de villageois, de mères de famille "portant à leurs bras chacune en enfant à la mamelle", de jeune filles offrant sur un plat de porcelaine un couple de tourtereaux, de bergers "les chacuns avec leur agneau attaché d'un ruban rose", ces troupes légères échappées de l'Astrée avec leurs carquois et leurs houlettes, les voici enfin sorties des pages des livres et mariant leur grâce à la robustesse des beaux noms du terroir français. Quel enchantement, quand Galatée se nomme Marie Fenouillet! (*Fête révolutionnaire*, 134)

These spectacular *fêtes*, these "Arcadies incarnées", themselves part and parcel of the social upheaval that accompanied the end of the century, would have been unthinkable without Rousseau's literary prescriptions. The Lacademonian "feast" that he describes at the end of the *Lettre à d'Alembert*, with its emphasis on the creation of a utopian atmosphere predicated on the reduction of the individual to the biological chain of generations, anticipates these rather pastoral, para-literary moments of the feast of the Supreme Being.

The French Revolution, obsessed as it was with the "sincerity" of its participants, implies aims not far removed from those of the author of *Julie*, the *Lettre à d'Alembert* and the discourses. Indeed, as Hannah Arendt points out, the rhetoric of the revolutionaries implied, "that the Revolution offered the opportunity of tearing the mask of hypocrisy off the face of French society, of exposing its rottenness, and, finally, of tearing the façade of corruption down and of exposing behind it the unspoiled, honest face of the *peuple*."[45] The Revolution was eminently literary in its functioning,

---

[44] Cf. Trilling, 68-74.

[45] Arendt, *On revolution*, 102.

turning the likes of Molière's Alceste into political superheroes. The very form of the link between authority and desire metamorphoses the image of the leader from the loveable monarch (Louis le bien aimé) into the solid, respectable revolutionary who substitutes ideological authenticity for royal pomp and circumstance, and who dominates the social imaginary while demystifying and denouncing the false pretenses of his predecessors. The new political leader has a right to rule no less divine than the divine right of kings, mostly because his mode of operation is that of the legislator—using the statue of the mute God as a theatre prop and claiming to be its oracle. The mere fact that he does not belong to the social order (which is corrupt by definition) renders the revolutionary leader a "saint", one who can do no wrong, because he is closer to the innocent, uncorrupted state of nature described by Rousseau, where he can forge his own "divinity".[46]

The authentic individual who, like Rousseau, is good by virtue of the fact that he opposes the status quo, is he who plays his own part, translating his "conscience de lui-même" into political action. But this consciousness is itself an artifice, a collage of citations culled from various literary works. It would be no exaggeration to say that the sort of authenticity and self-consciousness that Rousseau's legacy engenders is quixotic first and foremost; that the French Revolution marks the spilling over of the histrionic sensibility to areas of human behaviour far removed from the space of literature. The literary imagination—be it oratorical or *romanesque*—becomes the authentic individual's imaginary space, which space he then projects onto the world outside in accordance with the revolutionary ethic of Rousseau.

The coincidence of socio-political action and internal individual motivation is one of the key definitions of modernity: this is presumably the age when putatively free individuals, living under the auspices of the legislator, are free to do as they choose, which is to say to be themselves, to act (in every sense of the term) as themselves by enacting themselves in accordance with the dictates of their "consciences d'eux-mêmes". Hence the myth of the reign of "reason" understood as the identity of theory and action, desire and knowledge (as opposed to desire and authority, the frivolous reasoning advocated by Rousseau's enemies), individual consciousness and universal law (set by the legislator, i.e. the impostor). Modernity is the age when people's life becomes a permanent festival,

---

[46] Or rather the revolutionary is a sort of secular saint, bringing absolute, universal values to bear on quotidian matters. For an enlightening discussion of the relationship between sanctity, renunciation and individuality, see Louis Dumont's fine discussion of the *individu-hors-du-monde* and the *individu-dans-le-monde* in his *Essais sur l'individualisme*, 33-67 and 95-114.

where they are always actors and spectators to and for each other, where it no longer makes sense to pose the question of hypocrisy because dissemblance cannot be detected in the ubiquitous theatre of the political.[47]

Nor is this all. In locating the source of the role that one will play, the identity that one will enact, internally rather than externally, as a "conscience de soi-même", Rousseau effectively reverses the trend that has dominated literature (as traced in this study) since Corneille and classicism. There, as we saw, the role that one played was a function of social rank and of the mirror-image against whom one pitted oneself: Chimène tells Rodrigue; "Tu n'as fait le devoir que d'un homme de bien/ Mais aussi ce faisant tu m'as appris le mien," and Horace's entire existence as "le bras de Rome" is spanned by the operation of "s'attacher au combat contre un autre soi-même." Emulation and conformity were the order of the day. Rousseau reverses the vector: rather than take his cue from *le roi soleil* he will take it from *le moi soleil* in a process whereby the profound, individual self is crowned the alpha and omega of his existence.[48] Small wonder that, in so doing, he created generation upon generation of narcissistic, novel-gazing romantics.

Rather than pride himself on having served his king, the individual now prides himself on serving his conscience. Henceforth, Hamlet and Oedipus will replace Rodrigue as archetypes to be emulated. The quest for plenary self-deification gives way to the search for the absolute as practiced by the German Romantics and as documented by Balzac. The theatre, and theatricality, now extend their hold to the production of the nineteenth century's "discovery", lyric poetry (as witness Shakespeare's impact on everyone from Hugo to Mallarmé), as well as the novel (Hugo defined his novels as "des drames qu'on ne peut pas jouer.") Finally, the importance of self-consciousness gives rise to the very theatrical concept of political and social *engagement*, as enshrined by Sartre and the many warring factions in what has come to be known as the politics of cultural identity.[49]

---

[47] Cf. Arendt: "If, in the words of Robespierre, 'patriotism was a thing of the heart' then the reign of virtue was bound to be at worst the rule of hypocrisy, and at best the never-ending fight to ferret out the hypocrites, a fight which could only end in defeat because of the simple fact that it was impossible to distinguish between true and false hypocrites... In politics, more than anywhere else, we have no possibility of distinguishing between being and appearance. In the realm of human affairs, being and appearance are indeed one and the same." (*On Revolution*, 93-94)

[48] Cf. Taylor, 355-363. Corneille, too, was concerned with *le moi soleil*, but Rousseau expands Corneille's model: while Corneille's was "played" before the relatively limited audience of Parisian society, Rousseau's plays out to the entire world.

[49] There are, of course, several other cases of interest, notably Stendhal and Baudelaire, both of whom are treated along with Sartre in Shattuck's "The Prince, the Actor

The cult of the self—for that is what it is—is now protected by an institution and accompanied by a discursive practice known as "literature" that tells its tales and frames its genealogies. Unlike the "arts and the sciences" that corrupted people by making them more sociable, which is to say conformable,[50] literature celebrates uniqueness, non-conformity and the like. Among its many products we can list the outcast, the *solitaire*, the *flâneur*, the *bohème*, the dandy, the "existentialist", the Marxist (in non-Communist countries before 1989), and the "oppositional" writer. And just as it is impossible to tell the legislator from the impostor, it is impossible to draw a real distinction between the *littérateur* and the fictions through which he creates himself.

\*

\*  \*

This attitude constitutes the *Weltanschauung* that prevails during the second half of the twentieth century. The tendency peaks with Sartre, the philosopher who seems to define the entire postwar ethical agenda, whose stand on literary and social issues proved exemplary for half a century, and who was himself a man of the theatre, in more than one respect. In *Les Mains sales*, Sartre's theatrical meditation on leftist politics, Hugo, a "gosse des riches," devotes a great deal of time and energy to re-inventing himself and reconciling his aristocratic origins with his place in the Illyrian Communist Party. Called upon to prove his revolutionary mettle by killing Hoederer, another member of the party and a solid, respectable revolutionary in his own right. Hugo spends a great deal of time pondering the reality of this act, and whether he has the courage to pull it off. Once he does, he spends even more time wondering whether it was a "real" act or a theatrical one, whether it was a revolutionary assassination or a crime of passion. For Hugo, the style of the killing matters far more than the killing itself. Indeed, Hugo's entire revolutionary project, through which he hopes to become a man, is shot through with theatricality: he poses as Hoederer's secretary, agonises endlessly that he does not look like a killer ("Une gueule d'assassin... ça devrait se voir"), he compares himself to canonical literary revolutionaries like Julien Sorel and Raskolnikov, his wife Jessica taunts him that he is simply playing at being a revolutionary, and all the proletarians in the Illyrian communist party assume that his flirtation with communism is just a game he plays while trying to work out his identity.

---

and I." On the ambiguities of conflating politics and philosophy, see Descombes, *Philosophie par gros temps* (Paris: Minuit, 1989), 9-27.

[50] Cf. Trilling, 58.

The assumption is correct, of course, but Sartre's point in *Les Mains sales* seems to be that this is the sort of game that one cannot help playing, that it is an integral part of the formation of the self. Even afterwards, Hugo muses, "Oui. J'ai remué le doigt. Les acteurs aussi remuent les doigts, sur les planches... C'est le même geste. Peut-être que ce n'était pas moi qui étais vrai. Peut-être c'était seulement la balle."[51] This unreality emphasises the fact that for Hugo, there is no possible distinction between acting and being, between real and theatrical murder. So much so that even the facticity of Hoederer's murder dissolves completely: just before the end of the play he says, "Je n'ai pas encore tué Hoederer." The only way out of the dilemma comes with Hugo throwing himself at the party's shooting squad shouting "non-récuperable": if his life was a farce then perhaps his death won't be. Perhaps. Sartre is clever enough to leave the question open.

Hugo's case is a rather dramatic instance of a leitmotiv that recurs with surprising frequency in Sartre's work. The existential definition of the subject as a linear combination of project and history owes much to Rousseau's combination of theatrical and narratological behaviour. His analysis of bad faith in *L'Etre et le néant* brings to light several examples of people who play at what they are in an effort to be what they are, to the point of reducing themselves to the role in question. His lengthy analysis of the "garçon de café" is especially revealing in no small part because of his adopting the pronoun "je" in speaking of the waiter:

> Il joue, il s'amuse. Mais à quoi donc joue-t-il? Il ne faut pas l'observer longtemps pour s'en rendre compte: il joue *à être* garçon de café... Et c'est précisément ce sujet que *j'ai à être* et que je ne suis point... Il est une "représentation" pour les autres et pour moi-même, cela signifie que je ne puis l'être qu'*en représentation*.[52]

Sartre's diction recalls the theology of the middle ages: we all have our pre-ordained roles to play, and we have to play them to death. Our being only comes about insofar as it is represented, which is to say theatrically enacted, before another.

This theme is also found in Sartre's literary biographies. The development of Jean Genet's identity and literary "project" recalls Rotrou's Saint Genêt, who, it will be remembered, converted to Christianity while playing the part of a Christian martyr onstage, much as the café waiter becomes a café waiter by playing the part of a café waiter. Similarly, Jean Genet, in Sartre's view, becomes what he is by assuming a role—the thief, the

---

51 *Les Mains sales* (Paris: Gallimard, 1948), VII.i, 247.

52 *L'Etre et le néant* 2nd. ed. (Paris: Gallimard, 1970), 95-96.

*méchant*—that society imposes upon him, and playing that role endlessly. They say to him, "Tu es un voleur", and he responds, "Je serai le voleur." His entire life becomes one big gesture, a moment at which he assumes his being, ready-made, like a pre-fabricated role, from the "honnêtes gens";

> [L]'être que Genet croit avoir reçu des grandes personnes est *déjà fait*... [C]'est une *personne* au sens latin de *persona*—je veux dire un masque et un rôle dont les conduites et les répliques sont déjà fixées...Un acte qu'on accomplit pour être, ce n'est plus un acte; c'est un geste. Genet ne fait pas le Mal, il n'est pas méchant, il *fait* le méchant.[53]

It is not insignificant that the scheme by which Sartre explains Genet's pschology is not backed up by any solid, empirical evidence: it simply fits the Sartrean conception of the formation of the writer's identity, which is theatrical through and through.[54]

Of even greater interest in this respect is the trajectory traced by young Sartre himself, as it is narrated in *Les Mots*. Like Genet, he too seems to have decided to be what others have made of him ("ce que les autres ont fait de moi"): his grandfather declares his phrenological outlook promising ("Il a la bosse de la littérature"), and Jean-Paul proceeds to construct an identity composed of literary clichés. He, like Genet, receives his "being" ready-made, like a role, from the world around him and the books that he reads. His entire childhood becomes a rehearsal for the literary life to come. When his mother catches him reading *Mme Bovary* at the age of eight and wonders what he will do when he grows up, given that he is reading such scandalous texts at such a tender age, Sartre responds, "Je les vivrai!"[55] So much so that he writes in the dark, in order to be seen doing so and to leave a lasting memory for posterity (Sartre assumes that one day a great-nephew will read about moments like these with tears in his eyes and sigh, "C'est pourtant vrai... il a écrit dans les ténèbres." (*Les Mots*, 171)) For Sartre, writing—his project, the activity that makes him what he is—is an activity that starts with his playing parts scripted by others and

---

[53] *Saint Genet, Comédien et martyr* in Jean Genet, *Oeuvres complètes* (Paris: Gallimard, 1951-1986), 1:75-76.

[54] This tendency can also be seen in *L'Idiot de la famille*, where Sartre openly owns up to what he is doing: "Je l'avoue: c'est une fable. Rien ne prouve qu'il en fut ainsi. Et, pis encore, l'absence de ces preuves—qui seraient nécessairement des faits singuliers—nous renvoie, même quand nous fabulons, au schématisme, à la généralité: mon récit convient a *des* nourrissons, non pas à Gustave en particulier." (*L'Idiot de la famille* (Paris: Gallimard, 1971) 1:139)

[55] *Les Mots* (Paris: Gallimard, 1964), 87.

ends with his taking his place alongside other famous men in books like *L'Enfance des hommes illustres*. The theatricality of everyday life is an axiom that regulates the young Polou's conduct even before he finds the words that would express and invest it with a political dimension of its own:

> J'étais préparé à admettre—si seulement j'eusse été en âge de les comprendre—toutes les maximes de droite qu'un vieil homme de gauche m'enseignait par ses conduites: que la Vérité et la Fable sont une même chose, qu'il faut jouer la passion pour la ressentir, que l'homme est un être de cérémonie. (*Les Mots*, 69)

Sartre knew very early on that without an audience he himself would not become anything, would fail to exist. Moreover, by going beyond the immediate context of his activity (namely, that of a child dabbling about in literary creation), by becoming a Hegelian hero in miniature, one whose actions bring about unforeseen but momentous results, the sense of whose each and every gesture transcends the confines of the task at hand, Sartre brings about the moment where habit hardens into character trait, where formative neurosis becomes proper idiosyncrasy. His tendency to see himself as someone who belongs in the lineage of illustrious men soon becomes his *raison d'être*. Sartre lives to play the part of that which he will grow up to be, to set a precedent, to provide a suitably sustaining fiction for his future self. The histrionic sensibility thus becomes something of which he cannot rid himself, a process by which a meaningful form is imposed upon what would otherwise have been mere scribbles filling up one notebook after another with a childhood hero's adventures. Playing the writer leads to Sartre's being the writer; neither his past nor his future are in any way independent of one another, mediated as they are by the theatrical space that allows their merging.

*
*   *

We have now come full circle: the frantically conformist ethics that animated Rodrigue and enabled his reincarnation as *Le Cid* lead to the anti-conformist ethics that motivate our modern search for individuality. And yet, Marivaux's questions are still with us: how can one be what one is, especially in an epoch where authenticity only obeys the maxims of inauthenticity? Curiously enough, the many social and historical changes that separate us from Rousseau have only deepened our histrionism: we now live in an age where playing one's part and "doing one's own thing" are ethical ideals to which nearly everyone aspires, ones which are accepted and adopted uncritically. And the theatrical ethics described in this study seem to hold sway not only in French cafés, but in American social life as well. Political campaigns are basically a televised popularity contest, whose principles are derived from the *Lettre à d'Alembert* where "les elections se font dans les loges des Actrices" (5:112). Furthermore, contemporary ethnically-based group politics bear out Sartre's dicta that we can never be ourselves enough, so we keep playing our parts endlessly in a desperate attempt to coincide with our irrecuperable "being" (the hidden implication of this social system is that one must play one's group ethnic identity endlessly; one can never be "man" enough, "black" enough, "gay" enough and so on). Furthermore, the categorical imperative to superstardom in any undertaking, no matter how trivial, coupled with the mania for overawarding and overachievement is symptomatic of our living in an unprecedented age where the individual reigns as a god (to borrow a phrase from a recent book title, this is the age of *l'homme dieu*).

We have yet to leave this framework. Recent political developments—notably the collapse of the former Soviet Union—have only added to the wholesale adoption of this philosophy on a global scale. Much of the world's population now subscribes, volens nolens, to what Christopher Lasch called the culture of narcissism, where one can only be socially integrated by playing oneself. It is well worth wondering what kind of an individuality it is that is predicated on our being actors and actresses, and whether this individuality amounts to something more than the empty gestures that are required for its implementation.[56] Moreover, it remains to be seen whether this culture will end in fire or in ice, whether we are inadvertently paving a path for some social paroxysm that will dissolve our enacted selves back into some primordial horde or whether we will each end up living—and dying—separately, in a wasteland of solipsism where no human contact is possible.

---

[56] Some of these questions are treated very suggestively through a more analytic philosophical idiom in Vincent Descombes' recent work. Cf. "L'Esprit comme esprit des lois" in *Le Débat*, 90 (1996), 89-92.

# Bibliography

**Abbreviations:**

| | |
|---|---|
| *MLN* | Modern Language Notes. |
| *PFSCL* | Papers on French Seventeenth-Century Literature. |
| *SVEC* | Studies on Voltaire and the Eighteenth Century. |

Abraham, Claude. *On the Structure of Molière's Comédie-Ballets.* Paris: PFSCL, "Biblio 17", 1986.

Apostolidès, Jean-Marie. *Le Roi-Machine. Spectacle et politique au temps de Louis XIV.* Paris: Minuit, 1981.

-. *Le Prince sacrifié. Théâtre et politique au temps de Louis XIV.* Paris: Minuit, 1985.

-. "Corneille, Tite-Live et la fondation de Rome" *Poétique* 82 (1990).

Arendt, Hannah. *On Revolution.* New York: Viking, 1963 rpt. 1977.

Auerbach, Erich. *Scenes from the Drama of European Literature.* New York: Meridian Books, 1959.

-. *Mimesis.* Princeton: Princeton University Press, 1974.

Barthes, Roland. *S/Z.* Paris: Seuil, 1971.

Bennington, Geoffrey. *Dudding. Des noms de Rousseau.* Paris: Galilée, 1991.

Benrekassa, Georges. *Le Concentrique et l'excentrique. Marges des lumières.* Paris: Payot, 1980.

Benveniste, Emile. *Problèmes de linguistique générale I.* Paris: Gallimard, 1966.

Bercé, Yves-Marie. *La Naissance dramatique de l'absolutisme.* Paris: Seuil, 1992.

Bollème, Geneviève, *et al. Livre et société dans la France du dix-huitième siècle.* Paris: Mouton, 1965-70.

Brooks, Peter. *The Novel of Worldliness: Crébillon fils, Marivaux, Laclos, Stendhal.* Princeton: Princeton University Press, 1969.

-. "Psychoanalytic Constructions and Narrative Meanings." *Paragraph* 7 (Spring 1986).

Bürger, Peter. *Die frühen Komödien Pierre Corneilles.* Frankfurt: Athenäum, 1971.

Butor, Michel. *Répertoire II.* Paris: Minuit, 1964.

Canary, Robert H. and Henry Kozicki, eds. *The Writing of History: Literary Form and Historical Understanding*. Madison, WI: University of Wisconsin Press, 1978.

Carré, Marie-Rose. "Mots en échange, mots en liberté: Molière devant les théories littéraires de son temps." *Dix-septième siècle* 104 (1974).

Casanova de Seingalt, Giacomo. *Histoire de ma vie*, suivie de textes inédits. Francis Lacassin ed. 3 vols. Paris: Robert Laffont, 1993.

Charron, Pierre. *De la sagesse trois livres*. Amsterdam: Louys et Daniel Elzevier, 1662.

Cioranescu, Alexandre. *Le Masque et le visage. Du baroque espagnol au classicisme français*. Genève: Droz, 1983.

Coleman, Patrick. *Rousseau's Political Imagination: Rule and Representation in the Lettre à d'Alembert*. Genève: Droz, 1984.

Collins, David. *Thomas Corneille, Protean Dramatist*. The Hague: Mouton, 1966.

Conroy, P.V. *Crébillon fils: Techniques in the Novel*. *SVEC* 99 (1972).

-. "Real Fiction: Authenticity in the French Epistolary Novel." *Romanic Review* 72:4 (1981).

Corneille, Pierre. *Œuvres complètes*. Alain Niderst ed. Paris: Editions du Seuil, 1963.

-. *Œuvres complètes*. 3 vols. Paris: Gallimard, "Bibliothèque de la Pléiade", 1980.

Corneille, Thomas. *Œuvres*. 9 vols. Paris, 1758. rpt. Genève: Slatkine, 1970.

Coulet, Henri. *Le Roman jusqu'à la révolution*. 2 vols. Paris: Armand Colin, 1967.

-. & Michel Gilot. *Marivaux. Un humanisme expérimental*. Paris: Larousse, 1973.

-. & Jean Ehrard, Françoise Rubellin eds. *Marivaux d'hier, Marivaux d'aujourd'hui*. Paris: Editions du CNRS, 1991.

Couton, Georges. *La Vieillesse de Corneille*. Paris: Deshayes, 1949.

Crébillon, Claude-Prosper Jolyot de. *Œuvres complètes*. 11 vols. Maestricht: Dufour and Roux, 1779.

-. *Les Egarements du cœur et de l'esprit*. Etiemble ed.. Paris: Gallimard, 1977.

-. *Le Sopha*. Paris: Garnier-Flammarion, 1995.

-. *La Nuit et le moment*. Paris: B. Laville, "Erotika Biblion" 4, 1981.

Crocker, Lester G. *Jean-Jacques Rousseau*. 2 vols. New York: Macmillan, 1968-73.

Curtius, Ernst R. *European Literature and the Latin Middle Ages*. Willard Trask trans. New York: Pantheon, 1953.

Darnton, Robert. "Reading, Writing and Publishing in Eighteenth-Century France" *Daedalus* 100 (1971).

Defaux, Gerard. *Molière ou les metamorphoses du comique.* Lexington, KY: French Forum Publishers, 1980.

Deloffre, Fréderic. *Une nouvelle préciosité. Marivaux et le marivaudage.* Paris: Les Belles Lettres, 1955.

De Man, Paul. *Allegories of Reading: Figural Language in Rousseau, Nietzsche, Rilke and Proust.* New Haven: Yale University Press, 1979.

-. *The Rhetoric of Romanticism.* New York: Columbia University Press, 1984.

Derrida, Jacques. *De la grammatologie.* Paris: Minuit, 1967.

-. *La Dissémination.* Paris: Seuil, 1972.

Descombes, Vincent. "La Vérité du vrai." *Critique* 369 (1978).

-. *Philosophie par gros temps.* Paris: Minuit, 1989.

-. "L'Esprit comme esprit des lois." *Le Débat* 90 (1996).

Diderot, Denis. *Œuvres.* Paris: Gallimard, "Bibliothèque de la Pléiade", 1951.

Doubrovsky, Serge. *Corneille et la dialectique du héros.* Paris: Gallimard, 1963.

-. *Autobiographiques: de Corneille à Sartre.* Paris: Presses Universitaires de France 1989.

Dort, Bernard. *Théâtres.* Paris: Seuil, 1986.

Dumont, Louis. *Essais sur l'individualisme. Une perspective anthropologique sur l'idéologie moderne.* Paris: Seuil, 1983.

Du Plaisir. *Sentiments sur les lettres et sur l'histoire avec des scules sur le style.* Philippe Hourcade ed. Genève: Droz, 1975.

Duvignaud, Jean. *L'Acteur. Esquisse d'une sociologie du comédien.* Paris: Gallimard, 1965.

Ehrmann, Jacques. "Structures of Exchange in *Cinna*" in *Yale French Studies* (1965).

Elias, Norbert. *Die höfische Gesellschaft: Untersuchungen zur Soziologie des Königtums und der höfischen Aristoktratie.* Darmstadt: Suhrkamp, 1983.

Ellrich, Robert. "Rousseau's Androgynous Dream: The Minor Works of 1752-62." *French Forum* 13:3 (1988).

Emelina, Jean. *Les Valets et les servantes dans le théâtre comique en France de 1610-1700.* Grenoble: Presses Universitaires de Grenoble, 1975.

Epictetus. *Handbook.* Nicholas White trans. Indianapolis, IN: Hackett, 1986.

Felman, Shoshana. *Le Scandale du corps parlant: Don Juan avec Austin ou la séduction en deux langues.* Paris: Seuil, 1980.

Fergusson, Francis. *The Idea of a Theater.* Princeton: Princeton University Press, 1949.

Fleck, Stephen. *Music, Dance and Laughter: Comic Creation in Molière's Comedy-Ballets*. Paris: PFSCL, "Biblio 17" 1995.

Fleming, John A. "Textual Autogenesis in Marivaux's *Paysan Parvenu*." *SVEC* 189 (1980).

Forestier, Georges. *Le Théâtre dans le théâtre sur la scène française du XVIIᵉ siècle*. Genève: Droz, 1981.

-. *Esthétique de l'identité dans le théâtre français (1550-1680). Le Déguisement et ses avatars*. Genève: Droz, 1988.

Forster, Robert and Jack P. Greene eds. *Preconditions of Revolution in Early Modern Europe*. Baltimore: The Johns Hopkins Press, 1970.

Foucault, Michel. *Histoire de la folie à l'âge classique*. Paris: Plon, 1961.

-. "Un si cruel savoir" *Critique* 18:182 (1962).

-. *Les Mots et les choses*. Paris: Gallimard, 1966.

-. *Le Souci de soi*. Paris: Gallimard, 1984.

-. *L'Usage des plaisirs*. Paris: Gallimard, 1984.

Fried, Michael. *Absorption and Theatricality: Painting and Beholder in the Age of Diderot*. Berkeley, CA: University of California Press, 1980.

Fumaroli, Marc. "Microcosme comique et macrocosme solaire: Molière, Louis XIV et *L'Impromptu de Versailles*." *Revue des sciences humaines* 145 (1972).

-. ed. *Critique et création littéraire au dix-septième siécle*. Paris: Editions du CNRS, 1977.

-. "Aveuglement et désabusement dans *Le Malade imaginaire*" in M-T. Jones-Davies, ed. *Vérité et illusion dans le théâtre au temps de la Renaissance* Paris: Jean Touzot, 1983.

-. *Héros et orateurs. Rhétorique et dramaturgie cornéliennes*. Genève: Droz, 1990.

Gagnebin, Bernard. "Le rôle du législateur dans les conceptions politiques de Rousseau" in *Etudes sur le Contrat social de Jean-Jacques Rousseau*. Paris: Les Belles Lettres, 1964.

Gaines, James F. *Social Structures in Molière's Theater*. Columbus, OH: Ohio State University Press, 1984.

Gearhart, Suzanne. *The Open Boundary of History and Fiction: A Critical Approach to the French Enlightenment*. Princeton: Princeton University Press, 1984.

Genet, Jean. *Œuvres complètes*. Paris: Gallimard, 1951-1986.

Gide, André. *Dostoievsky: articles et causeries*. Paris: Plon, 1923.

Gilot, Michel. "Sur la composition du *Paysan parvenu*" *Dix-huitième siècle* 2 (1970).

Girard, René. "Marivaudage and Hypocrisy" *American Society Legion of Honor magazine* 34:3 (1963).

-. *Mensonge romantique et vérité romanesque.* Paris: Grasset, 1961.

-. *La Violence et le sacré.* Paris: Grasset, 1972.

-. *William Shakespeare: A Theatre of Envy.* Oxford: Oxford University Press, 1991.

Gossman, Lionel. *Men and Masks: A Study of Molière.* Baltimore: The Johns Hopkins University Press, 1963.

-. "Literature and Society in the Early Enlightenment: The Case of Marivaux." *MLN* 82:4 (1967).

-. *French Society and Culture: Background for Eighteenth-Century Literature.* Englewood Cliffs, NJ: Prentice-Hall, 1972.

Grosrichard, Alain. "'Où suis-je?', 'Que suis-je?' (Réflexions sur la question de la *place* dans l'œuvre de Jean-Jacques Rousseau, à partir d'un texte des *Rêveries*)" in *Rousseau et Voltaire en 1978. Actes du colloque international de Nice, 1978.* Genève: Slatkine, 1981, 338-365.

Guicharnaud, Jacques. *Molière. Une aventure théâtrale.* Paris: Gallimard, 1963.

Gutwirth, Marcel. *Molière ou l'invention comique. La métamorphose des thèmes et la création des types.* Paris: Minard, 1966.

Hadot, Pierre. *Exercises spirituels et philosophie antique* 2nd. ed. Paris: Etudes Augustiniennes, 1987.

Hagstrum, Jean. *Sex and Sensibility: Ideal and Erotic Love from Milton to Mozart.* Chicago: University of Chicago Press, 1980.

Harari, Josué V. *Scenarios of the Imaginary: Theorizing the French Enlightenment.* Ithaca: Cornell University Press, 1987.

Harth, Erica. *Ideology and Culture in Seventeenth-Century France.* Ithaca: Cornell University Press, 1983.

Heckman, John. "Marianne: The Making of an Author." *MLN* 86:4 (1971).

Hubert, J.D. *Molière and the Comedy of Intellect.* Berkeley, CA: University of California Press, 1962.

Huet, Marie-Hélène. *Le Héros et son double. Essai sur le roman d'ascension sociale au XVIIIᵉ siècle.* Paris: Corti, 1975.

Huizinga, Jakob. *Rousseau, The Self-Made Saint.* New York: Grossman, 1976.

Jeanneret, Michel. "Rabelais et Montaigne: l'écriture comme parole." *L'esprit créateur* 16.4 (1976) 78-94.

Jeanson, Francis. *Sartre par lui-même.* Paris: Seuil, 1955.

Kantorowicz, Ernst. *The King's Two Bodies: A Study in Mediaeval Political Theology.* Princeton: Princeton University Press, 1957.

Kapp, Volker ed. *Le Bourgeois gentilhomme. Problèmes de la comédie-ballet.* Paris: PFSCL, "Biblio 17" 1991.

Kavanagh, Thomas. *Writing the Truth: Authority and Desire in Rousseau* Berkeley, CA: University of California Press, 1987.

Kempf, Roger. *Sur le corps romanesque.* Paris: Seuil, 1968.

Kibédi Varga, Aron. "La Désagrégation de l'idéal classique dans le roman français de la première moitié du dix-huitième siècle." *SVEC* 25 (1963).

-. "Le Roman est un anti-roman." *Littérature* 48 (1982).

Keohane, Nannerl O. *Philosophy and the State in France: The Renaissance to the Enlightenment.* Princeton: Princeton University Press, 1980.

Koch, Philip. "On Marivaux's Expression, 'se donner la comédie'" *Romanic Review* 56:1 (1965).

Krailsheimer, A.J. *Studies in Self-Interest: Descartes to La Bruyère.* Oxford: Oxford University Press, 1972.

Krauss, Werner. ed. *Roman et lumières au dix-huitième siècle.* Paris, Editions sociales, 1970.

Laclos, Choderlos de. *Œuvres complètes.* Paris: Gallimard, "Bibliothèque de la Pléiade" 1979.

Laden, Marie-Paule. "The Pitfalls of Success: Jacob's Evolution in Marivaux's *Le Paysan parvenu.*" *Romanic Review* 74:2 (1983).

-. *Self-Imitation in the Eighteenth-Century Novel.* Princeton: Princeton University Press, 1987.

Lafarge, Catherine ed. *Dilemmes du roman: Essays in Honour of Georges May.* Saratoga, CA: Anma Libri, 1990.

Lancaster, Henry C. *A History of French Dramatic Literature in the Seventeenth Century.* 5 vols. Baltimore: The Johns Hopkins University Press, 1929-1942.

Leiner, Wolfgang. ed. *Onze études sur l'image de la femme dans la littérature française au dix-septième siècle.* Tübingen: Gunter Narr, 1984.

Lenglet-Dufresnoy, N-A. *De l'usage des romans, où l'on fait voir leur utilité et leurs différents caractères.* Paris, 1734, reprinted Genève: Slatkine 1970.

Levin, Lubbe. "Masque et identité dans *Le Paysan parvenu.*" *SVEC* 79 (1971).

Lough, John. *An Introduction to Eighteenth-Century France.* London: Longmans, 1960.

Lyons, John D. *A Theatre of Disguise: Studies in French Baroque Drama 1630-1660.* Columbia, S.C.: French Literature Publications Company, 1978.

MacBride, Robert. *The Skeptical Vision of Molière.* New York: Barnes & Noble, 1977.

Malandain, Pierre. "Corneille ou la modification." *Revue des sciences humaines* 215 (1989).

Marin, Louis. *Le Récit est un piège*. Paris: Minuit, 1978.

Marivaux, Pierre Carlet de Chamblain de. *Romans*. Paris: Gallimard, "Bibliothèque de la Pléiade", 1949.

-. *Théâtre complet*. Paris: Gallimard, "Bibliothèque de la Pléiade", 1949.

-. *La Vie de Marianne, ou les aventures de Madame la Comtesse de *****. Frédéric Deloffre ed. Paris: Garnier Frères, 1957.

-. *Le Paysan parvenu*. Deloffre ed. Paris: Garnier Frères, 1959.

-. *Journaux et œuvres diverses*. Deloffre ed. Paris: Garnier, 1969.

-. *Œuvres de jeunesse*. Deloffre ed. Paris: Gallimard, "Bibliothèque de la Pléiade", 1972.

-. *Théâtre complet*. 2 vols. Deloffre & Françoise Rubellin eds. Paris: Bordas, 1989.

Marshall, David. *The Surprising Effects of Sympathy: Marivaux, Rousseau, Diderot and Mary Shelley*. Chicago: University of Chicago Press, 1988.

Maurens, Jean-Jacques. *Une tragédie sans tragique. Le Neo-stoicisme dans l'œuvre de Pierre Corneille*. Paris: A. Colin, 1966.

May, Georges. "L'Histoire a-t-elle engendré le roman?" *Revue de l'histoire littéraire de France* 55 (1955).

-. *Le Dilemme du roman au dix-huitième siècle. Etude sur les rapports du roman et de la critique 1715-1761*. Paris: Presses Universitaires de France, 1963.

Mercier, Louis-Sebastien. *Tableau de Paris*. 8 vols. Amsterdam: 1783-1789.

Méré, Antoine Gombeaud, chevalier de. *Œuvres*. Charles-Henri Boudhors, ed. Paris: François Roche, 1930.

Molière. *Œuvres complètes*. 2 vols. Paris: Gallimard, "Bibliothèque de la Pléiade", 1980.

Molina, Tirso de. *El Burlador de Sevilla y convidado de piedra, Don Gil de las calzas verdes, La Prudencia en la mujer*. Madrid: Aguilar, 1964.

Montaigne, Michel de. *Les Essais*. 2 vols. Pierre Villey ed. Paris: Presses Universitaires de France, 1924.

Moore, W.G. *Molière: A New Criticism*. Oxford: Oxford University Press, 1949.

Mousnier, Roland. *Histoire générale des civilisations*. Paris: Presses Universitaires de France, 1962.

-. *Etat et société en France aux dix-septième et dix-huitième siècles*. Cours de Sorbonne; Paris: Centre de documentation universitaire, 1968.

-. "The Fronde" in Robert Forster and Jack Greene, eds., *Preconditions of Revolution in Early Modern Europe*.

-. *Les Institutions de la France sous la monarchie absolue: 1598-1789.* 2 vols. Paris: Presses Universitaires de France 1974.

-. ed. *L'Age d'or du mécénat:1598-1661.* Paris: Editions du CNRS, 1985.

Murray, Geoffrey. *Voltaire's Candide: The Protean Gardener, 1755-1762.* Genève: Institut Voltaire, 1970.

Mylne, Vivienne. *The French Eighteenth-Century Novel: Techniques of Illusion.* Cambridge: Cambridge University Press, 1965.

Nancy, Jean-Luc. *Ego sum.* Paris: Aubier-Flammarion, 1979.

Nelson, Robert J. *Play within a Play: The Dramatist's Conception of his Art from Shakespeare to Anouilh.* New Haven: Yale University Press, 1958.

Niderst, Alain. ed. *Pierre Corneille. Actes du colloque tenu à Rouen du 2 au 6 octobre 1984.* Paris: Presses Universitaires de France, 1985.

*Obliques.* "Don Juan. Analyse d'un mythe" special issue 1:4 1974.

Ozouf, Mona. *La Fête révolutionnaire, 1789-1799.* Paris: Gallimard, 1976.

Pascal, Blaise. *Œuvres complètes.* Lafuma ed. Paris: Seuil, 1963.

Perrault, Charles. *Parallèle des anciens et des modernes.* Max Imdahl and Hans-Robert Jauss eds. Munich: Eidos, 1964.

Pire, Georges. "Du bon Plutarque au citoyen de Genève." *Revue de littérature comparée* 32:4 (1958) 510-547.

Pomeau, René. ed. *Laclos et le libertinage. 1782-1982, Actes du colloque du bicenténaire des Liaisons dangereuses.* Paris: Presses Universitaires de France, 1983.

Pontalis, J-B. Preface. *Les Confessions.* By Jean-Jacques Rousseau. Paris: Gallimard, 1973. 7-26.

Poulet, Georges. *La Distance intérieure.* Paris: Plon, 1952.

-. *Les Métamorphoses du cercle.* Paris: Flammarion, 1979.

Prévot, Jacques. "*L'Amphitryon* de Molière, ou ce que parler veut dire." *Dix-septième siècle* 125 (1979).

Raymond, Marcel. *Jean-Jacques Rousseau. La quête de soi et la rêverie.* Paris: Corti, 1962.

Reichler, Claude. *La Diabolie. La séduction, la renardie, l'écriture.* Paris: Minuit, 1979.

-. *L'Age libertin.* Paris: Minuit, 1987.

Reiss, T.J. *Toward Dramatic Illusion: Theatrical Technique and Meaning from Hardy to Horace.* New Haven: Yale University Press, 1971.

Restif de La Bretonne. *Œuvres complètes.* Henri Bachelin ed. Genève: Slatkine, 1971

*Revue des sciences humaines.*, nos. 145 "Le Théâtre dans le théâtre" (1972) and 158 "Aspects de l'humanisme jésuite au XVIIᵉ siècle" (1975).

Reynier, Gustave. *Le Théâtre de Thomas Corneille*. Paris: Hachette, 1892. rpt. Genève: Slatkine, 1971.

Robert, Marthe. *Roman des origines et origines du roman*. Paris: Grasset, 1972.

Roche, Daniel. *Les Républicains des lettres. Gens de culture et lumières au dix-huitième siècle*. Paris: Fayard, 1988.

Romanowski, Sylvie. "Le Rôle du langage dans le *Dom Juan* de Molière." *Neophilologus* 59 (1975).

Rougemont, M de. *et al.. Dramaturgies, langages, dramatiques. Mélanges pour Jacques Scherer*. Paris: Nizet, 1986.

Rousseau, Jean-Jacques. *Œuvres complètes*. 5 vols. Paris: Gallimard, "Bibliothèque de la Pléiade", 1959-95.

Rousset, Jean. *Forme et signification: Essais sur les structures littéraires de Corneille à Claudel*. Paris: Corti, 1962.

-. *L'Intérieur et l'exterieur: Essais sur la poésie et le théâtre au dix-septième siècle*. Paris: Corti, 1968.

-. *Narcisse romancier: Essai sur la première personne dans le roman*. Paris: Corti, 1973.

Roustang, François. *Un Destin si funeste*. Paris: Minuit, 1976.

Sacy, Silvestre de. *Descartes par lui-même*. Paris: Seuil, 1956.

Saint-Amand, Pierre. *Séduire ou la passion des lumières*. Paris: Méridiens Klincksieck, 1987.

Sartre, Jean-Paul. *Les Mains sales*. Paris: Gallimard, 1948.

-. *Saint Genet, comédien et martyr*. Paris: Gallimard, 1952.

-. *Les Mots*. Paris: Gallimard, 1964.

-. *L'Être et le néant*. 2nd. ed. Paris: Gallimard, 1970.

-. *L'Idiot de la famille*. Paris: Gallimard, 1971.

Scherer, Jacques. ed. *Théâtre du dix-septième siècle*. 2 vols. Paris: Gallimard, "Bibliothèque de la Pléiade", 1975.

-. *La Dramaturgie classique en France*. Paris: Nizet, 1950.

Serres, Michel. *Hermès I: La communication*. Paris: Minuit, 1968.

Shattuck, Roger. *The Innocent Eye*. New York: Washington Square Press, 1986.

Shklar, Judith N. *Men and Citizens: A Study of Rousseau's Social Theory*. Cambridge: Cambridge University Press, 1969.

Siemek, Andrzej. *La Recherche morale et esthétique dans le roman de Crébillon fils*. Oxford: Voltaire Foundation, 1981.

-. "Crébillon précurseur de Laclos?" in René Pomeau ed. *Laclos et le libertinage* Paris: Presses Universitaires de France, 1983.

Spitzer, Leo. "A propos de *La Vie de Marianne*." *Romanic Review* 44 (1953).

Stanton, Domna. *The Aristocrat as Art: A Study of the honnête homme and the Dandy in Seventeenth- and Nineteenth-Century French Literature.* New York: Columbia University Press, 1980.

Starobinski, Jean. *L'Œil vivant.* Paris: Gallimard, 1961.

-. *L'Invention de la liberté, 1700-1789.* Paris: Skira, 1964.

-. *La Transparence et l'obstacle.* Paris: Gallimard, 1971.

-. *La Relation critique.* Paris: Gallimard, 1972.

-. *Montaigne en mouvement.* Paris: Gallimard, 1982.

Steiner, George. *The Death of Tragedy.* New York: Knopf, 1961.

Stendhal. *La Chartreuse de Parme.* Paris: Gallimard, 1964.

-. *Œuvres intimes.* Paris: Gallimard, "Bibliothèque de la Pléiade", 1981.

Stegmann, André. *L'Héroïsme cornélien: genèse et signification.* Paris: Armand Colin, 1968.

Stewart, Philip. *Le Masque et la parole. Le Langage de l'amour au dix-huitième siècle.* Paris: Corti, 1973.

Sturm, Ernest. *Crébillon fils et le libertinage au dix-huitième siècle.* Paris: Nizet, 1970.

Sturzer, Felicia. "*Marivaudage* as Self-Representation." *French Review* 49:1 (1975).

-. "Exclusion and Coquetterie: First-Person Narrative in Marivaux's *L'Indigent philosophe.*" *French Review* 55:4 (1982).

Taylor, Charles. *Sources of the Self: The Making of the Modern Identity.* Cambridge, MA: Harvard University Press, 1989.

Tomlinson, Robert. *La Fête galante. Watteau et Marivaux.* Genève: Droz, 1983.

Trilling, Lionel. *Sincerity and Authenticity.* Cambridge, MA: Harvard University Press, 1972.

Ubersfeld, Anne. *Lire le théâtre.* Paris: Editions sociales, 1977.

-. *L'Ecole du spectateur Lire le théâtre II.* Paris: Editions sociales, 1981.

-. "Corneille: Du roi au tyran, un itinéraire." in *Actes de Wake Forest.* Paris: PF-SCL "Biblio 17", (1987).

Valéry, Paul. *Cahiers.* Paris: Gallimard, "Bibliothèque de la Pléiade", 1973.

Viala, Alain. *La Naissance de l'écrivain. Sociologie de la littérature à l'âge classique.* Paris: Minuit, 1985.

-. *Racine. La Stratégie du caméléon.* Paris: Seghers, 1990.

Voltaire. *Essai sur les mœurs.* 2 vols. Paris: Garnier, 1963.

-. *Correspondance I.* T Bestermann ed. Paris: Gallimard, "Bibliothèque de la Pléiade", 1977.

Wald Lasowski, Patrick. *Libertines*. Paris: Gallimard, "Les Essais", 1980.

Wald Lasowski, Roman. "Crébillon fils, ou le libertinage galant." Dissertation, Catholic University at Nijmegen, 1984.

Waterson, Karolyn. "Du héros guerrier au fourbe héroïque: La transmutation des valeurs héroïques cornéliennes dans le théâtre de Molière." *Dix-Septième siècle* 113 (1976).

Woshinsky, Barbara. "The Discourse of Disbelief in Molière's *Dom Juan*" *Romanic Review* 72:4 (1981).

Zerilli, Linda M.G. *Signifying Woman: Culture and Chaos in Rousseau, Burke and Mill*. Ithaca: Cornell University Press, 1994.

Zizek, Slavoj. *Looking Awry: An Introduction to Jacques Lacan through Popular Culture*. Cambridge, MA: MIT Press, 1991.

# *études littéraires françaises*

Philippe-Joseph Salazar

## 'La Divine Sceptique'. Ethique et Rhétorique au 17ᵉ siècle
Autour de La Mothe Le Vayer

études littéraires françaises 68, 2000, 130 Seiten, DM 56,–/ÖS 409,–/SFr 53,– ISBN 8-8233-5581-3

On a parfois tendance à oublier que le scepticisme occupa une place de choix dans l'élaboration des discours sur l'éthique à l'Age classique. La Mothe Le Vayer emblématise cette option sceptique, s'étant trouvé à la charnière du mouvement des idées et de la solidification de la monarchie. Courtisan, praticien des affaires, et savant, il développe une éthique de mise à distance par le biais d'une mise en valeur et d'un questionnement des moyens rhétoriques mis à la disposition de ceux qui veulent bien y prendre garde. Autour de lui et de ses amis se façonne ainsi une contre-culture classique qui voile sa violence critique derrière les sourires de l'éloquence.

Betty Halpern-Guedj

## Le temps et le transcendant dans l'œuvre de Simone de Beauvoir

études littéraires françaises 67, 1997, XIV, 278 Seiten, DM 78,–/ÖS 569,–/SFr 74,– ISBN 3-8233-5580-5

Où faut-il chercher la vérité de Beauvoir? Dans "la gaieté d'exister" ou dans "l'horreur de finir"? Comment s'articulent ces deux extrêmes dans une œuvre où éclate le parti-pris de l'autobiographie? Si l'on reprend chacune des phases de l'écriture de Beauvoir dans l'éclairage du concept du "transcendant" – l'entreprise de se dépasser indéfiniment – on s'aperçoit qu'il constitue la clé de voûte d'une thématique qui pourrait se résumer au slogan de mai 1968 cité dans *Tout compte fait*: "Vivre sans temps morts". Entre la vie et la mort, il y a les instants à sauver de l'anéantissement.

## Gunter Narr Verlag Tübingen
Postf. 2567 · D-72015 Tübingen · Fax (0 70 71) 7 52 88
Internet: http://www.narr.de · E-Mail: narr-francke@t-online.de

# Biblio 17 – Suppléments aux *Papers on French Seventeenth Century Literature*

Emmanuèle Lesne-Jaffro (éd.)

## Fléchier et les Grands Jours d'Auvergne

Actes d'une Journée d'étude, Université Blaise Pascal – Clermont-Ferrand, 3 octobre 1997

Biblio 17, Bd. 122, 2000, 137 Seiten, DM 38,–/ÖS 277,–/SFr 38,– ISBN 3-8233-5534-1

Les Mémoires sur les Grands-Jours d'Auvergne, d'Esprit Fléchier sont le prétexte d'une réflexion pluridisciplinaire, qui permit de réunir, à l'Université de Clermont-Ferrand, autour d'un récit exeptionell, des spécialistes de l'histoire politique, religieuse, juridique et littéraire du XVIIᵉ siècle: Pierre Charbonnier, Arlette Lebigre, Robert Sauzet, Bernard Dompnier, Jean Garapon, Agnès Fontvieille, François-Xavier Cuche, Constance Cagnat, Emmanuèle Lesne-Jaffro. Les études réunies dans ce volume permettent de mesurer l'exacte place d'un texte discret mais essentiel pour la connaissance de l'histoire et de la littérature du XVIIᵉ siècle.

Yvan Loskoutoff

## L'armorial de Calliope

L'œuvre du Père Le Moyne S.J. (1602–1671): littérature, héraldique, spiritualité

Biblio 17, Bd. 125, 2000, 360 Seiten, DM 86,–/ÖS 628,–/SFr 77,– ISBN 3-8233-5537-6

Cette étude sur le goût héraldique du poète et moraliste jésuite Pierre Le Moyne (1602-1671), replace l'auteur du *Saint Louis* dans la double tradition fondant sa poétique de la noblesse, celle de la Compagnie de Jésus et celle de l'Hôtel de Rambouillet. Elle analyse l'emploi de l'image armoriale, encomiastique ou satirique. Elle aborde enfin le regard d'un moraliste sur les fascinations du blason au XVIIᵉ siècle.

**Gunter Narr Verlag Tübingen**
Postf. 2567 · D-72015 Tübingen · Fax (0 70 71) 7 52 88
Internet: http://www.narr.de · E-Mail: narr-francke@t-online.de